RESTORATIVE ART: FOUNDATION & PRACTICE

Funeral Service Education Resource Center

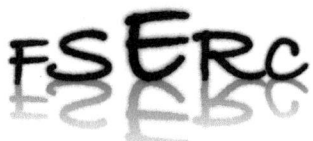

Dedicated to the Advancement of Funeral Service Education

JOHN B. FRITCH, PH.D.

Copyright © 2020 by

Funeral Service Education Resource Center

All rights reserved. No part of this publication may be reproduced, distributed, or transmitted in any form or by any means, including photocopying, recording, or other electronic mechanical methods, without the prior written permission of the publisher, except in the case of brief quotations embodied in critical reviews and certain other noncommercial uses permitted by copyright law. For permission requests, write to the publisher, addressed "Attention: Permissions Coordinator," at the address below.

Funeral Service Education Resource Center
3000 W Memorial – STE 123, Box 241
Oklahoma City, OK 73120

First Publication 2020, Printed in the U.S.A.

ISBN: 978-0-9979261-6-3

Published by:
Funeral Service Education Resource Center
3000 W Memorial – STE 123, Box 241
Oklahoma City, Oklahoma 73120
Phone: 405-226-3155
Email: fnrleducation@gmail.com
Website: www.fserc.com

About the Author

John B. Fritch, Ph.D.

Dr. Fritch holds a B.A. in Economics from the University of Kansas, a B.S. in Funeral Service from the University of Central Oklahoma, an M.Ed. also from the University of Central Oklahoma, and a Doctor of Philosophy specializing in Higher Education Leadership and Policy Studies from Oklahoma State University. He is also a licensed funeral director, embalmer, and has been certified as a crematory operator.

Fritch is the chairperson for the University of Central Oklahoma, Department of Funeral Service Education. Although his full-time position at the university demands the majority of his time, he has remained committed to staying current in the funeral service profession and continues to practice as a funeral director and embalmer when possible. His research focus centers on quality funeral service education and what elements define such classification. In addition to his leadership role at Central, and practicing as a funeral director and embalmer, he is also the founder of the Funeral Service Education Resource Center, a company dedicated to the advancement of funeral service education. In addition to this text he has also co-authored three other books; Fires of Change: A Comprehensive Examination of Cremation, One World: Sociology & Funeral Service and Fundamentals of Funeral Directing: Building a Professional Cornerstone.

Acknowledgments

Leslie Similly, Ph.D., Book Editor

American Board of Funeral Service Education – Content Contributor

Sydney Baumeister – Image Contributor

Martha Cansler – Illustration Contributor

The Dodge Company – Image Contributor

Doug Ferrin – Content Contributor

Anthony Fleege, MBA – Image Contributor

Cody Lopasky, M.A. – Chapter Author & Content Contributor

Gary Sokoll, J.D. – Content Contributor

Steve Spann, M.S. – Chapter Author

RESTORATIVE ART: FOUNDATION & PRACTICE

Contents

Preface	vi

Unit 1, Introduction to Restorative Art

Chapter 1: Introduction to Restorative Art	2
Chapter 2: Professional Instruments & Necessary Supplies	13
Chapter 3: Modeling Techniques & the Art of Facial Reconstruction	25

Unit 2, Elements of Human Form

Chapter 4: Skeletal Anatomy and Restorative Art	67
Chapter 5: Muscular Anatomy and Restorative Art	86
Chapter 6: Subcutaneous Tissues, Integument, and Facial Markings	104
Chapter 7: Value and Interpretation of Photographs, Facial Proportions, Facial Profiles, Facial Shapes, & The Bilateral Appearance of Facial Features	118

Unit 3, Understanding Specific Features and Associated Restorative Techniques

Chapter 8: Facial Features and Associated Restorations	138
Chapter 9: Hair and Hair Restorations	160

Unit 4, General Restorative Treatments

Chapter 10: General Restorative Treatments	171
Chapter 11: Sutures	210

Unit 5, Color Theory and Mortuary Cosmetology

Chapter 12: Color Theory	221
Chapter 13: Mortuary Cosmetology	232
Glossary	248
Index	270

Preface

The primary function of a preface is to answer two fundamental questions, why this book and why now? The answers are quite clear in this case. The funeral service profession is changing and evolving rapidly, and funeral service education resources are not keeping up with the pace. Restorative art represents a cornerstone of the profession. The ability to present human remains in a natural and peaceful manner requires the unique skillset of this discipline. Unfortunately it can be decades between quality funeral service textbooks. With respect to restorative art, funeral service education is in dire need of a new textbook. This book is more than an outline, it is a book. The decision was to make this a hardback text as this material will serve as a reference for students well after they have graduated and been licensed. This book is meeting the demands and requirements of funeral service educators and students alike. This is a comprehensive text published to assist educators in preparing students for a successful professional career. Consistent with other publications of the Funeral Service Educational Resource Center, experts in various fields were identified, and consulted to provide their expertise in assisting with writing this book

UNIT 1

AN INTRODUCTION TO RESTORATIVE ART

•

Chapter 1:

Introduction including Restorative Art defined, major vs. minor restorations, anatomical terminology, and brief history

•

Chapter 2:

Professional Instruments/Necessary Supplies

•

Chapter 3:

Modeling Techniques, including the Art of Facial Reconstruction

Chapter One

Introduction to Restorative Art

Chapter Learning Objectives

Upon completion of the study of this chapter students should:

- Understand the two main elements associated with the definition of restorative art, form, and color
- Be able to analyze the meaning of physiognomy and how it relates to restorative art
- Be able to demonstrate the elements of classical anatomical position and how it relates to the study of restorative art
- Understand the difference between minor and major restorations
- Recognize features and characteristics not to be restored or altered
- Be able to demonstrate an understanding of the history of restorative art

Introduction

Restorative

adjective

re • stor • ative

of or relating to restoration – having power to restore

Art

noun

ärt

skill acquired by experience, study, or observation

Restorative art, defined as the care of the deceased to recreate natural form and color is in essence all work associated with the care of the dead human body from the time of removal until final disposition. As families are selecting fewer service options that include embalming and visitation, one would be tempted to minimize the importance of restorative art. We believe the opposite is true, it has never been more important to achieve proficiency regarding this skillset. Whenever the opportunity arises to care for the deceased and present a loved one to the surviving family, the funeral service professional must be up to the task. As people outside of the funeral service profession are offering to assist with memorial services and prepare folders and videos to memorialize the deceased, as true funeral service professionals, we remain the only option for families that desire actual care of the deceased. It is imperative that we seek to exceed the expectations of client families and deliver when it counts most -when a family desires an open casket and viewing.

The definition of restorative art provided above demands further examination. Included in this definition is the care of the deceased to recreate natural **form** and **color**. **Form** refers to general shape; it includes various dimensions such as length, width, and projection. The restorative artist must think in three dimensional (3D) terms if they are to be successful at restoring remains to a pleasant state, suitable for viewing. **Color** refers to those rays of light reflected from the surface. It is important to be mindful that skin color is determined by its spectral composition and the impact of highlights and shadows resulting from variations in surface form.

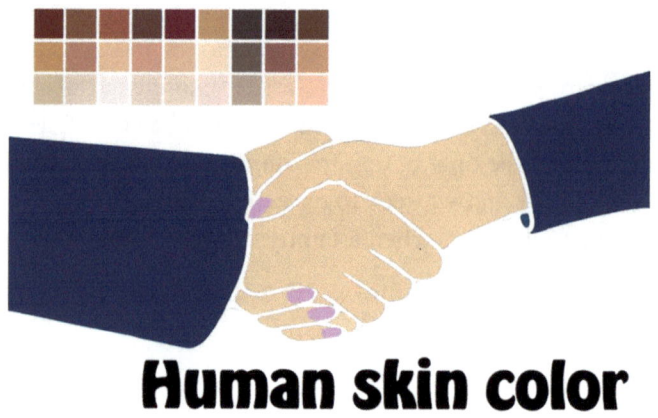

A common misunderstanding is that the embalmer only restores features with wax when performing restorative art. This is simply not true. Any procedure, treatment, or application when dealing with human remains that serves to aid in the process of recreating natural form and color is in fact restorative art. This includes something as simple as removing the cot cover as soon as possible to avoid pressure directly on the nose of the deceased, or adding appropriate dye to the arterial fluid to impart more life-like color to the deceased. Furthermore, consider treatments to maintain moisture balance in tissues or cosmetic applications, all of which function as features of restorative art. Of course, when the embalmer restores features with wax, this too is an element of restorative art. As we have already indicated, all actions taken by funeral service professionals to recreate natural form and color, from the first call until final disposition, are considered elements of restorative art. It is valuable to remember that this work requires the embalmer to embrace an unbiased attitude when conducting restorations. Do not associate what happened to the deceased, but focus on the goal of presenting the body in a desirable manner to the family. As the funeral service student considers the implications of restorative work, remember that achieving proficiency in this skillset is our professional responsibility. Our client families expect us to be able to present their loved ones in a favorable light regardless of the cause, manner, or time of death. The contemporary funeral service professional accepts this challenge and should always seek to exceed family expectations regarding the presentation of the body. Furthermore, we believe it is our ethical responsibility to always do all we believe is possible or within our capabilities with respect to restorative work. Recall the psychological effect on family and friends when it is possible to view a loved one. Mayer (2012) claimed that honest confrontation of the reality of death requires the mourners to see the deceased or a symbol of the deceased. Viewing and touching a dead human body is the best way for the bereaved to overcome any death denial. In a time when we are witnessing a decline in services that include embalming, visitation, and viewing we argue now is the most important time in the profession's history to excel in restorative treatments, we believe it separates true funeral service professionals from the imposters; just ask a mourning mother who desperately wants to see her child one more time.

Physiognomy

A critical element in the examination of restorative art is **physiognomy**, the study of the structures and surface markings of the face and features. It is through physiognomy we learn about facial form.

The study of the face and facial features are essential for the restorative artist
Photo courtesy of Charles G. Fritch

Part of the study of the face and associated features is the dedication to discover the **norm**, the most common characteristics of each feature (the embalmer is typically most concerned with the face). As part of this discovery process, the funeral service student must study elements that contribute to human form. In the second unit of this text, students will explore this reality as they investigate elements of human form and the relationship they share related to personal appearance. In unit two, you will study skeletal and muscular anatomy and make connections to how this development relates to the surface form. These items collectively, along with life experiences, influence individual appearance.

Anatomical Position

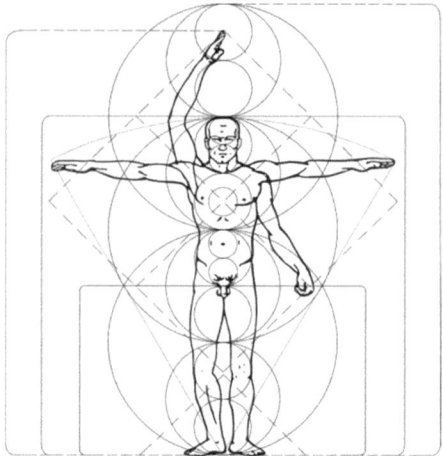

If one is to study human form, it is necessary to have a basic understanding of terms of form, position, and or direction as related to the human form. **Anatomical position**, the erect position of the body with the face directed forward, the arms at the side, and the palms of the hands facing forward, is used as a reference in describing the relation of body parts to one another. For the study of restorative art, we believe it is necessary to understand the following terms of form, position, and/or direction.

Anterior vs. Posterior

Anterior (or ventral): Describes the front or direction toward the front of the body. The toes are anterior to the foot.

Posterior (or dorsal): Describes the back or direction toward the back of the body. The popliteus is posterior to the patella.

Superior vs. Inferior

Superior (or cranial): Describes a position above or higher than another part of the body proper. The eyes are superior to the mouth.

Inferior (or caudal): Describes a position below or lower than another part of the body proper; near or toward the tail. The pelvis is inferior to the abdomen.

RESTORATIVE ART: FOUNDATION & PRACTICE: CHAPTER 1

Medial vs. Lateral

Medial: Describes the middle or direction toward the middle of the body. The hallux is the medial toe.

Lateral: Describes the side or direction toward the side of the body. The thumb (pollex) is lateral to the digits.

Superficial vs. Deep

Superficial: Describes a position closer to the surface of the body. The skin is superficial to the bones.

Deep: Describes a position farther from the surface of the body. The brain is deep to the skull.

Concave vs. Convex

Concave: Exhibiting a depression, a hollow surface; a surface exhibiting an inward curve.

Convex: Having an outline or surface curved like the exterior of a circle or sphere.

Projection vs. Recession

Projection: A feature or part extending beyond the level of its surroundings.

Recession: A feature or part withdrawn within the level of its surroundings.

Depression vs. Protrusion

Depression: A hollow or shallow concave area in a surface.

Protrusion: The state of being projected beyond a surrounding surface.

Bilateral vs. Frontal vs. Profile

Bilateral: Having or relating to two sides.

Frontal: Of or at the front.

Profile: an outline of something, especially a person's face, as seen from one side.

Inclination

Inclination: A slope or a slant; deviation from the vertical or horizontal.

Body Planes to Consider

Consistent with the need to grasp an understanding of terms related to form, position, and/or direction as related to the human form, it is necessary for the successful restorative artist to understand various planes associated with the human body.

Median Plane (mid-sagittal)

The median vertical longitudinal plane that divides the bilaterally symmetrical human body into right and left halves.

Horizontal

The horizontal plane (also called the axial plane or transverse plane) is an imaginary plane that divides the body into superior and inferior parts.

Oblique

Slanting; deviating from the perpendicular, horizontal, sagittal, or coronal plane of the body.

Frontal

A vertical plane at right angles to a sagittal plane, dividing the body into anterior and posterior portions, or any plane parallel to the central coronal plane.

Classification of Restorations

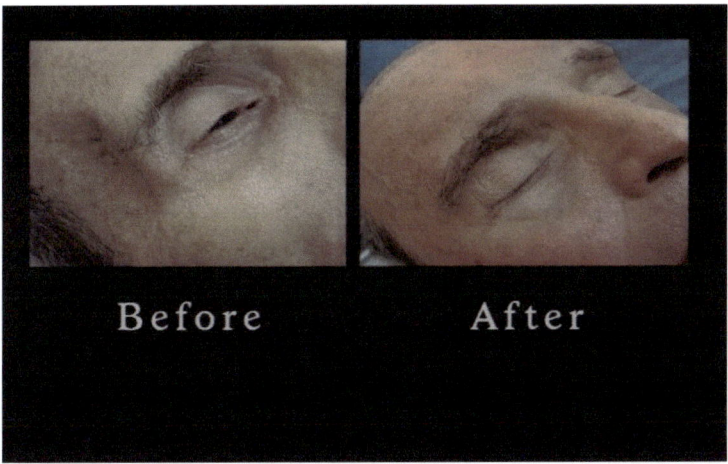

Hypodermic Tissue Building and Cosmetic application of the eye, major or minor? Image Courtesy of The Dodge Company.

Much attention is commonly given to the discussion regarding if any specific restoration would be classified as "major" or "minor". The truth is that various restorations are relative to the funeral service professional carrying out the treatment. Although it is quite predictable that correcting a small line of separation gap would be a minor restoration, and completing an entire head of hair restoration would be a major restoration, the definitive truth is that classification depends on the extensive nature of the restoration and the amount of time and skill-level required for performing the treatment. A **major restoration** is formally defined as one requiring a long period of time, extensive in nature, and requiring advanced technical skill. A **minor restoration** is one that requires minimum time, effort, and skill to complete. It is important to note that no specific restoration is mentioned in these definitions. This means that what may be classified as a major restoration for one person, may indeed be a minor restoration for another. Furthermore, we do not specify which classification of restoration should require appropriate authorization as the definitions are relative in nature. The reality is that it is critical to discuss all restorations with families and receive appropriate authorizations. Mayer (1980) suggested that authorization should be secured if one is going to undertake a major or minor restoration, especially before making any incisions or excisions, as either can be classified as mutilation. He furthermore indicates that the only restorations for which authorization is not required are those incurred during the embalming of the remains such as swelling, leakage, or tissue discoloring. Note here that authorization to embalm the remains has already been received; therefore, the embalmer has actually received authorization for these treatments.

RESTORATIVE ART: FOUNDATION & PRACTICE: CHAPTER 1

Distinguishing Characteristics Not to be Altered or Concealed

Recall the term *norm* mentioned above. Recreating natural form and color require an embalmer to seek to recreate the "norm," representing the most common characteristics of a feature or of the face. As funeral service professionals, we must constantly remind ourselves that our goal is to recreate a natural appearance, and this often includes analysis to determine if certain characteristics are indeed part of the norm and therefore should not be altered or concealed. Consider an old scar from a childhood accident that over time has become part of a person's natural appearance and therefore should not be concealed. Other common items that may fall into this same category include birthmarks, warts, moles, and age spots. Although we have the ability to conceal most any discoloration or abnormality, we must remember that we are attempting to recreate that which was the person's natural appearance. If at any point an embalmer is unsure if it is appropriate or desired to conceal any specific discoloration, feature, or skin abnormality it is our professional responsibility to discuss this directly with the next-of-kin or authorizing agent. Communication is key. No one expects a funeral director to be able to read minds, just to act in a responsible and professional manner.

Asymmetry

As funeral service students advance in their training and professional development, many times it is necessary to keep in mind the obvious. Here, we recall the reality of the asymmetric nature of the human face. Recall the definition of **symmetry**, correspondence in size, shape, form, and relative position of parts that are on opposite sides of the face. Yes, a skilled restorative artist always keeps a keen eye on the bilateral reality of the face and the similarity of paired features. But, we must also remain cognizant that the face exhibits a lack of true symmetry, balance, and proportion. As funeral service professionals work to recreate natural form and color, and present human remains in a dignified and familiar fashion, it is important to revisit this reality.

RA – A Brief History

Like so many funeral traditions, the roots of restorative art can be traced back to ancient Egypt. Evidence indicates that the Egyptians practiced a range of restorative techniques with the goal to care for the whole remains. Throughout historical periods and various cultures, we witness the evidence of restorative art. Whether physicians caring for the remains of the privileged in the 13th and 14th centuries or the practice of creating death masks during the Italian Renaissance, we find evidence of elements related to restorative techniques related to death practices (Mayer, 1980).

Modern restorative techniques in North America were influenced by the result of the embalming techniques developed by Dr. Thomas Holmes. In the late 1800s, soldiers that died on the battlefield would be able to be embalmed and returned to their respective hometowns. Although the remains could now be returned, the conditions for viewing were often less than ideal; this necessitated the need for improved restorative techniques (Mayer, 1980). Johnson, Johnson, and Williams claim that the science of restorative art as we know it today was founded by one man, Joel E. Crandall, and that 1912 marks the establishment of the modern era of what is known as restorative art. Crandall published information about new techniques and included before and after photographs of mutilated remains. These publications generated great interest and influenced others in the death care profession to achieve proficiency in the area. Although techniques, materials, and instruments have been modified and improved throughout the years, a significant development took place in the mid-1920s when embalming chemical companies made available restorative waxes. Prior to the introduction of these products, items like Plaster of Paris, clay, putty, and soap were being utilized for restorative purposes. The new waxes allowed embalmers the ability to restore, conceal, and apply cosmetics in order to achieve a desirable appearance of the deceased. These developments set the course for the evolution of restorative treatments and had a significant impact on modern services offered by funeral service professionals (Mayer, 2012).

Chapter Conclusion

This chapter has served to introduce many key elements of the successful restorative artist. These included a formal definition of restorative art and an examination of certain elements of that definition. Following this information, many terms associated with the practice of restorative art were introduced including anatomical terminology and specific terms unique to this discipline, such as *physiognomy* and the *norm*. This was followed with a short section that discussed the classification of various restorative treatments as well as the reality that not all distinguishing features are to be altered or concealed. The chapter then provided a reminder to the reader that the embalmer must always remember the asymmetric nature of the human face; our goal is to recreate, not to create. The chapter concluded with a very brief history of restorative art.

References

Professional Experience and Educational Presentations:
A great deal of the content of this book has been derived from years of professional experience as an embalmer, funeral director, and funeral service educator.

Klicker, R. (2002). *Restorative art and science*. Buffalo, NY: Thanos Institute.

Mayer, J. S. (1980). *Restorative art*. Dallas, TX: Professional Training Schools.

Mayer, R. G. (2012). *Embalming: History, theory, and practice* (5th ed.).

New York, NY: McGraw-Hill.

Prager, G. J. (1955). *Postmortem restorative art*. Amelia, OH: G. Joseph Prager.

Spriggs, A.O. (1964). *Champion restorative art* (6th ed.). Springfield, OH: The

Champion Company.

Chapter Two

Professional Instruments/Necessary Supplies

All images contained in this chapter were provided courtesy of The Dodge Company

Chapter Learning Objectives

Upon completion of the study of this chapter students should:

- Understand wax and other media utilized during restorative work
- Be able to identify the process of applying skin texture to various media
- Understand the tissue that provides for the best application of wax media
- Recognize the various instruments and supplies typically associated with restorative art

In an effort to fully introduce the principles of restorative art, we have elected to familiarize our audience with many of the instruments and supplies typically associated with this practice. Please note that instruments and supplies specific to cosmetics will be discussed in Chapter Thirteen, Mortuary Cosmetology. Here, we focus on elements such as wax and other modeling media, elements related to preparing human skin for restorative techniques, and provisions utilized for general restorative treatments. We begin this examination with the presentation of various wax media.

Wax Media

Although we emphatically stated in chapter one that it is not true to say that the embalmer only restores features with wax when performing restorative art, here we fully acknowledge that the use of various wax media are central to the practice of restorative art. In this section, we introduce various types of waxes and common uses as well as methods for altering consistency and coloring of these waxes.

Typically wax is categorized with respect to how soft or firm the media is. This is important, as various restorative techniques work best when a specified type of wax is utilized. The continuum below represents the classifications of waxes commonly used with respect to firmness.

RESTORATIVE ART: FOUNDATION & PRACTICE: CHAPTER 2

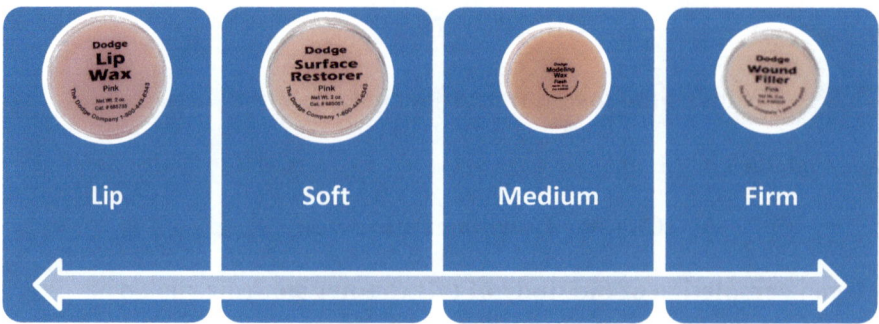

Lip wax is a very soft restorative wax that is commonly tinted to assist embalmers with matching various skin colors. This wax is used to smooth areas of the mucous membranes or to correct separations of the lines of closure of the lips and eyes. It is also sometimes used to fill in gaps that are common in the area around the medial canthi. **Surface restorer** is a soft wax that is used to fill in shallow depressions; this is softer and more malleable than wound filler. **Restorative** or **derma-surgery** wax is of medium firmness. This consistency of wax is intended for small feature restoration as well as shallow surface repairs. **Wound filler,** is a firm wax and is considered the most dense and least adhesive type of wax. It is used to fill large cavities (typically requiring a basket-weave suture to anchor the wax filler) or to model features.

Altering Wax Media

It will not take the restorative art student long to realize the importance of understanding the various methods of altering the consistency of wax media. In order to effectively apply waxes to achieve lifelike appearances, it is necessary to modify these products. Although cosmetics will be covered thoroughly in chapter thirteen, it is necessary to consider the implication of using various types of cosmetics with wax here. When conducting various restorative treatments, cosmetics may be applied under, mixed with, or applied over wax, but not all cosmetics are suitable for each application category. Certain cosmetics lend themselves best when used upon wax, while others are more suited to be mixed with cosmetics, and yet others can be applied as a concealing undercoat on a discolored area prior to wax treatment. Keep in mind that with all restorative work the embalmer should always perform treatments that will provide the best results and impart the most favorable color with respect to the specific body. As we consider cosmetics and wax, it is good to note that regarding cream cosmetics, they are suitable for mixing with wax or applied on top of a wax restoration. Transparent and semi-opaque cream cosmetics may also be applied upon or mixed with wax, but water soluble types will not be effective. Liquid tints will not work on wax, as the cosmetic will not have the ability to infiltrate and impart color to the wax. Opaque paints can be applied to tissue as an undercoating and will adhere to wax after the restoration, but these products will not mix well with wax. Powder cosmetics can be mixed with wax, but the consistency that results may not adhere well to body tissue. The professional embalmer knows that anytime you mix anything with wax it will have an impact on the color and consistency of the wax media. Here we consider coloring, softening, and firming waxes.

Coloring Wax

Funeral service professionals often mix various cosmetics with wax to impart color in order to better match the skin color of the deceased. It is important to realize that anytime you mix something with wax, not only the intended effect will be realized, but other results may also be encountered. For example, when an embalmer mixes a pigment powder with wax to enhance the color of the wax, the media will naturally become more firm as a result of mixing with the powder.

Softening Wax

It is standard practice to soften wax when an embalmer is preparing to conduct a restoration with wax. Numerous methods are effective to temper the wax including warming by mixing with a spatula on the embalmer's hand which utilizes friction and body heat, mixing with massage cream or petroleum jelly, mixing with a cream cosmetic (bear in mind that the wax will adopt the coloring of the cosmetic), as well as direct applied heat (electric spatula, blow dryer, curling iron). Although all of these items will indeed soften wax, the most common method utilized in our profession is mixing the wax with a spatula on the embalmer's hand. It is important to note that depending on the initial firmness of the wax, the restoration to be performed, and embalmer preference will determine how soft or firm an operator may desire the wax consistency.

Firming Wax

It is also possible that an embalmer may need to apply treatments that require one to firm the wax media. The three recognized methods to firm wax are cooling the wax (i.e. Refrigeration), the addition of a drying powder (i.e. talcum or cosmetic powder), and the addition of starch (corn starch) to the wax. If you are going to firm the wax by the addition of some media (powder or starch), it is recommended to add small amounts, and gradually increase the amount until the desired firmness is achieved. Also, note that any color that a powder contains will impart color to the wax and change the appearance.

Other Modeling Media

The reality is that once mortuary waxes were introduced sometime during the early 1900s, they have remained as the most desired media for modeling and restorative treatments. Other media that have been utilized for modeling and other repairs include clay, specialized latex and silicone products, as well as cotton and collodion. As new products are introduced intended for modeling and restorative purposes, it is common for funeral service professionals to try these products and ultimately defer back to the familiarity and predictability of wax media.

Smoothing Wax Surfaces

In the section below, we present techniques used for the application of skin texture, as it is often quite easy to conceal a problem area but quite challenging to make the area look natural as if the problem never existed. It is also true that many times, in order to achieve a natural skin texture, we are required to smooth wax surfaces. The most common method used for smoothing wax surfaces is hand/finger smoothing. Simply coating fingers with water or a thin film of massage cream will allow the fingers to glide over the wax surfaces and reduce any rough areas. It is also common to utilize the brush smoothing method; saturate a half-inch sable brush with acetone, chloroform, or trichloroethylene and proceed with brushing the wax to achieve a surface of desired smoothness. Here, we can note that acetone (or chloroform if available) may be used to remove residue from tissue when oil or petroleum jelly is used.

Applying Skin Texture

As mentioned above, it can be quite easy to conceal various problems associated with restoring human remains; the challenge is often to make it appear as if the problem area never existed. A crucial element in achieving a natural, peaceful appearance is to make sure appropriate skin texture has been secured prior to final cosmetic applications. This includes the application of pores, associated facial markings, paying strict attention to detail regarding the various planes of the restoration, and also maintaining smooth surfaces in order to reproduce correct surface detail and contour.

RESTORATIVE ART: FOUNDATION & PRACTICE: CHAPTER 2

Common treatments for the application of pores include:

- Stipple brush
- Lintless gauze
- Paper hand towel imprint to provide an irregular pattern
- Terry cloth or other material with raised irregular patterns

Common practices to achieve appropriate wrinkles (furrows) include:
- Draw in the wax with a blunt edge instrument
- Place wax paper or plastic wrap on the wax, then draw in with an appropriate instrument
- Moisten and rub a piece of ligature into the wax surface
- Elevate adjacent areas with cylinders of wax and feather into the surfaces

Tissue Best for Wax Restorations

- **Preparation of Tissue for Wax Restoration**

    - Results will be best when wax is applied to FIRM & DRY tissue.

        Methods to achieve firm and dry tissue

        - Arterial embalming (preservative)
        - Hypodermic injection (preservative or cauterizing agent)
        - Surface compress (preservative or cauterizing agent)
        - Cauterizing agents
        - Electric spatula
        - Sealer (binding agent)

    - In order for wax to adhere to skin surfaces it is necessary to clean the surface, a good solvent to remove residue is acetone for oil-based residues

Instruments & Supplies

A professional embalmer will quickly realize that it is virtually impossible to develop a list of all instruments and supplies used during restorative work. The truth is that each restoration is unique and may require specific instruments and supplies not necessary on previous restorations. Although this is true, it is also factual that certain instruments and supplies are commonly utilized when performing restorations. In order to introduce restorative art students to certain elementary aspects of this skillset, this section presents instruments and supplies that are frequently used when conducting restorative treatments. This list is intended to familiarize students with certain commonly used items, but the list is not exhaustive, nor does it contain supplies and instruments directly related to cosmetic applications and hair products as many of these will be covered later in this book.

Common Restorative Instruments

- Scalpel - a knife with a small, sharp, sometimes detachable blade, as used by an embalmer/restorative artist

- Flat Spatula - a flat, knife-like instrument used for wax applications, modeling, and mixing cosmetics; a palette knife

- Hypodermic Needle - a hollow needle commonly used with a syringe to inject substances into the body or extract fluids from it

- Syringe - a device used to inject fluids into or withdraw them from something (such as the body or its cavities)

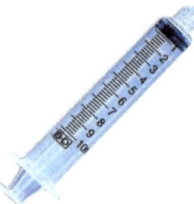

Restorative Art: Foundation & Practice: Chapter 2

- Electric Spatula – an electrically-heated blade used to dry moist tissues, reduce swollen tissues, and restore contour to normal form

- Suture Needle - a needle designed to carry sutures when sewing tissues

- Scissors- a cutting instrument having two blades whose cutting edges slide past each other

- Forceps - an instrument for grasping, holding firmly, or exerting traction upon objects especially for delicate operations

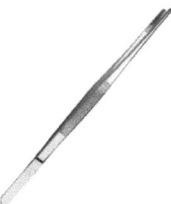

- Aneurysm Hooks and Needles – instruments used for blunt dissection (aneurysm needle has an eye in the hook portion for the placement of ligature)

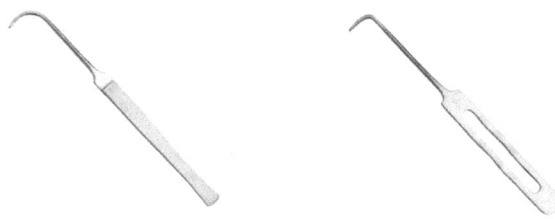

RESTORATIVE ART: FOUNDATION & PRACTICE: CHAPTER 2

- Pneumatic and Water Collars – instruments designed to fit around the neck to reduce neck swelling that work by inflating with air or water.

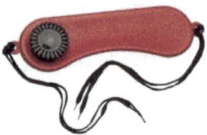

- Razors - an instrument with a sharp blade, or combination of blades, used to remove unwanted hair from the face or body
- Brushes
    - Stipple – small, rounded, with stiff bristles all the same length, used to simulate skin pores on wax; stencil brush; could be used for cosmetic application

    - Spreading – instrument designed to spread various cosmetics

    - Powder – an instrument containing hairs or bristles set in a handle used to apply and/or remove powder

- Tinting – instruments designed to add color to specific features

- Lining & Highlighting – instruments designed for use when addressing meticulous areas such as lips, eyes, hairline, and other areas that require extra-fine details

Common Restorative Supplies

- Eyecaps – thin, dome-shaped items designed to be placed beneath the eyelids to restore natural curvature and to maintain the position of the closed eye

- Head and Positioning Blocks – equipment designed to maintain the head, arms, and legs in an appropriate viewing position

- Mouth Former – device used in the closed mouth to shape the contour of the lips

- Cotton Rolled and Sheet – material well-suited for various applications during the restoration process

- Feature Builder – a product used to provide natural form to emaciated tissues by hypodermic injection
- Bleaching Agents – chemical agents that act to lighten a discolored area by surface compress or hypodermic injection
- Cauterizing Agents – chemicals that possess the capacity to dry tissues by searing; caustic agent
- Adhesive – agent which may be applied in order to sustain contact of two surfaces
  Common adhesives used by the restorative artist:
    - Rapid Bonding Cement - very strong quick-setting adhesive; based on cyanoacrylates or similar polymers
    - Rubber Cement - a cement or adhesive containing rubber in a solvent
- Ligature – thread used for suturing.

- False Hair – A covering or bunch of human or artificial hair used for restorative purposes
- False Nails – Extensions placed over fingernails for restorative purposes
- Preservative Gel – Chemical in gel form, typically used for surface embalming and bleaching of human remains
- Stain Removers – any substance or agent that will remove or lessen an external discoloration

RESTORATIVE ART: FOUNDATION & PRACTICE: CHAPTER 2

Common Discolorations and Recommended Stain Remover, adapted from Klicker (2002)

Surface Stain	Suggested Stain Remover
Adhesive tape	Rubbing alcohol, ether
Blood	Cold water, ammonia
Paint	Turpentine, paint thinner
Nicotine	Lemon juice, household bleach
Tar/varnish	Acetone, commercial remover, liquid shampoo
Iodine	Alcohol
Mercurochrome	Household bleach
Grease	Ether, acetone, liquid shampoo
Oil	Ether, kerosene, carbon tetrachloride
Wax	Ether
Urine	Ammonia
Ink	Lemon juice, petroleum jelly
Glue	White vinegar, glue solvent
Lipstick	Dry cleaning solvent

Note: Many of these chemicals may be difficult or impossible to purchase for use in the contemporary funeral home. It is also necessary to mention that many of these chemicals are dangerous and should always be used as directed.

- Massage Cream – restorative oily product used as a protective coating for external tissues; prepares a suitable base for cream cosmetics and may also be used to soften wax; an emollient
- Mortuary Putty (mastic) – puttylike substance that can be injected under skin or applied to surfaces to establish natural form; this product also has absorbent and sealing qualities
- Body Tape – adhesive tape specifically designed for use on human remains

Chapter Conclusion

This chapter introduced various materials associated with restorative work. This included both wax and other media utilized for restorations as well as means to manipulate and adapt these media including how to soften, firm up, or impart skin texture on the media. Also, the best tissue for employing wax restorations was discussed, followed by a presentation of various instruments and supplies used when performing restorative art.

References

Professional Experience and Educational Presentations:
A great deal of the content of this book has been derived from years of professional experience as an embalmer, funeral director, and funeral service educator.

Klicker, R. (2002). *Restorative art and science.* Buffalo, NY: Thanos Institute.

Mayer, J. S. (1980). *Restorative art.* Dallas, TX: Professional Training Schools.

Mayer, R. G. (2012). *Embalming: History, theory, and practice* (5th ed.).

New York, NY: McGraw-Hill.

Spriggs, A.O. (1964). *Champion restorative art* (6th ed.). Springfield, OH: The

Champion Company.

Chapter Three

Modeling Techniques & The Art of Facial Reconstruction

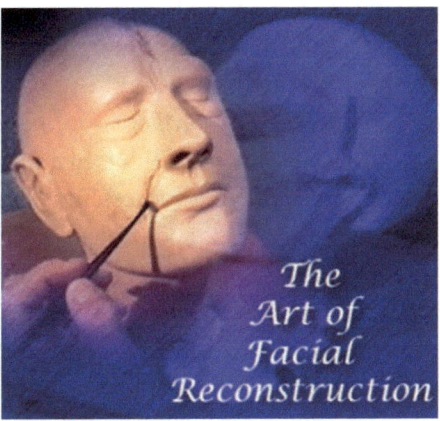

Chapter Learning Objectives

Upon completion of the study of this chapter students should:

- Understand the importance of form, size, and location with respect to modeling techniques
- Recognize the importance of varied perspectives, including the profile view, when performing restorative treatments
- Be able to explain the importance of working in stages and implementing rest periods when conducting restorative work
- Comprehend the elements associated with wax modeling and understand how this process works

Although one quickly learns that restorative art is more than wax restorations, it is true that wax restorations and modeling techniques have become synonymous with the practice. In order to fully grasp the necessary qualifications required of a restorative artist, one must nurture the skillset associated with wax and modeling techniques. In this chapter, we introduce elements associated with modeling techniques, followed by an instructional segment that presents step-by-step procedures for the creation of an entire face wax replication as presented by Gary Sokoll in The Art of Facial Reconstruction, 2nd ed.

RESTORATIVE ART: FOUNDATION & PRACTICE: CHAPTER 3

Elements Associated with Successful Modeling Techniques

Form, Size, & Location

The successful restoration must replicate the form, size, and location of the feature or features being replicated. Recall from the definition of restorative art the term "form", referring to the shape of a surface structure (i.e. head, face, & hands) which are recognized by outline and impacted by surface movement. When considering modeling techniques the restorative artist must think in a three dimensional (3D) manner in order to prepare for and achieve a successful restoration. Thinking in this way will involve considering length, width, and projection. For our considerations, length is a vertical measurement, width represents a horizontal measurement, and projection refers to how various features extend beyond the level of its surroundings. It is critical to utilize 3D visualization, as form without appropriate size and location will fail to meet the RA "norm" standard. Through this arduous process it is made possible to determine the appropriate size of various features, as well as ascertaining the exact location the feature should be placed. Always remember that a modeled feature that is not accurate on all three fronts will not meet expectations. Achieving correct measurements by utilizing facial proportions, paired features, calculating size using photographs, or by other means is a critical step in order to achieve a positive result when performing restorative work.

Varied Perspectives & Profile View

Individuals new to the practice of restorative art might find it common to enthusiastically work on modeling with great care and skill only to realize at the conclusion that the final product is lacking. This is commonly due to a failure of the practitioner to change their operating perspective. The successful restoration typically involves an operator that is careful to view their work from multiple perspectives and varied distances. This practice will aid in assuring the restoration will be successful with respect to form and size and will enhance location placement. This process will reduce distortions of the restoration resulting in a more natural appearance. It is recommended that views include frontal, profile, as well as viewing the restoration from both the superior and inferior positions. The restorative artist will discover that it is through this process one can identify a misrepresentation of the feature that would have been missed if the perspectives were limited. These varied observations allow the artist to compare features that are viewed simultaneously and make detailed modifications to most fully represent the planes and surface contours of the subject of the restoration. One view, the profile, has the significant impact of allowing the embalmer to grasp the amount of anterior projection a feature possesses.

RESTORATIVE ART: FOUNDATION & PRACTICE: CHAPTER 3

Work in Stages/Rest Periods

An element important to the successful restoration is working in stages and including rest periods while conducting the work. Some minor restorations may not require this time implementation plan, but most major restorations will ultimately benefit from NOT taking on the entire project at once, but rather to work in stages and take time to rest. Not only will this allow the embalmer time to rejuvenate, but it will also provide the opportunity to reenter the preparation room with a new perspective and be able to evaluate the progress of the restoration with a more clear perception. Implementing work in stages and including rest periods can be significant when completing restorative work.

The following section was adopted from

The Art of Facial Reconstruction, 2nd ed. by Gary Sokoll

Modeling the Nose

Glossary of Terms

Dorsum - The anterior ridge of the nose

Root - The concave recession located along the superior portion of the dorsum, immediately below the forehead

Bridge - Supported by the nasal bones, the bridge forms the arched portion of the nose

Lobe - Located along the inferior part of the dorsum, the lobe appears spherical in shape and adjoins both the columna nasi and the wings of the nose

Wings - Located between the nasal sulcus and the lobe of the nose, each wing lies along the inferior margin of the side of the nose

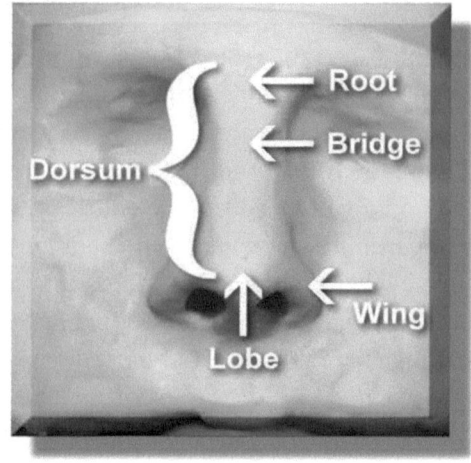

Columna Nasi - The skin partition located between the nostrils

Glabella - Located superior to the root of the nose, the glabella is an eminence of the forehead found between the eyebrows

Sides - Located between the bridge and each wing of the nose, the sides comprise the lateral walls

Nasal Sulcus - The angular depression located between the anterior cheek and the wing of the nose

Nostrils - The external openings of the nose located between the columna nasi and each wing

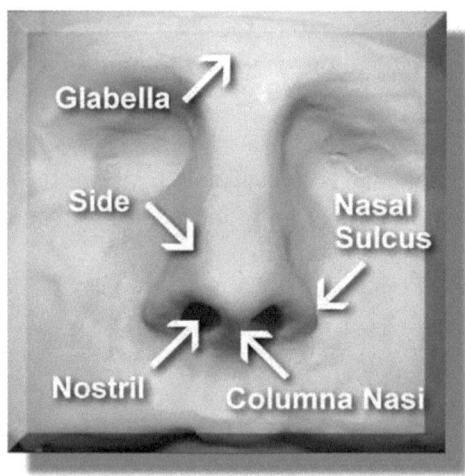

RESTORATIVE ART: FOUNDATION & PRACTICE: CHAPTER 3

Modeling the Nose

Create a sheet of wax four inches wide and three inches long with a thickness of one-fourth inch.

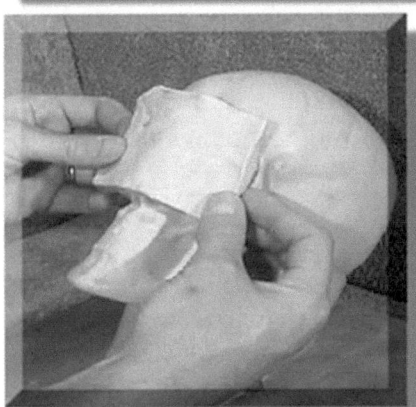

Place the sheet of wax on the skeletal armature covering the brow, nasal bones, eye sockets, and part of the anterior cheeks. Do not completely cover the nasal spine of the maxilla.

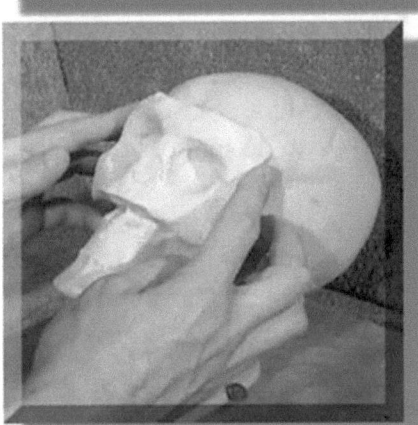

Anchor the wax to the skeletal armature.

RESTORATIVE ART: FOUNDATION & PRACTICE: CHAPTER 3

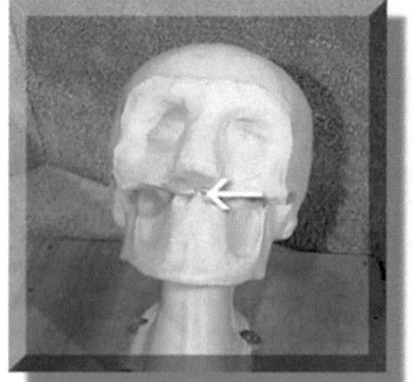

Again, do not completely cover the nasal spine with wax.

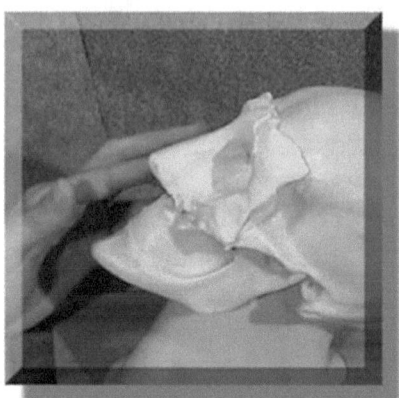

Blend this form into the surrounding wax.

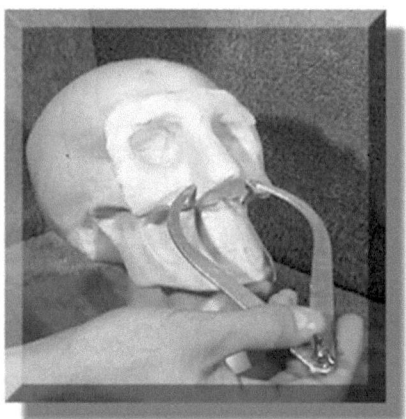

Compare the nose width to that of your subject's.
Add or remove wax as needed.

RESTORATIVE ART: FOUNDATION & PRACTICE: CHAPTER 3

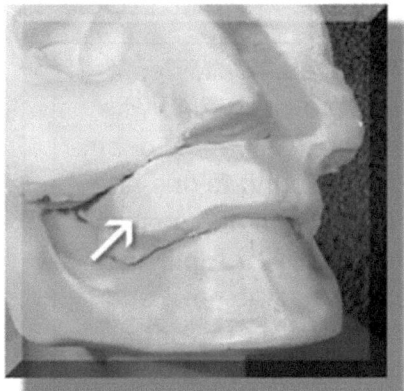

The upper integumentary lip is the skin region bordering the orifice of the mouth at its superior aspect. It includes the skin area below the nose and extends to (but does not include) the mucous membrane.

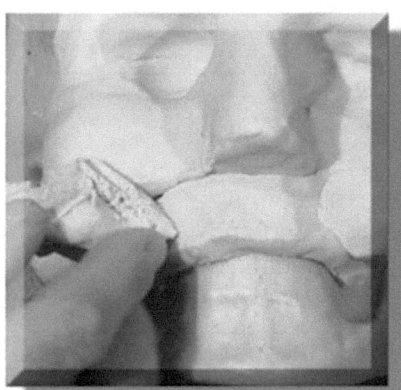

Add more wax to the anterior cheek areas.

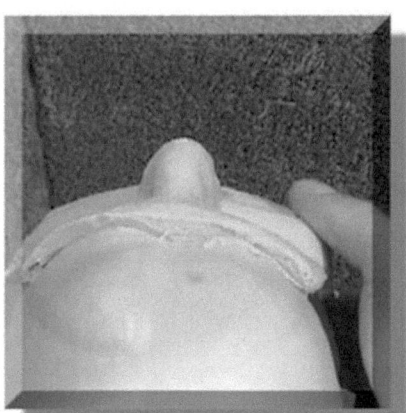

Again, determine symmetry of the anterior cheeks by observing the area from the top view.

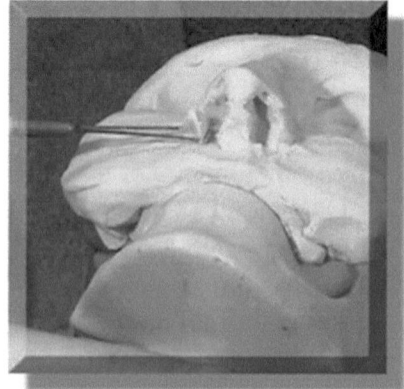

To create nostril depth, remove wax with a wire end tool. Carve to a depth of one-fourth to one-half inch. Often, the nostrils are close in proximity near the tip of the nose and further apart near the integumentary lip.

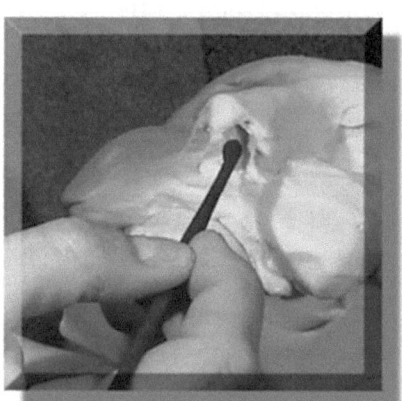

Increase the depth with a small to medium size round end modeling tool.

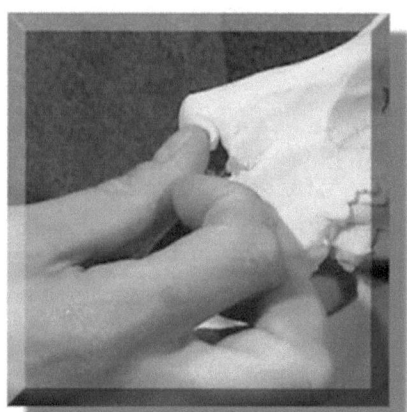

Add wax to the inferior margins of each wing.

RESTORATIVE ART: FOUNDATION & PRACTICE: CHAPTER 3

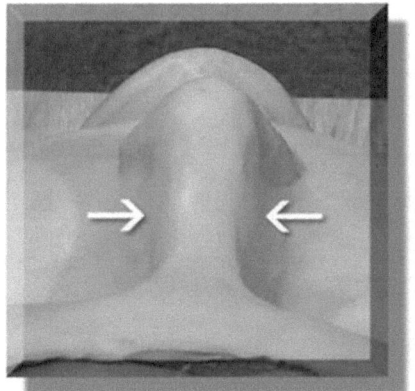

Add or remove wax from the sides and bridge of the nose, as needed.

Review the front, profile, top, and bottom views of the nose.

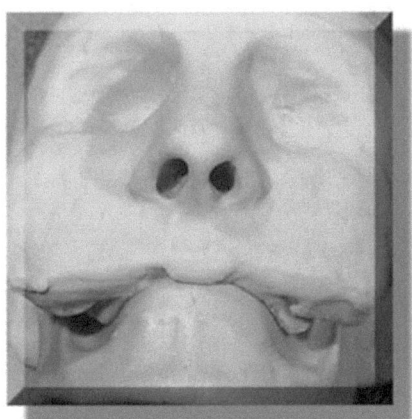

Make corrections as needed.

Restorative Art: Foundation & Practice: Chapter 3

Modeling the Mouth

Glossary of Terms

Angulus Oris Eminence - The small eminence lateral and slightly superior to the corner of the mouth

Angulus Oris Sulcus - The sulcus or furrow at the corner of the mouth. It extends from the corner both laterally and inferiorly

Integumentary Lips -
a) **Upper Integumentary Lip** - The skin that surrounds the orifice of the mouth region superiorly. It includes the area from the base of the nose to the upper mucous membrane

b) **Lower Integumentary Lip** - The skin region that surrounds the orifice of the mouth inferiorly. It includes the area from the lower mucous membrane to the labiomental sulcus

Labiomental Sulcus - The furrow along the superior border of the chin

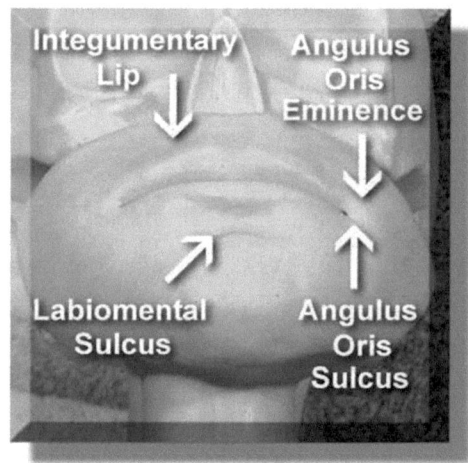

Mucous Membranes - The red surface of the lips

Nasolabial Fold - The elevation of tissue that begins at the nasal sulcus and proceeds inferiorly and laterally to the corner of the mouth

Nasolabial Sulcus - The furrow medially adjacent to the nasolabial fold

Philtrum - The depression along the median line found on the upper integumentary lip

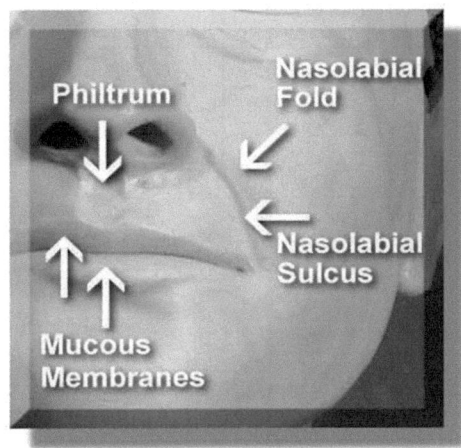

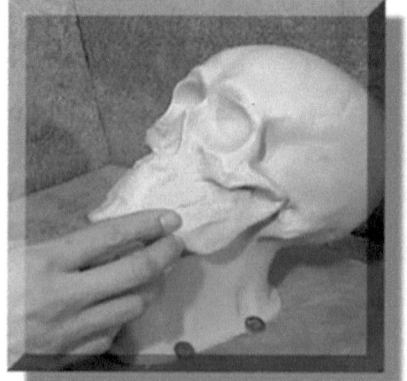

Apply wax over molar teeth

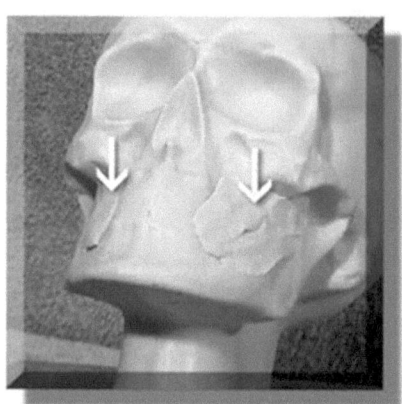

If your subject's face is full or heavy, add a larger volume of wax to this area. Alternately, less wax is added when duplicating the mouth of a thin subject.

Create a cylinder shaped piece of wax approximately one inch in diameter. This wax represents the upper mucous membrane (red lip).

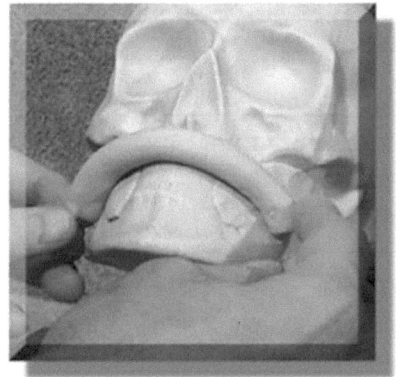

Place the cylinder on the skeletal armature, as shown here. To achieve a relaxed appearance, turn the ends downward.

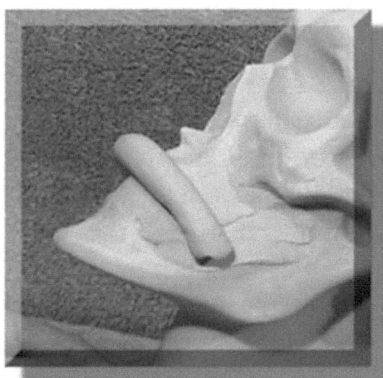

Normally, this cylinder covers the top row of teeth.

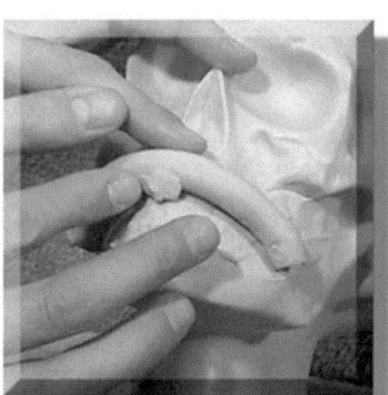

To create a central lobe, add a small pellet of wax on the inferior surface (along the median line) of the cylinder.

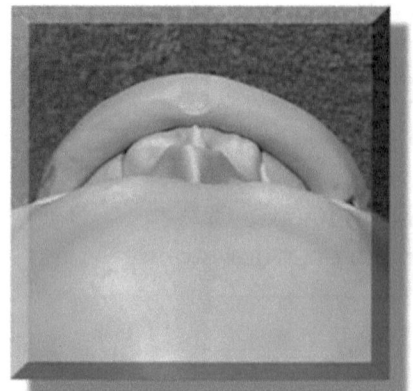

Inspect the upper mucous membrane. Is it symmetrical?

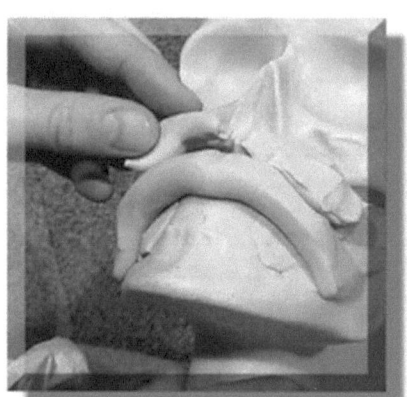

To create the remainder of the upper integumentary lip, add a sufficient amount of wax to the area immediately superior to the upper lip.

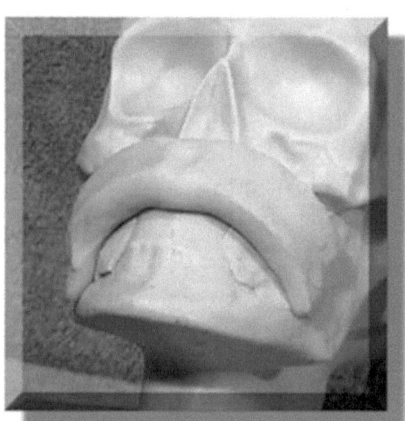

Blend together both pieces of wax.

RESTORATIVE ART: FOUNDATION & PRACTICE: CHAPTER 3

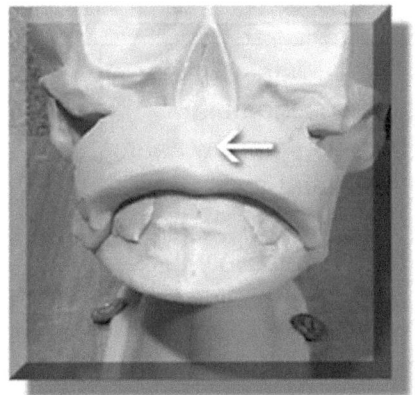

Extend the philtrum into the upper integumentary lip.

The Lower Mucous Membrane

Create a cylinder of wax representing the lower mucous membrane.

The diameter is slightly less than that of the previous cylinder.

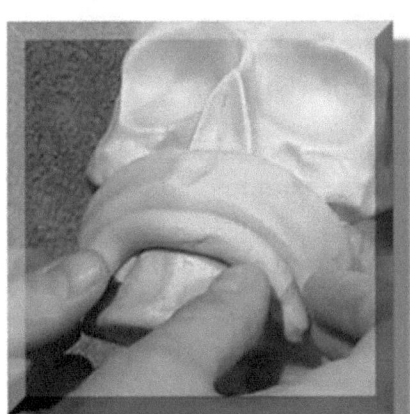

Place the cylinder of wax below the upper mucous membrane, as shown here.

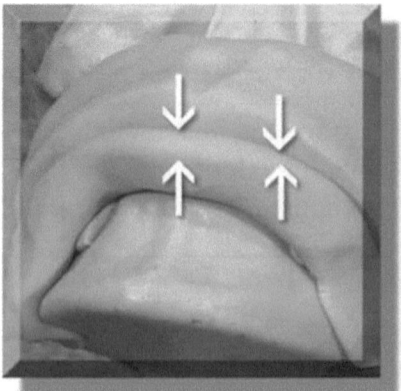

The thickness of the mucous membrane becomes narrow near the lateral ends (lateral arrows). The area is relatively thick along the midline (middle arrows).

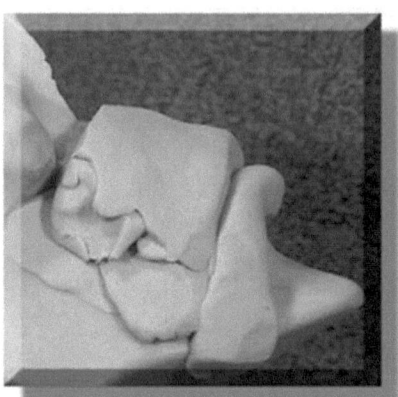

From the profile view, inspect the fullness of the mucous membrane. Compare this to the fullness of your subject's bottom lip.

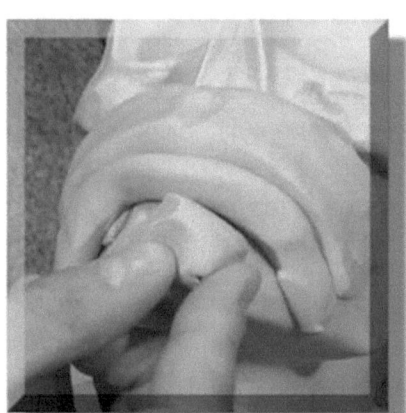

Adding the Lower Integumentary Lip

Create the remainder of the lower integumentary lip by adding a sufficient amount of wax to the area above the chin.

RESTORATIVE ART: FOUNDATION & PRACTICE: CHAPTER 3

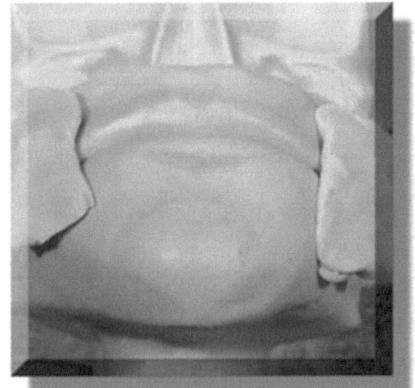

Here, the wax additions define the location of the mouth corners.

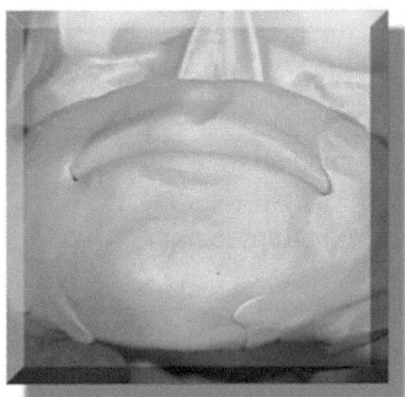

Blend the wax into the surrounding integumentary lips and cheeks.

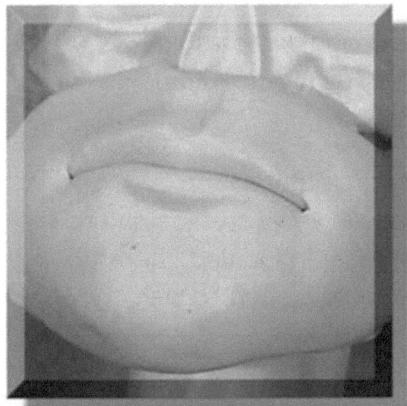

All but the immediate corners are smoothed.

RESTORATIVE ART: FOUNDATION & PRACTICE: CHAPTER 3

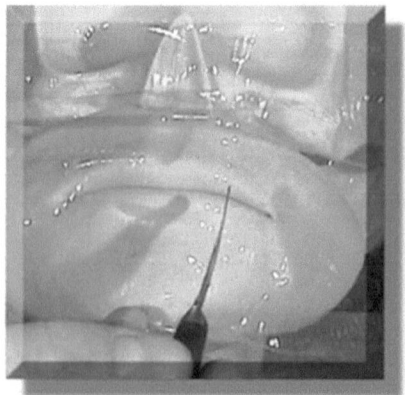

Creating Facial Markings

Vertical lines found on mucous membranes are carved with a spatula. To create soft margins, plastic or wax paper is first applied to the lip surfaces.

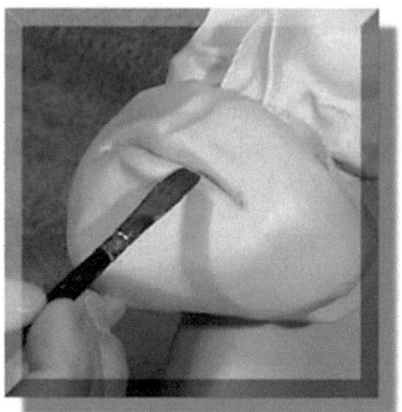

Remaining sharp lines are smoothed with a solvent saturated flat brush.

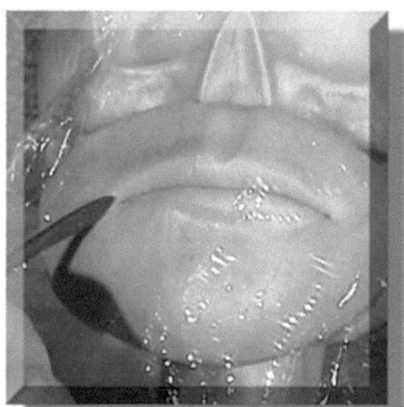

The angulus oris sulcus is made using the same method.

Here, a flat wooden modeling tool creates a faint depression located lateral and below each corner.

RESTORATIVE ART: FOUNDATION & PRACTICE: CHAPTER 3

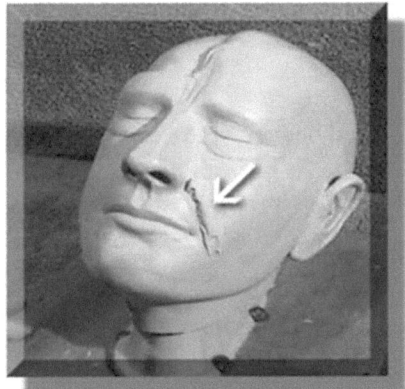

Adding the Nasolabial Fold

Place a flat piece of wax on the anterior cheek, lateral to the corner of the mouth. This wax represents the nasolabial fold.

With a small rounded modeling tool, attach the wax to the upper integumentary lip.

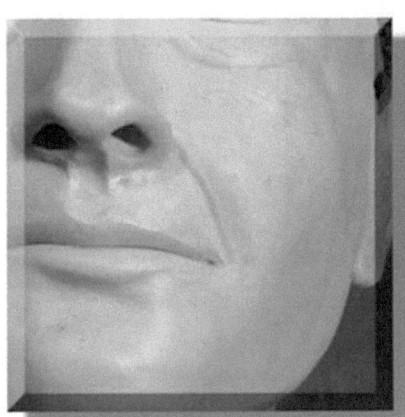

Notice how the nasolabial sulcus runs along the length of the medial margin of the nasolabial fold.

Restorative Art: Foundation & Practice: Chapter 3

Modeling the Eyes

Glossary of Terms

Interciliary Sulci - Vertical or horizontal sulci located between the eyebrows

Line of Closure - The line formed between the two closed eyelids

Medial Canthus - Inner canthus; the medial corner of the eye

Naso-Orbital Fossa - The depression located medial and superior to the inner canthus

Oblique Palpebral Sulcus - The oblique furrow descending from the medial canthus and extending to a point below the middle of the eye

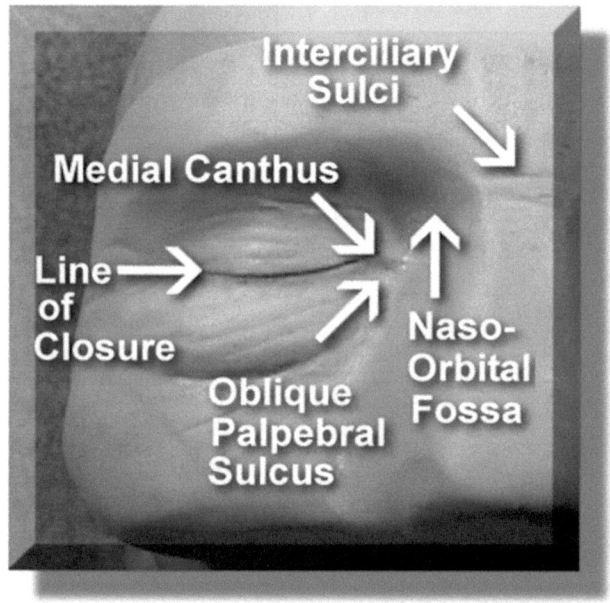

Optic Facial Sulci - Crow's feet; sulci found lateral to the outer corner of the eye

Orbital Pouch - A fold of skin located below the lower eyelid

Palpebra - Eyelid

Superior Palpebral Sulcus - A furrow located along the superior border of the upper eyelid

Supra-Orbital Area - The area located above the upper eyelid and below the eyebrow

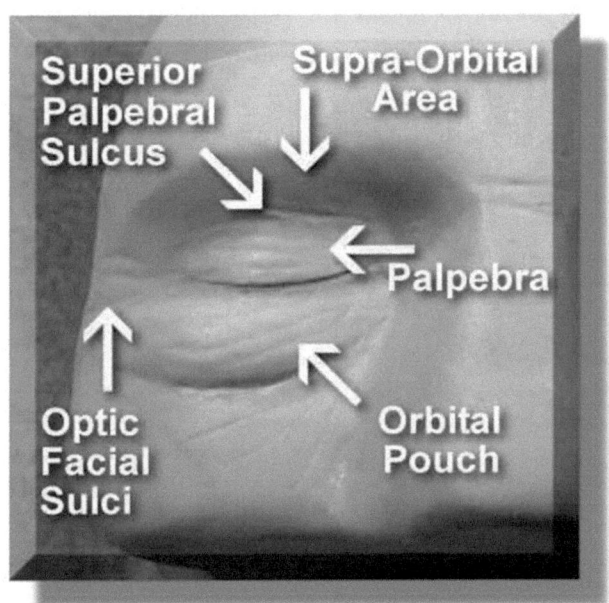

Restorative Art: Foundation & Practice: Chapter 3

Create a ball of wax for each eye. The diameter of each ball should measure approximately one inch.

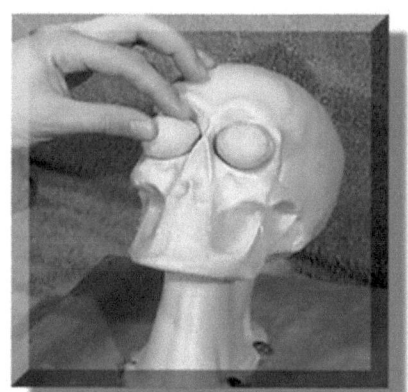

Place a ball of wax in each eye socket of the skeletal armature.

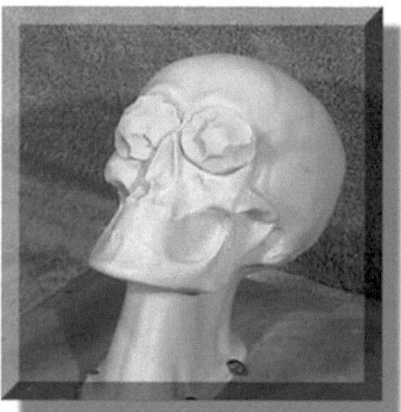

Attach the wax to the margins of the bony eye sockets.

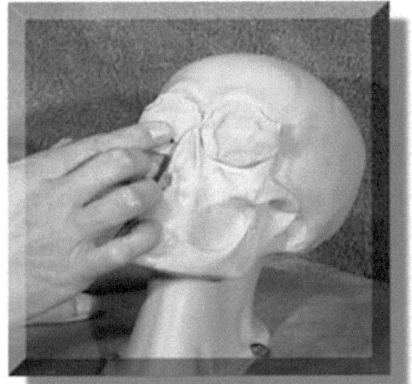

Flatten and smooth the remaining stalk of wax.

Do this for each eye.

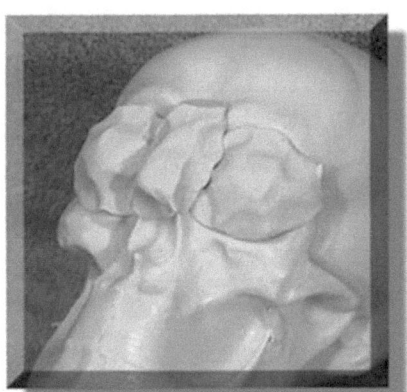

Attach wax to the surface of the armature's nasal bones. This wax represents the width of the nose.

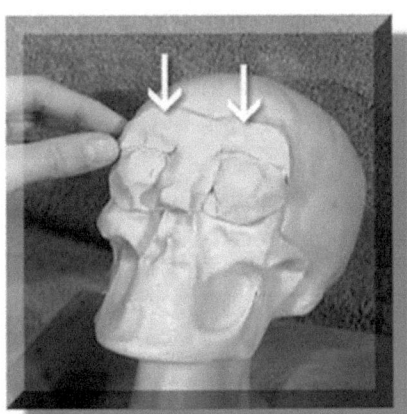

Attach wax along the inferior margin of the armature's frontal bone.

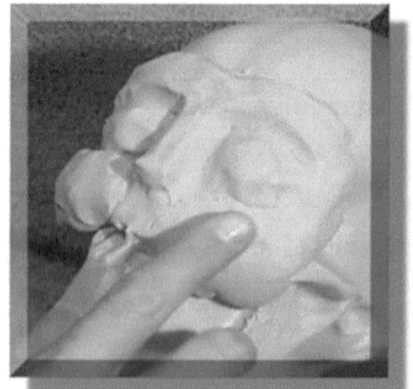

Smooth all wax representing the eyes, cheeks, and forehead.

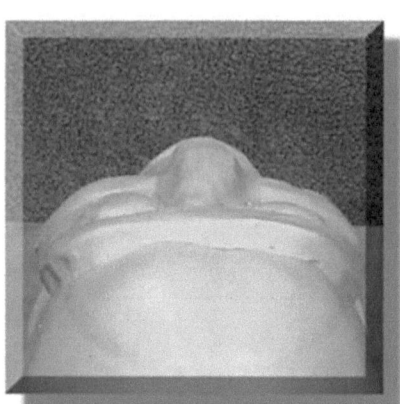

Again, check for symmetry of the eyes, cheeks, and forehead.

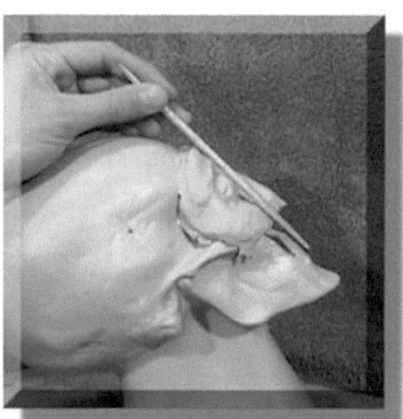

To determine the proper projection of the eye, place a straight modeling tool on the eyebrow and anterior cheek.

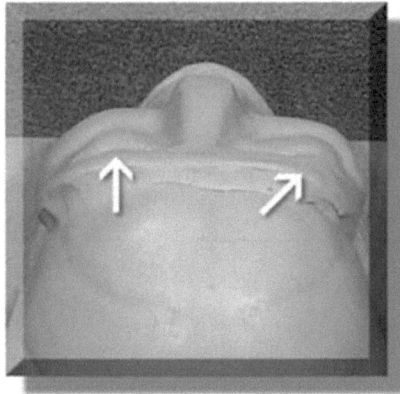

Here, the eyes appear to "look" in different directions.

This is not normal and should be corrected.

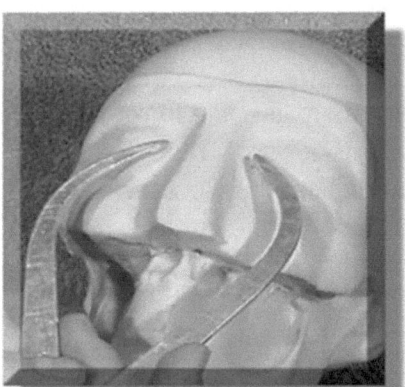

When shaping the eyelids, be aware that the distance between the eyes is equal to one eye width.

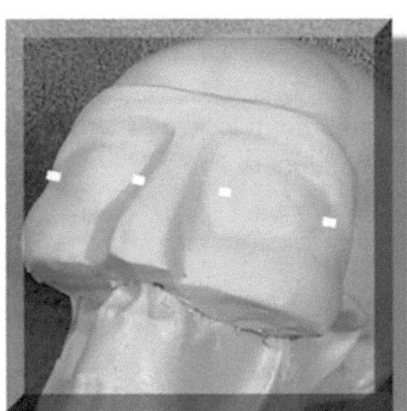

Before the lines of eye closure are carved, determine the location of both medial and lateral canthi.

Mark each canthus with a slight depression.

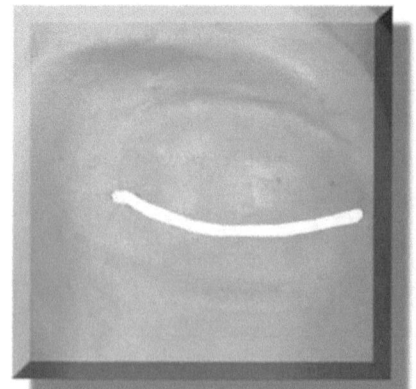

The line of closure locates along the lower one-third of the closed eye.

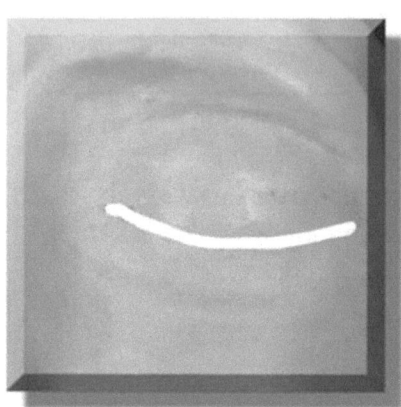

Normally, the line forms an inferior arc. Often, the medial canthus locates superior to the lateral canthus.

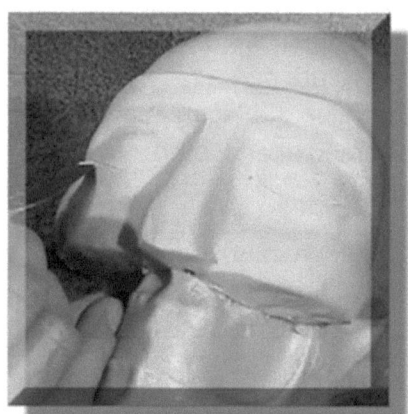

With a spatula, carve each closure line.

RESTORATIVE ART: FOUNDATION & PRACTICE: CHAPTER 3

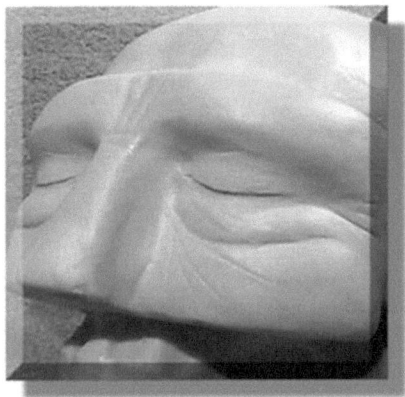

Inspect your work from the profile, front, top, and bottom views. To achieve exact duplication of your subject's eyes, follow the checklist below.

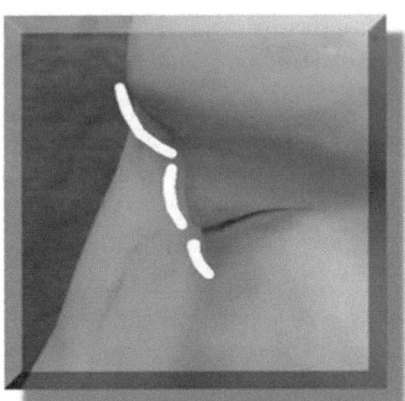

Observe the profile silhouette of the supraorbital area, upper eyelid, and lower eyelid.

Each should form a convex arc.

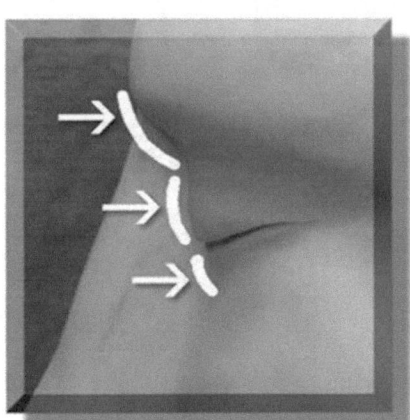

The arc of the upper eyelid posteriorly recedes from that of the supraorbital area.

Similarly, arc of the lower eyelid posteriorly recedes from that of the upper eyelid.

RESTORATIVE ART: FOUNDATION & PRACTICE: CHAPTER 3

Modeling the Ears

Glossary of Terms

The Depressions:

Auditory Meatus - Ear passage

Concha - The depression located superior, posterior, and inferior to the ear passage

Intertragic Notch - The notch located between the tragus and antitragus

Scapha - The long, slender depression located between the helix and antihelix

Triangular Fossa - The depression located between the crura of the antihelix

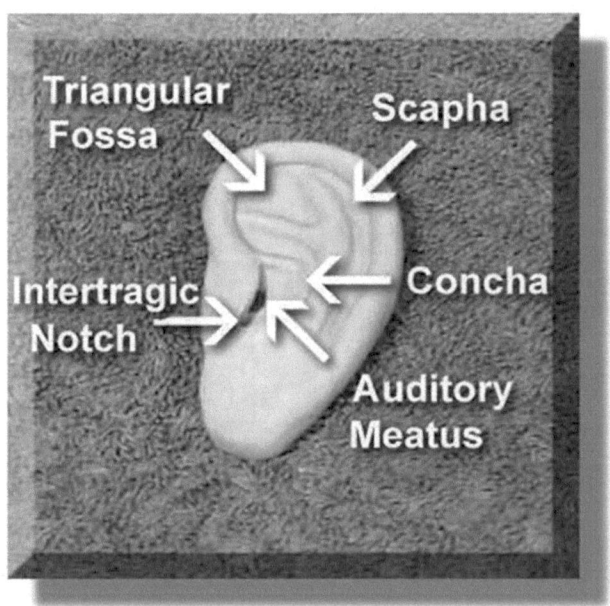

The Elevations:

Antihelix - The inner rim of the ear located adjacent to the scapha

Antitragus - The eminence located superior to the lobe of the ear and posterior to the intertragic notch

Helix - The outer rim of the ear

Lobe - The rounded portion of skin located inferior to the concha

Tragus - The prominence located anterior to the auditory meatus

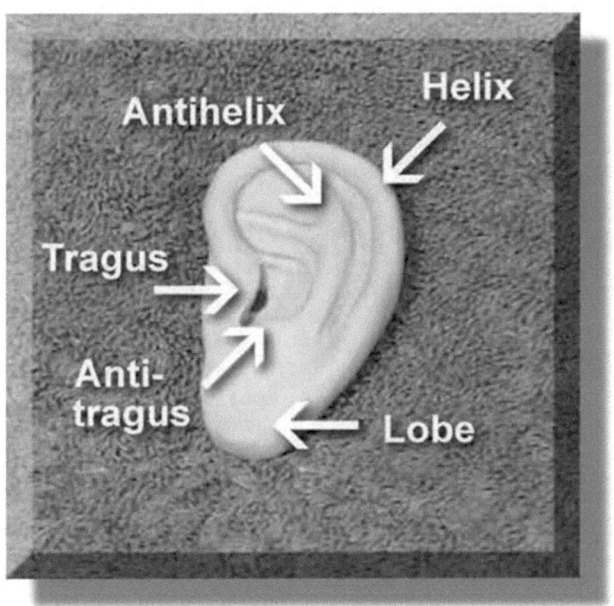

Several methods of modeling the ear exist. The method demonstrated in this manual may or may not be suited to each restorative artist.

Create a wedge of wax measuring approximately two and one-half inches wide and three inches long.

With a small, round-end modeling tool, depress the wax to create the auditory meatus.

This depression locates toward the anterior (thin side) margin of the wedge.

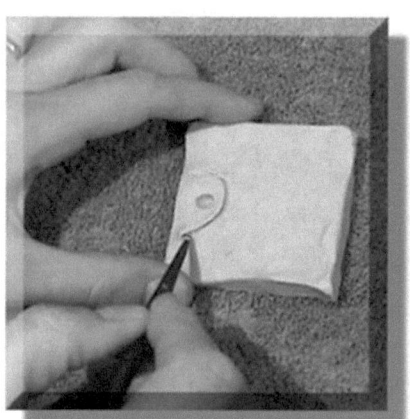

Carve the outline of the concha.

RESTORATIVE ART: FOUNDATION & PRACTICE: CHAPTER 3

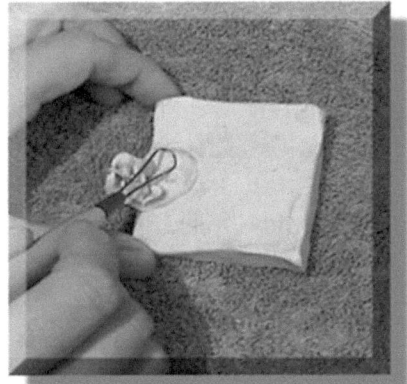

Using a wire end tool, remove wax to create the concha

Follow the outline you previously made. Observe the depth of your subject's ear. Carve at the same depth.

Smooth the area with a round end modeling tool.

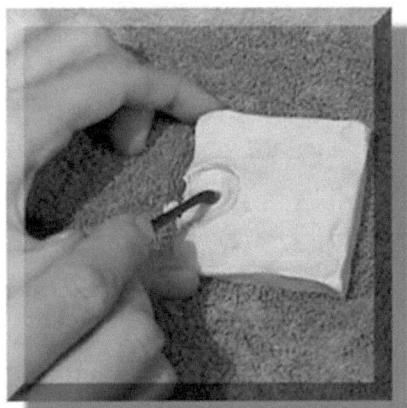

If necessary, re-create the auditory meatus.

Carve the outline of the triangular fossa. The size and shape of the fossa should duplicate that of your subject's ear.

With a wire end tool, remove the necessary amount of wax inside of the drawn outline.

Smooth the triangular fossa with a small round end modeling tool.

Carve the outline of the scapha.

Start above the triangular fossa and progress downward toward the lobe of the ear.

Remove the necessary amount of wax along the drawn outline.

Often, the scapha terminates slightly below the ear passage.

RESTORATIVE ART: FOUNDATION & PRACTICE: CHAPTER 3

Carve through the entire thickness of the wax and remove the excess.

Inspect the ridge of wax. This ridge forms the helix.

With your fingertips, shape the anterior-superior part of the helix.

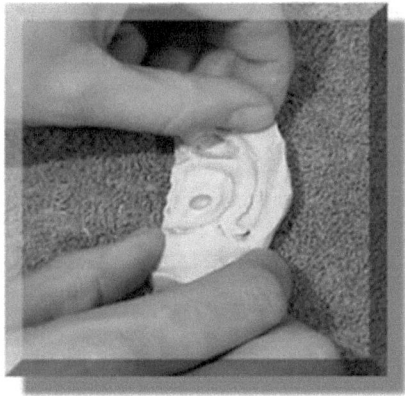

Smooth the ridge along the top and back side of the ear.

Use a small round end modeling tool to smooth the inner portion of the helix.

Smooth the concha, as shown here.

Also, smooth the triangular fossa.

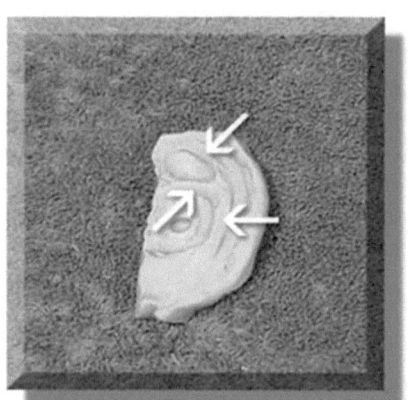

The ridge representing the antihelix and its crura may be smoothed at this time.

To complete the helix, add a small roll of wax to the anterior and superior portion of the ear.

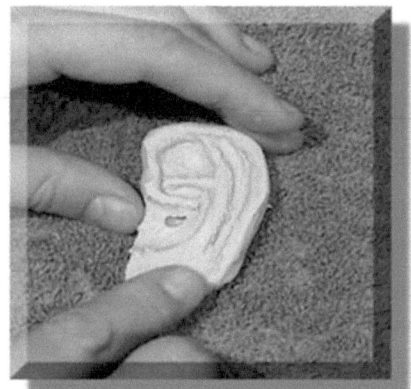

If necessary, add wax to the lobe of the ear.

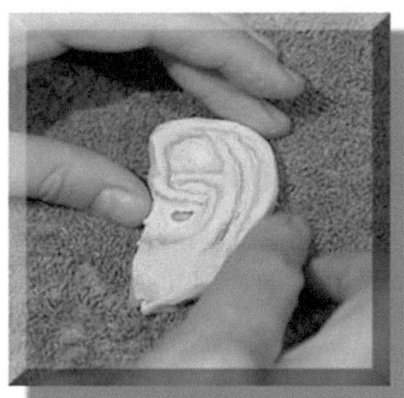

Blend this wax into the surrounding adjacent areas.

Inspect the side and back of the ear. Smooth the wax in these areas.

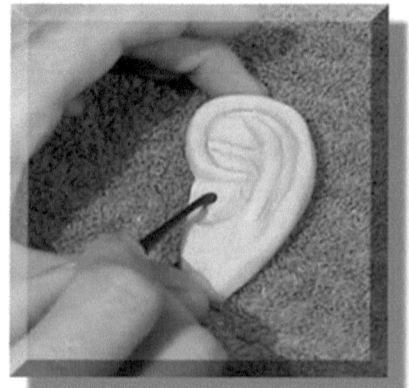

Again, check the location of the auditory meatus.

If necessary, relocate it to its proper position (along the anterior margin of the ear).

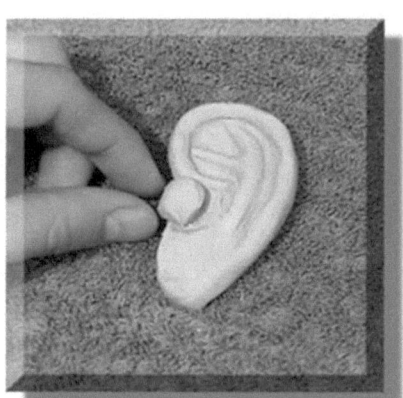

To create the tragus, add a pellet of wax along the anterior margin of the ear.

The tragus covers, but does not fill the auditory meatus.

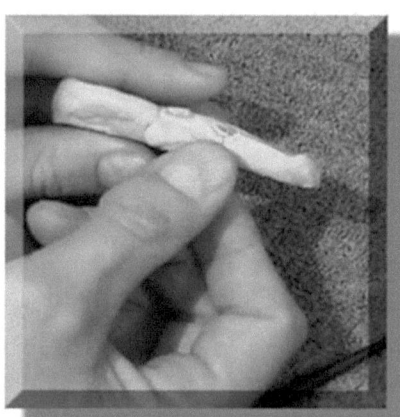

Connect the tragus to the anterior margin of the ear.

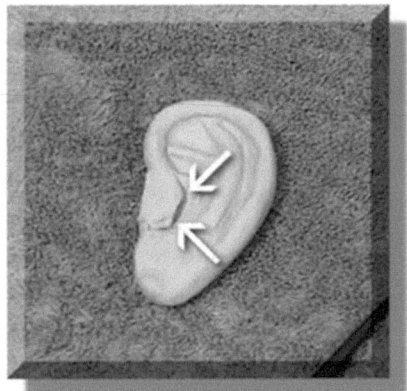

Form the proper shape along the posterior margin of the tragus.

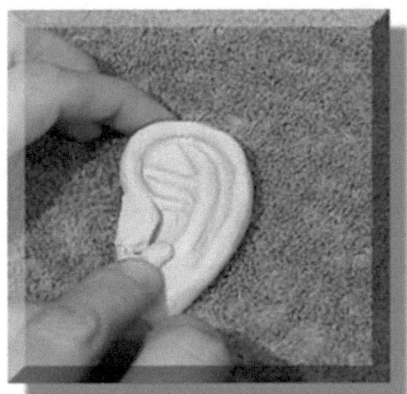

To create the antitragus, add a pellet of wax along the inferior margin of the concha.

To create the intertragic notch, depress the wax found between the tragus and antitragus.

A small round end modeling tool works well for this task.

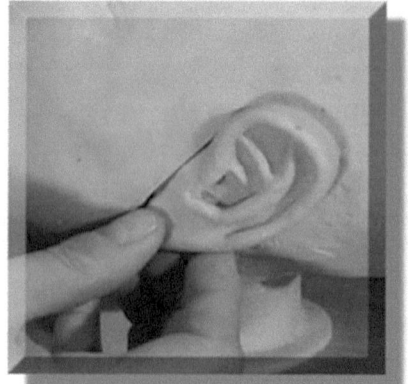

Align both ear passages as you place the ear on the side of the head.

The anterior margin of the ear rests flush with the lateral cheek.

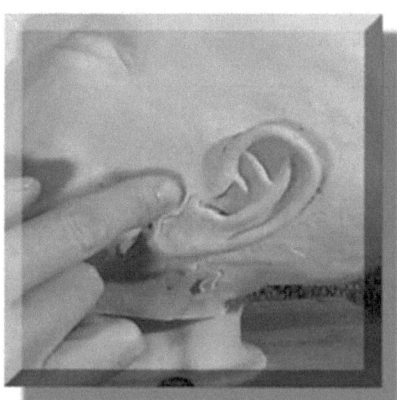

Blend the anterior margin of the ear into the lateral cheek.

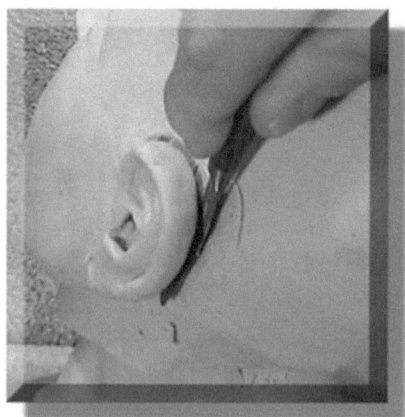

Attach the back side of the ear to the head.

Chapter Conclusion

This chapter introduced fundamental elements related to modeling techniques. This included the presentation of subject form, size, and location. Additionally, the importance of viewing your work from varied perspectives, including the profile view, was covered. The chapter also familiarized the reader with the importance of completing restorative work in stages and taking appropriate rest periods. The final section of the chapter delivered specific modeling techniques for modeling the nose, mouth, eyes, and ears. In totality, the chapter presented the central techniques utilized during the restorative process and specific techniques for the art of facial reconstruction.

References

Professional Experience and Educational Presentations:
A great deal of the content of this book has been derived from years of professional experience as an embalmer, funeral director, and funeral service educator.

Mayer, J. S. (1980). *Restorative art.* Dallas, TX: Professional Training Schools.

Sokoll, G. (2016). *The art of facial reconstruction.* Oklahoma City, OK:

Funeral Service Education Resource Center.

Spriggs, A. O. (1964). *Champion restorative art* (6th ed.). Springfield, OH: The

Champion Company.

Unit 2

Elements of Human Form

Chapter 4:

Skeletal Anatomy and Restorative Art

Chapter 5:

Muscular Anatomy and Restorative Art

Chapter 6:

Subcutaneous Tissues, Integument, and Facial Markings

Chapter 7:

Value and Interpretation of Photographs, Facial Proportions, Facial Profiles, Facial Shapes & the Bilateral Appearance of Facial Features

Chapter Four

Skeletal Anatomy and Restorative Art

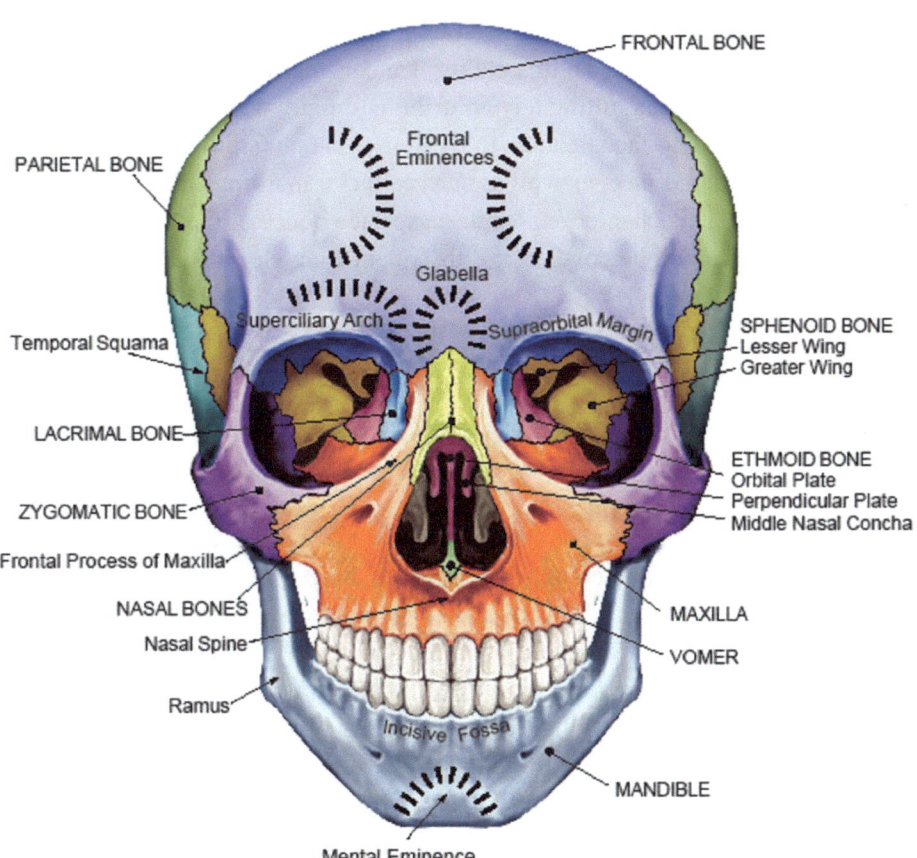

Image created and owned by Martha Cansler

Restorative Art: Foundation & Practice: Chapter 4

Chapter Learning Objectives

Upon completion of the study of this chapter students should:

- Understand the various elements of specific skulls
- Be able to identify the surface bones of the cranium and face
- Be able to identify specific parts of these bones and identify any connection they may have related to restorations

The practice of restorative art is enhanced by a basic understanding of elements that impact personal appearance. To this matter, we consider that the various components, when layered, ultimately contribute to individual appearance. Our focal point, the head and face, lead us to a discussion on cranial and facial bones, muscles of the head and face, as well as surface facial markings that impact natural form and contour. This chapter explores the surface bones of the head and face and the remaining topics will be covered in subsequent chapters.

Bones of the Head

Geometric Form of the Skull

As we begin to examine human appearance, note the geometric form of the skull is usually characterized as oval. This ovular shape may be viewed from multiple views including frontal, profile (side), and the superior view (crown or top). All views present a general oval formation of the skull but not an identical shape. The classical form is represented by the reality that the width is approximately two-thirds its length. Differences in form and size between individuals are related to variances in width and length of the skeletal formations. It is important to realize that common variations between male, female, and infant skulls exist.

The Infant Skull

One of the simple and central differences is that the infant skull has spaces called fontanels. These spaces exist to help babies be born physically, and these regions also permit growth of the brain and skull during early childhood. The infant skull has seven bones. The cranial sutures, made of strong, fibrous tissue, hold these bones together. Normally, the sutures remain flexible, giving the baby's brain time to grow until the bones fuse at about age two (Mayoclinic.org, 2019). They close through different stages of life, which may help medical examiners approximate the age of a skull. The entire infant skull is composed of numerous pieces that are essentially softer than the adult skull, and eventually fuse and increase in hardness.

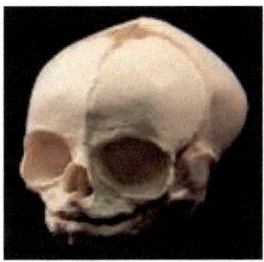

The Infant Skull

The Adult Skull

The male and female skulls remain similar in development until puberty.

The sutures, narrow junctions often found between two bones, within the adult skull are fused; the adult skull is much harder and exhibits more structural integrity compared to an infant skull.

The Major Sutures of the Cranium

Coronal – The junction between the frontal and parietal bones.

Lambdoidal – The junction between the parietal and occipital bones.

Squamosal – The junction between the parietal and temporal bones.

Three distinct areas present skull variations between the male and female; bone thickness, size, and the prominence of eminences. Generally, male skulls are heavier, the bone is thicker, and the areas of muscle attachment are more defined than in females. There are also key differences in the appearance of the forehead, eyes, and jaw between men and women that are used to determine the gender of a skull. Men generally tend to have thicker, heavier skulls. They are typically larger than female skulls. The part of the skull where the muscle attaches (the temporal line) often has a more pronounced ridge in males than females. In most cases, the adult female skull is lighter, smaller, exhibits thinner walls, and has less pronounced muscular ridges than that of the male counterpart. It is also characteristic for the adult female skull to have a more flattened vertex; overall, the female skull is more rounded. Before the presentation of the bones of the head, it is valuable to note the impact of the loss of teeth to the size and appearance of the adult skull. The reduction of the size of the superior and inferior jaws due to the loss of teeth and the absorption of the alveolar processes can be a significant sign of the aging process.

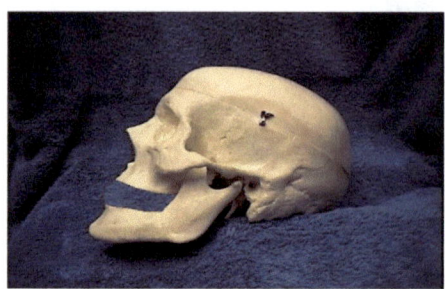 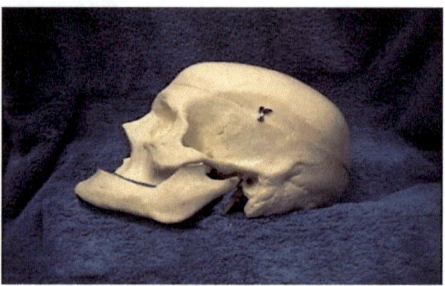

The reduction of the size of the superior and inferior jaws due to the loss of teeth and the absorption of the alveolar processes can no doubt be a significant sign of the aging process.

RESTORATIVE ART: FOUNDATION & PRACTICE: CHAPTER 4

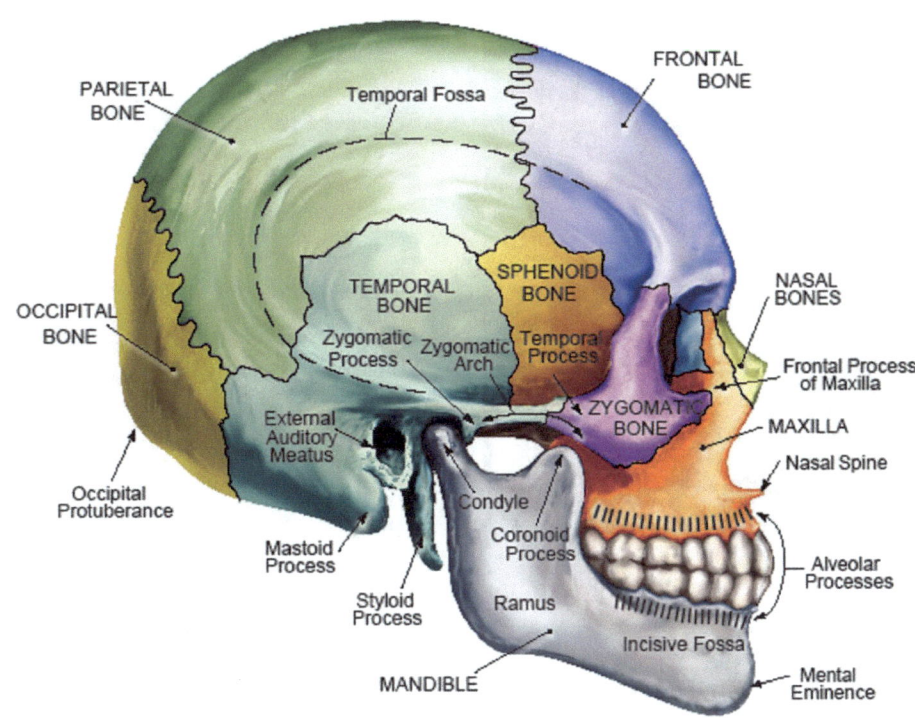

Image created and owned by Martha Cansler

Surface Bones of the Cranium

Occipital Bone (1 bone) – A single bone described as the lowest part of the back and base of the cranium, forming a cradle for the brain

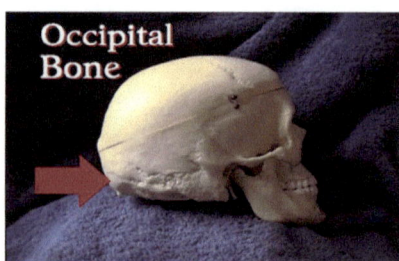
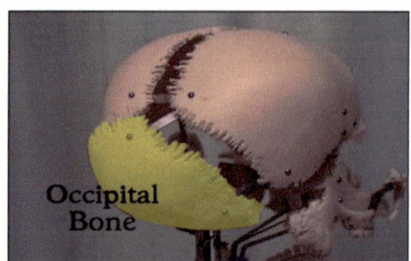
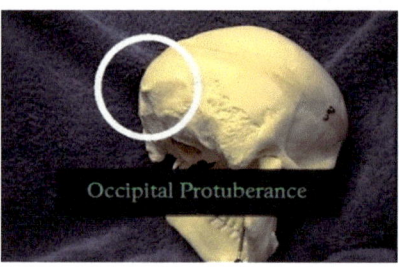

Occipital Protuberance – The prominence at the center of the external surface of the occipital bone

Foramen Magnum – An opening in the occipital bone through which the spinal cord passes from the brain (note the relevance of the foramen magnum when restoring the decapitated case. This larger opening may receive an appropriately sized PVC pipe or wooden dowel to assist in the reattachment of the head to the trunk.)

Occipital Condyles - Each of two rounded knobs on the occipital bone that form a joint with the first cervical vertebra (Image: Steve Smith, University of Central OK)

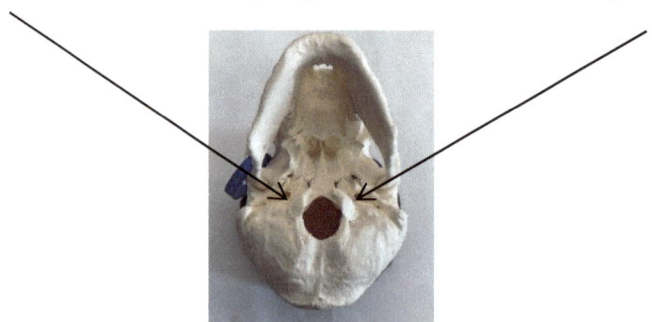

Parietal Bones (2 bones) – Two bones that form the posterior 2/3 of the vault of the cranium and part of the sides of the skull

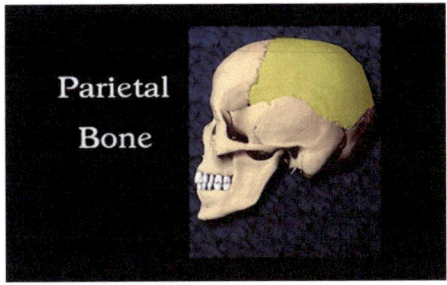
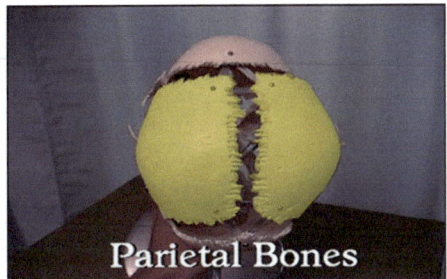

Parietal Eminence – The rounded peak of the external convexity of the parietal bones; determines the widest part of the cranium; note that the eminences are located a short distance above the posterior border of the ears. This may be helpful when attaching the modeled ear to the side of the cranium.

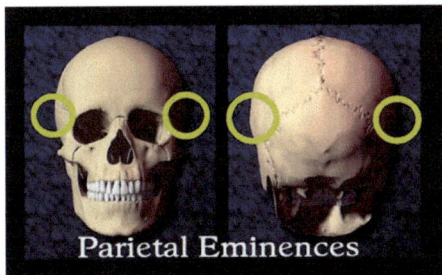
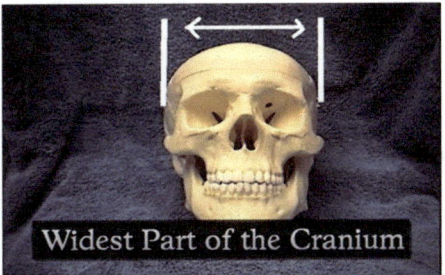

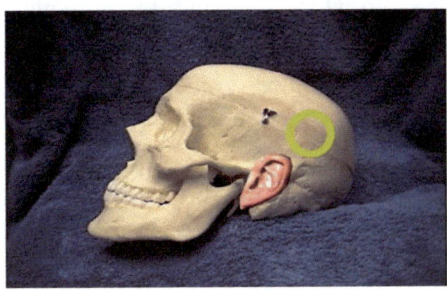

Temporal Bones (2 bones) – Inferior portion of the sides and base of the cranium, inferior to the parietal bones and anterior to the occipital bone

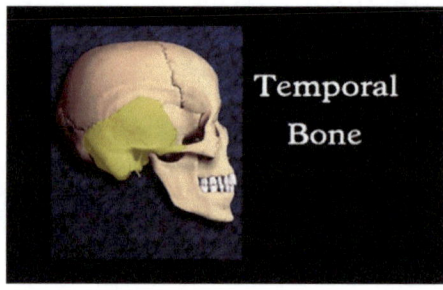

Associations of the Temporal Bone

Squama - The vertical surface of the temporal bone

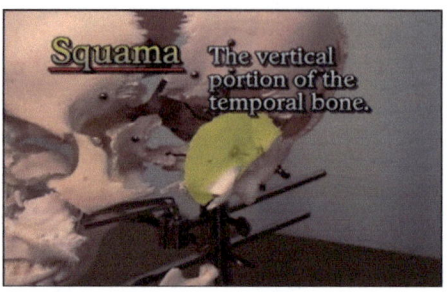

Temporal Cavity – The concave surface of the head overlying the temporal bone.

Anatomical Structures to Locate the Ear -

- External Auditory Meatus - The opening or passageway of the ear.
- Zygomatic Arch - The processes on the temporal and zygomatic bones; determines the widest part of the face
- Mandibular Fossa – The small oval depression on the zygomatic process of the temporal bone into which the condyle of the mandible articulates, just anterior to the external auditory meatus
- Mastoid Process – The rounded projection on the inferior portion of the temporal bones just posterior to the lobe of the ear

Zygomatic Arches - The processes on the temporal and zygomatic bones; determines the widest part of the face

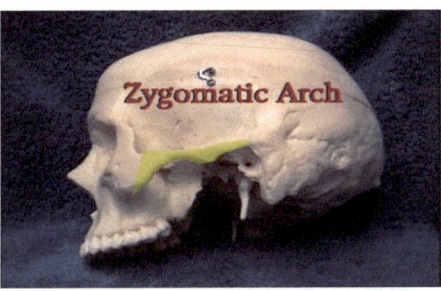

Mastoid Processes - The rounded projection on the inferior portion of the temporal bones just posterior to the lobe of the ear

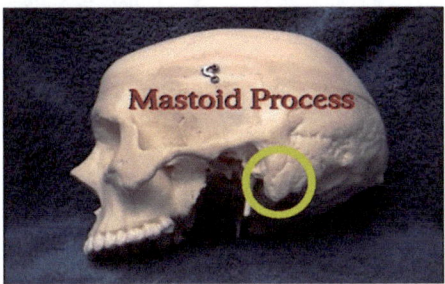

Frontal Bone (1 bone) – The anterior third of the cranium, forming the forehead and the anterior portion of the roof of the skull

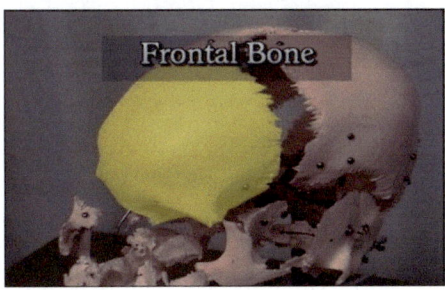

Surfaces of the Frontal Bone –

- **Vertical (forehead)** - This surface extends from the upper margin of the eye sockets to the level of the two frontal eminences. The forehead is defined as that part of the face above the eyes.

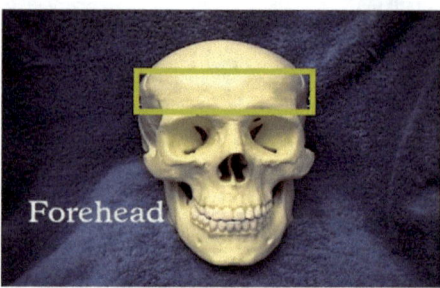

- **Horizontal (anterior portion of the crown)** - This surface continues to ascend superiorly until it reaches the parietal bones. The crown is defined as the topmost part of the head.

Eminences Associated with the Frontal Bone –

- Frontal Eminences – Paired, rounded, unmargined prominences of the frontal bone found approximately one inch beneath the normal hairline
- Supraorbital Margins – The superior rim of the eye socket
- Superciliary Arches – The inferior part of the forehead just superior to the median ends of the eyebrows

- **Glabella** – A single bony prominence of the frontal bone located between the superciliary arches in the inferior part of the frontal bone above the root of the nose

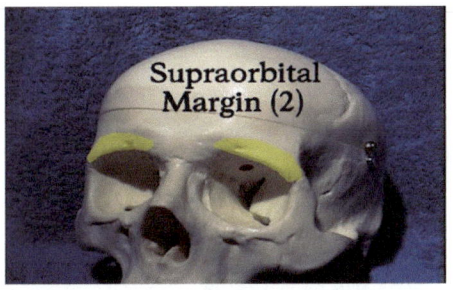

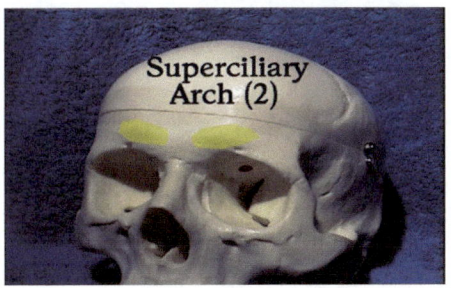
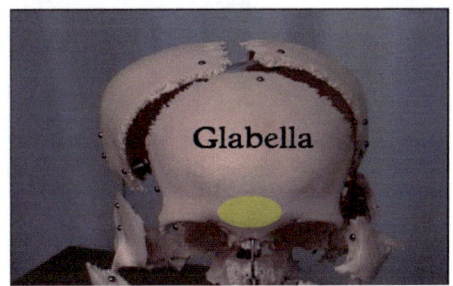

Two bones, the ethmoid and sphenoid, are indeed bones of the head. Nevertheless, they are not surface bones and therefore have little impact regarding restorative art. Regardless it is valuable to identify these two bones:

Sphenoid: An unpaired bone of the neurocranium. It is situated in the middle of the skull towards the front, in front of the basilar part of the occipital bone.

Ethmoid: This bone is an anterior cranial bone located between the eyes. It contributes to the medial wall of the orbit, the nasal cavity, and the nasal septum. The ethmoid bone has three parts: cribriform plate, ethmoidal labyrinth, and the perpendicular plate.

RESTORATIVE ART: FOUNDATION & PRACTICE: CHAPTER 4

Surface Bones of the Face

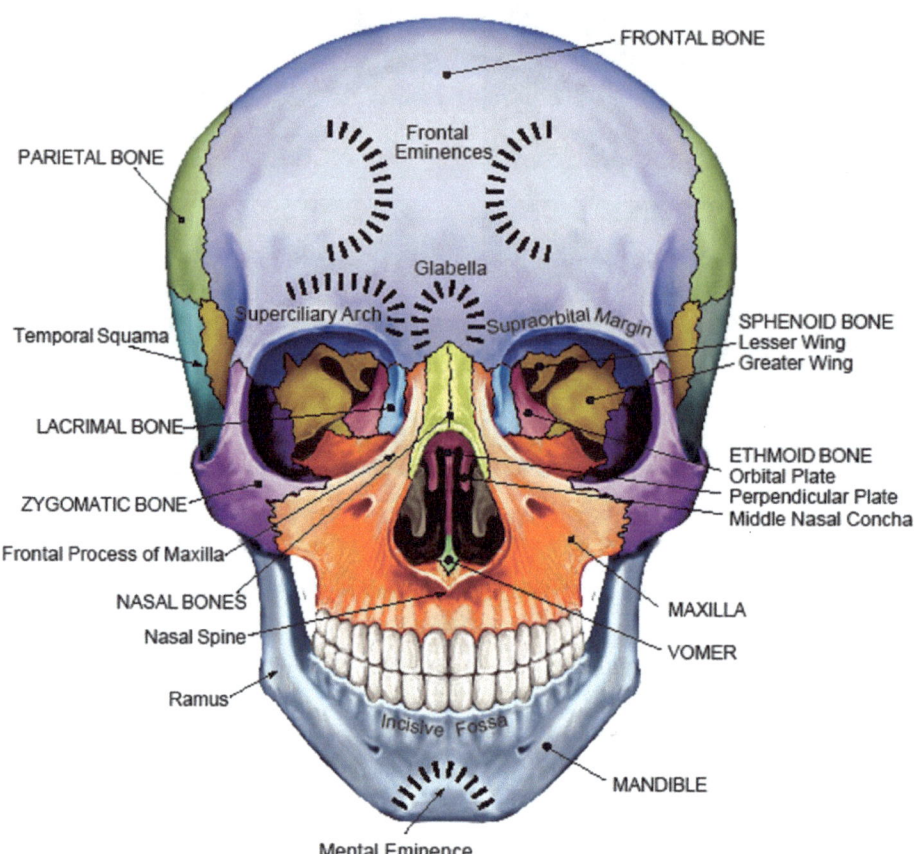

Image created and owned by Martha Cansler

Nasal Bones (2 bones) – Directly inferior to the glabella and forming a dome over the superior portion of the nasal cavity. Many indicate this structure to exhibit a triangular form. It is also valuable to note that the formation of the bridge of the nose is sustained by the articulation of the two nasal bones

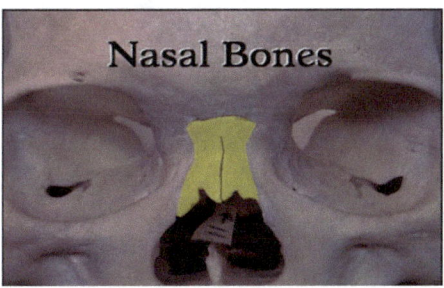

Nasal Cavity – The orifice in the bony face bounded by the margins of the nasal bones and the maxilla

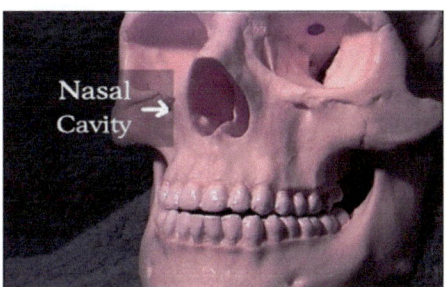

Zygomatic Bones (2 bones) – Bones of the cheek. Often described as being diamond shaped and forms the cheek bones, the surface of these bones is on both the frontal and lateral planes of the face.

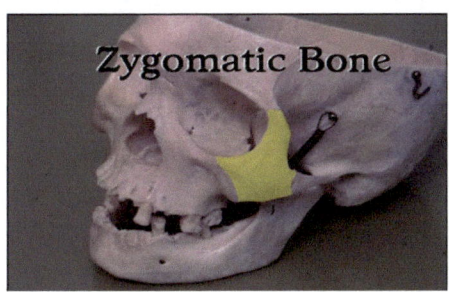

The surface of the zygomatic bone is convex in both an anterior and lateral direction. The change in direction of the bone occurs at the approximate center of the bone. It is important to practice caution when rouging the cheek as the prominence can create a highlight.

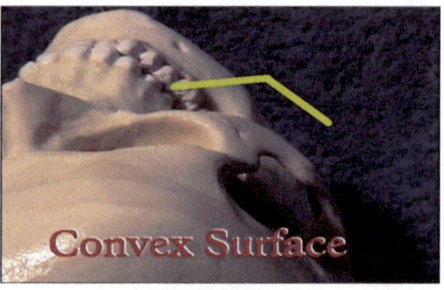

Associations of the Zygomatic Bone

Zygomatic Arch – The processes on the temporal and zygomatic bones; determines the widest part of the face

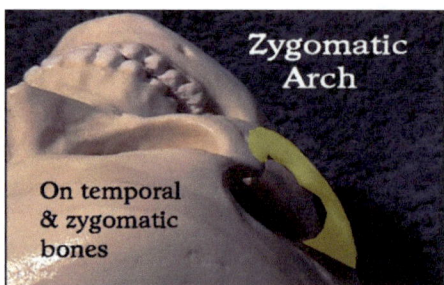

Zygomatic Arch Depression – One of the lesser concavities of the face located on the lateral portion of the cheek inferior to the zygomatic arch

Zygomaticofrontal Process – The lateral rim of the eye socket formed by a process of the frontal bone and a process of the zygomatic bone

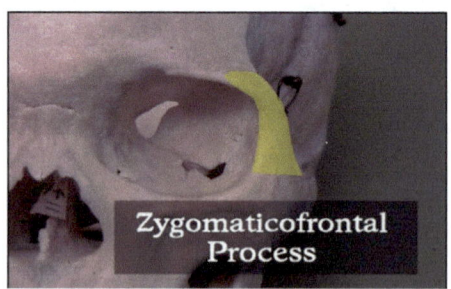

Maxilla Bones (2 bones) – A paired bone with several processes that form the skeletal base of most of the superior face, roof of the mouth, sides of the nasal cavity, and floor of the orbit

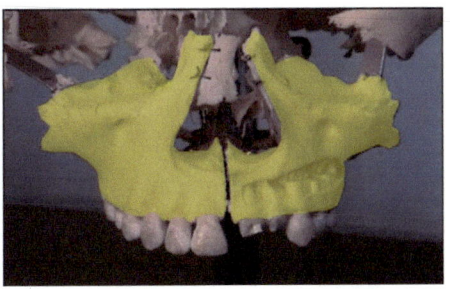

Eminences

- **Nasal Spine of the Maxilla** – The sharp, bony projection located medially at the inferior margin of the nasal cavity

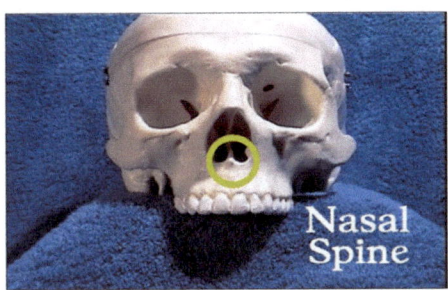

- **Alveolar Processes** – A bony ridge found on the inferior surface of the maxilla and the superior surface of the mandible which contain the sockets for the teeth
- **Frontal Process of the Maxilla** – The ascending part of the upper jaw which gradually protrudes as it rises beside the nasal bone to meet the frontal bone; the ascending process of the upper jaw

RESTORATIVE ART: FOUNDATION & PRACTICE: CHAPTER 4

Mandible (1 bone) – The horseshoe-shaped bone forming the inferior jaw

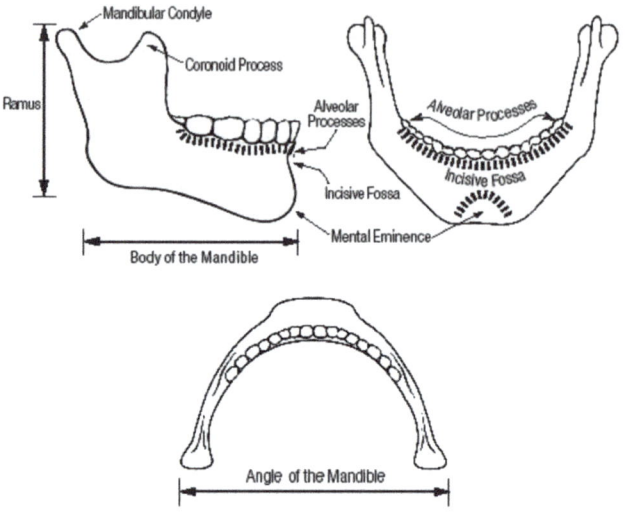

Illustration created and owned by Martha Cansler

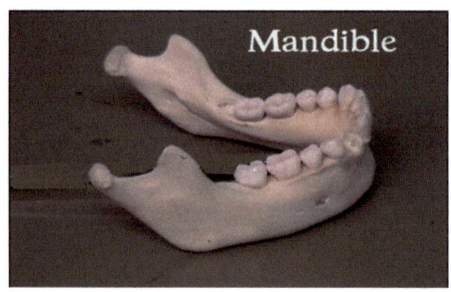

RESTORATIVE ART: FOUNDATION & PRACTICE: CHAPTER 4

Divisions of the Mandible

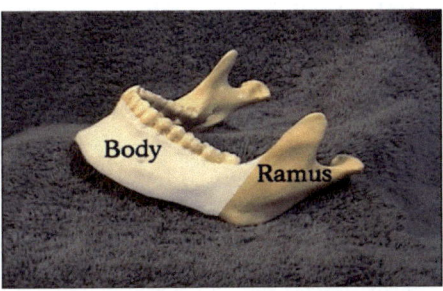

- Body of the Mandible
    - **Mental Eminence** – A triangular projection on the inferior portion of the anterior mandible
    - **Alveolar Processes** – A bony ridge found on the inferior surface of the maxilla and the superior surface of the mandible which contain the sockets for the teeth
    - **Incisive Fossa** – The depression between the mental eminence and the mandibular incisors

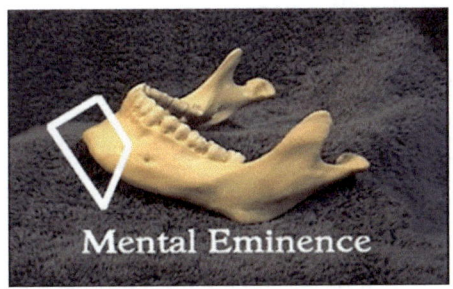
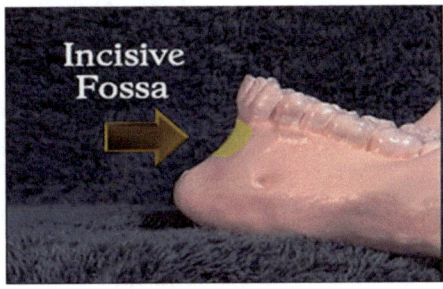

- Ramus
    - **Coronoid Process** – The anterior, non-articulating process of the ramus of the mandible which serves as the insertion for the temporalis muscle

    - **Mandibular Condyle** – A rounded prominence at the end of a bone forming an articulation; the posterior process of the ramus of the mandible

✓ **Mandibular Notch** – A relatively deep indentation between the condyle and coronoid process of the mandible

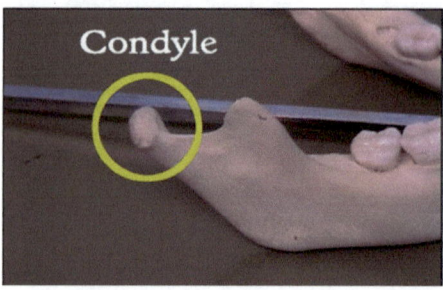

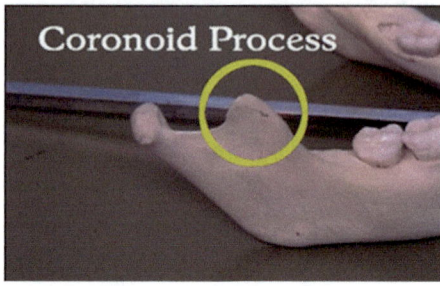

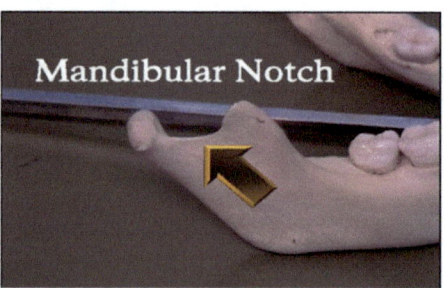

- **Angle of the Mandible** – A bony angle formed by the junction of the posterior edge of the ramus of the mandible and the inferior surface of the body of the mandible; marks widest part of the lower 1/3 of the face

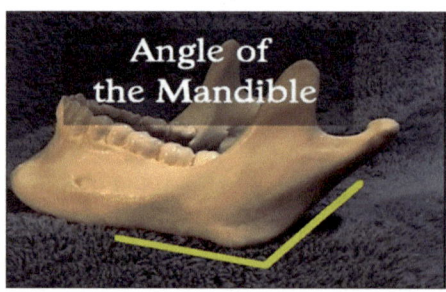

Chapter Conclusion

This chapter introduced specific skeletal anatomy that serves the restorative artist by providing foundational information with respect to various elements that contribute to personal appearance. Various skull types were discussed as well as specific characteristics associated with each type. After this introduction, the surface bones of the cranium and face were presented. In addition to general characteristics of these bones, any specific elements related to restorative work when dealing with the different structures were discussed. The fundamental purpose of this chapter was to establish a foundation as the restorative art student learns elements that contribute to personal appearance. In the next chapter, we expand on this study by introducing muscular anatomy as it relates to restorative art and how it impacts personal appearance.

References

Professional Experience and Educational Presentations:
A great deal of the content of this book has been derived from years of professional experience as an embalmer, funeral director, and funeral service educator.

Drake, R. L., Vogl, W., Mitchell, A. W. M., & Gray, H. (2005). *Gray's anatomy for students.* Philadelphia: Elsevier/Churchhill Livingstone.

Klicker, R. (2002). *Restorative art and science.* Buffalo, NY: Thanos Institute.

Mayer, J. S. (1980). *Restorative art.* Dallas, TX: Professional Training Schools.

Mayer, R. G. (2012). *Embalming: History, theory, and practice* (5th ed.). New York, NY: McGraw-Hill.

Mayo Clinic (2019). *Cranial sutures and fontanels.* Retrieved from Mayoclinic.org.

Chapter Five

Muscular Anatomy and Restorative Art

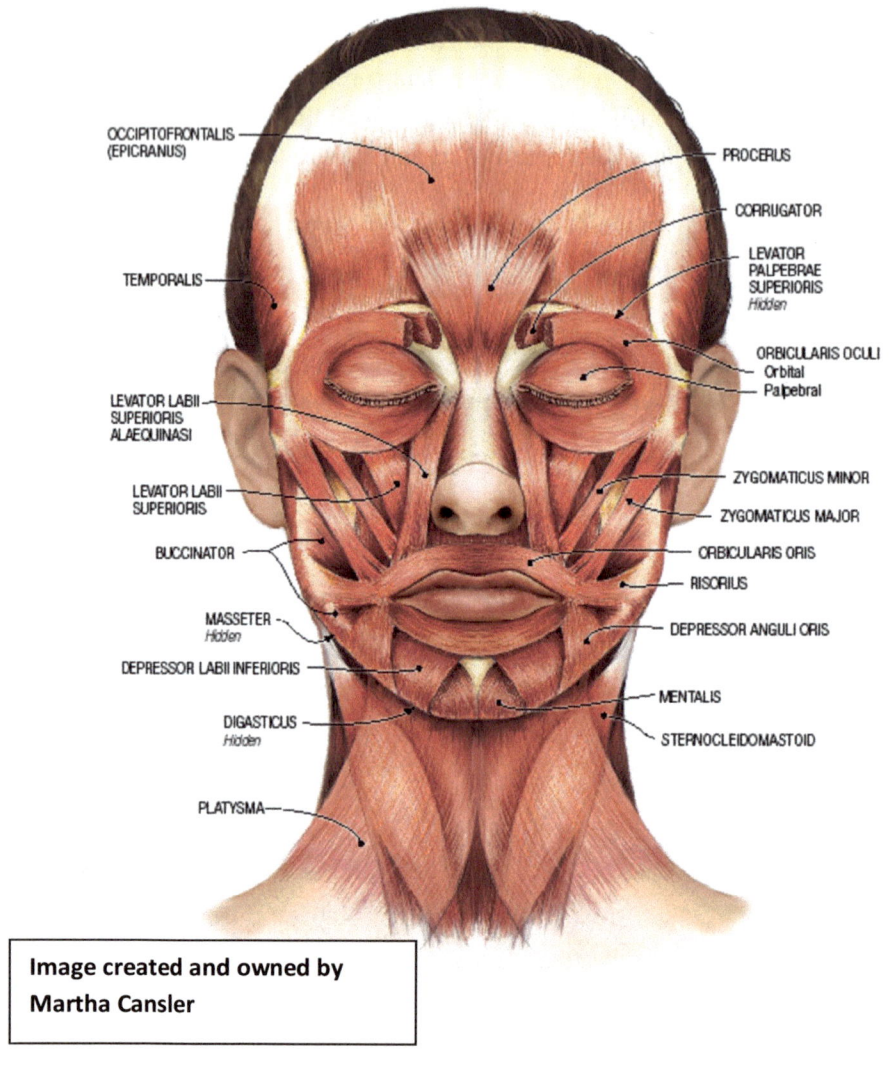

Image created and owned by Martha Cansler

RESTORATIVE ART: FOUNDATION & PRACTICE: CHAPTER 5

Chapter Learning Objectives

Upon completion of the study of this chapter students should:

- Understand the impact of muscular anatomy on personal appearance
- Be able to identify and describe the muscles of the cranium, facial expression, mouth, and anterior cheek
- Be able to demonstrate the influence on surface form for each muscle of the cranium and face
- Be able to identify the points of origin and insertion for this collection of muscles
- Understand the function associated with this collection of muscles

Grasping an understanding of what contributes to individual appearance is fundamental knowledge for a restorative artist. Chapter four presented the foundation regarding appearance and skeletal anatomy, as related to restorative art. This chapter introduces muscular anatomy as related to restorative art; the bones and muscles no doubt provide a base considering personal appearance. Some muscles have very specific functions while others may simply serve in a capacity to provide bulk and surface contour. This chapter continues the layering process that contributes to appearance. Our focal point, the head and face, lead us to a presentation of muscles of form and expression important to restorative art. It is essential to understand the impact of repetitive action of muscles on surface form. The continual contraction of muscles leaves markings on the face. These "wrinkles" run transverse to muscle fibers (see image on the following page). These markings will be more pronounced on emaciated individuals and less pronounced on people with large amounts of adipose tissue. Also, note that the loss of muscle tone will cause an increase in sagging tissues. An impact on our work may be the reality that the normal gravitational pull on living people is inferior, and when we place these individuals in a viewing position the gravitational pull tends toward a posterior direction. This can cause a change of appearance; in exaggerated cases, it may have a similar impact to a mini face lift, tightening the facial tissues of the deceased. This topic will be fully explored in Chapter Six, Surface Facial Markings. The current chapter explores muscles of the cranium, face, and neck that influence form.

RESTORATIVE ART: FOUNDATION & PRACTICE: CHAPTER 5

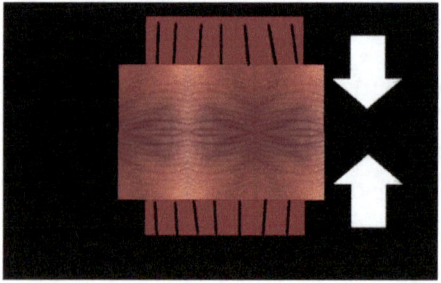

Wrinkles run transverse to muscle fibers

Origin versus Insertion

As one considers the impact of muscles on personal appearance, it is beneficial to recall that the muscle origin is the point that moves the least, and the insertion point, or attachment is the part that moves the most.

Muscles of the Cranium

Occipitofrontalis (Epicranius) –The muscle that draws the scalp posteriorly and anteriorly and raises the eyebrows.

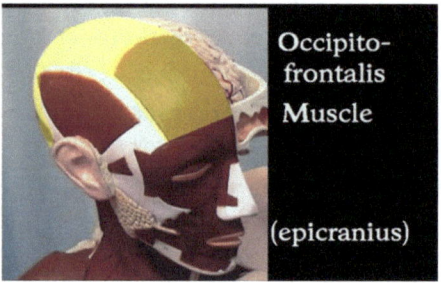

Component parts

- Frontal Belly – Muscle over the frontal bone
- Galea Aponeurotica – Tendonous sheet that connects the belly muscles
- Occipital Belly – Muscle over the occipital bone

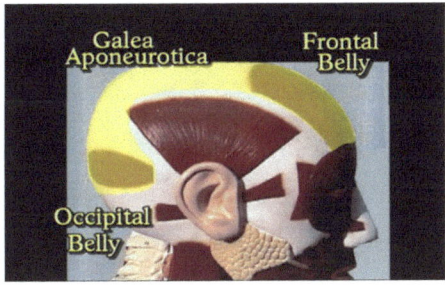

Important Information & Influence on Surface Form & Expression - Occipitofrontalis

- The two broad bellies of this muscle, located anterior and posterior, are connected by the flat fibrous connective tissue known as the galea aponeutrotica.
- Origin & Insertion – The occipital belly originates at the posterior base of the cranium, and inserts into the galea aponeurotica. The frontal belly originates with the galea aponeurotica and inserts into muscle fibers located above the eyes.

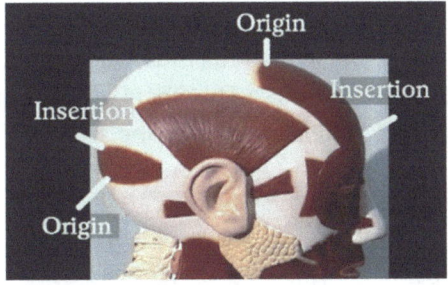

- Function – The occipitofrontalis muscle draws the scalp posteriorly and anteriorly and raises the eyebrows.
- Effect on Surface Form – The transverse frontal sulci result from continual contraction of this muscle.

RESTORATIVE ART: FOUNDATION & PRACTICE: CHAPTER 5

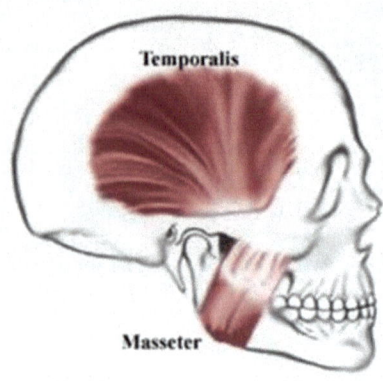

The Muscles of Mastication; Temporalis & Masseter

Temporalis Muscle (2) – Muscles of mastication, which help to close the mandible, are considered the strongest chewing muscles. The temporalis muscles are broad, fan-shaped muscles that are located along the temporal bone.

Important Information & Influence on Surface Form & Expression - Temporalis

- These muscles serve to raise the lower jaw (mandible) to contact the teeth of the maxilla. Although these muscles do not have a great impact on surface form, they do provide some bulk in the temporal cavity.
- Origin & Insertion – The temporalis muscles originate at along the temporal bone, the entire temporal fossa. The fibers of these muscles converge into tendon, which passes behind the zygomatic arch and insert into the coronoid process of the mandible.

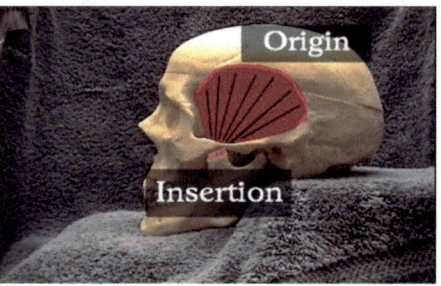

Masseter Muscle (2) – Muscles of mastication which close the mandible. The masseter muscles locate along the side of the face, below the zygomatic arch.

Important Information & Influence on Surface Form & Expression - Masseter

- These muscles serve to close the mandible (mastication) and provide bulk to the side of the cheek. The anterior borders are responsible for the

divisions of the lateral surface of the cheek. Also note that along the anterior border lies the buccofacial sulcus.
- The origin of the masseter is the anterior two-thirds of the zygomatic arch and the lower border of the cheekbone. The angle of the jaw and the lower half of the ramus serve as the insertion points of this muscle.

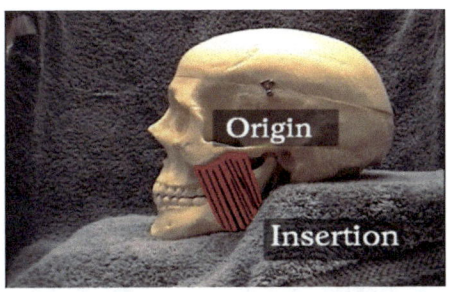

Muscles of Eyes and Facial Expression

Orbicularis Oculi Muscle (2) – The muscles that closes the eyelids; compresses the lacrimal sacs. These are sphincter muscles that surround the eyelids. The fibers merge with adjacent muscles of the forehead, temple, and cheek.

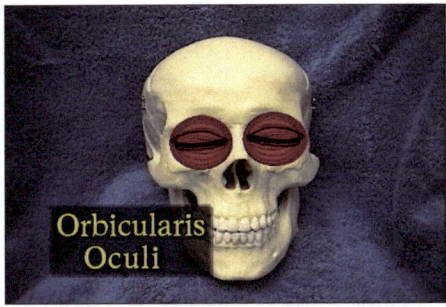

Important Information & Influence on Surface Form & Expression – Orbicularis Oculi

- These muscles serve to close the eyelids.
- Origin & Insertion – The orbicularis oculi muscles originate along the bony margins of the eyesockets; this includes both the frontal and maxillary bones. To insert, these muscles circle the orbit and extend within the eyelids.

- Through the continual contraction of these muscles during life, the skin at the lateral corner of the eye is folded which results in the development of the optic facial sulci (crow's feet).

Corrugator – Pyramid-shaped muscles of facial expression which draws the eyebrows inferiorly and medially. These muscles are located on the medial end of the eyebrows.

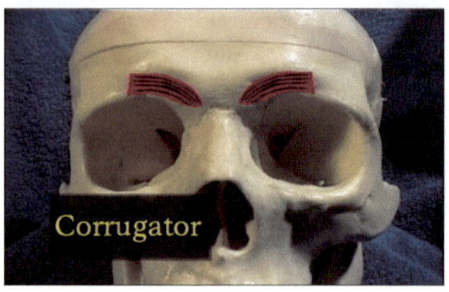

Important Information & Influence on Surface Form & Expression - Corrugator

- These muscles draw the eyebrows inferiorly and medially when contracted, sometimes referred to as the "frowning muscle."
- Origin & Insertion – The corrugator muscles originate near the root of the nose (at the bone) where it is covered by the frontalis and orbicularis oculi muscles. These muscles extend superiorly and laterally through the fibers of the orbicularis and frontalis muscles and insert into the skin at the middle of the eyebrow.
- The continual movement of these muscles produces the vertical interciliary sulci.

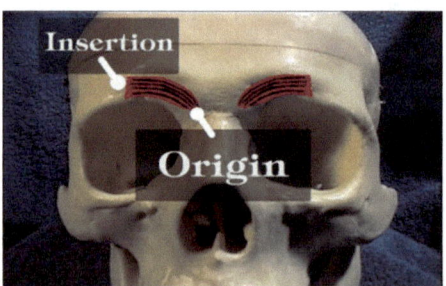

RESTORATIVE ART: FOUNDATION & PRACTICE: CHAPTER 5

Levator Palpebrae Superioris – Muscles of facial expression, which raises the upper eyelid. These are flat muscles that are located above the eyeball and serve to elevate the superior palpebrae.

Important Information & Influence on Surface Form & Expression – Levator Palpebrae Superioris

- These muscles elevate the superior palpebrae.
- Origin & Insertion – The levator palpebrae superioris originates deep in the roof of the orbit of the eye, and the fibers of these muscles extend inferiorly into the superior palpebrae and insert into the skin and superior tarsus.
- During the aging process, the continual movement of these muslces help form the palpebral fold across the superior palpebrae, along the superior tarsus.
- Restorative Note: When it becomes difficult to close the upper eyelid properly, this muscle may be severed from beneath the eyelid to offer more movement of the eyelid.

Muscles of the Nose

Procerus – The muscle that draws the skin of the forehead inferiorly and is located on the nasal bones

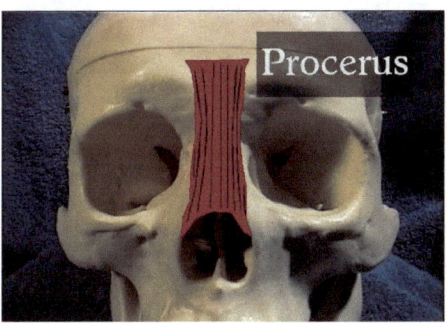

Important Information & Influence on Surface Form & Expression - Procerus

- This muscle, when contracted, draws the skin of the nose inferiorly. The muscle is located on the nasal bones.
- Origin & Insertion – The inferior margins of the anterior plane of the nasal bones serve as the muscle origin. The fibers extend superiorly and insert into the fibers of the frontalis muscle and the skin between the eyebrows.

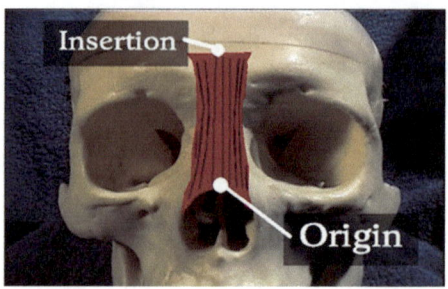

- When contracted, the muscle draws together skin on the nose to form the transverse interciliary sulci (transverse furrows across the bridge of the nose).

Muscles of the Mouth

Orbicularis Oris – The muscle that closes and puckers the lips. This muscle encircles the mouth and has many strands of fibers radiating in different directions.

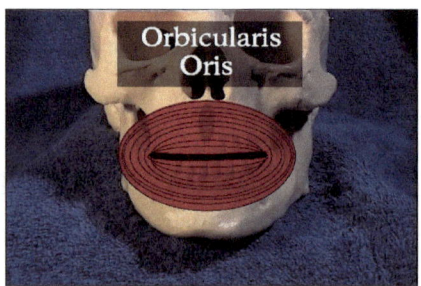

Important Information & Influence on Surface Form & Expression – Orbicularis Oris

- This muscle, which covers the entire area between the base of the nose and the top of the chin, when contracted, closes the mouth and can pucker the lips.
- Origin & Insertion – The muscle surrounding the mouth serves as both the origin and insertion points for the orbicularis oris
- This muscle is also sometimes referred to as the kissing or puckering muscle.

- The fibers interweave with all other muscles of the mouth. This reality explains the high degree of mobility of expression related to this part of the face, the mouth is known as the "Center of Expression" for the deceased.
- The Philtrum, the vertical groove located medially on the superior integumentary lip (a natural facial marking), is formed within the skin and the orbicularis oris muscle by the muscle fibers and their attachment to the skin.

Muscles Converging at the Corner of the Mouth

Zygomaticus Major (2) – The muscles of the face, which draw the superior lip posteriorly and superiorly.

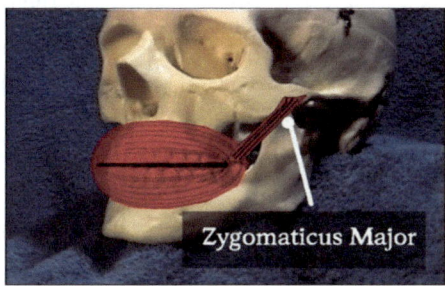

Important Information & Influence on Surface Form & Expression – Zygomaticus Major

- Located from the cheeks to the corner of the mouth, these muscles draw the superior lip posteriorly and superiorly.
- The function of this muscle is raising the corners of the mouth.
- The zygomaticus major is appropriately also known as "the laughing muscle".
- The posterior margin of the zygomatic bones serves as the origin of this muscle, and the muscle inserts into the skin and muscles at the angle of the mouth.
- This muscle creates the angulus oris eminence and also helps to produce the distinction of the nasolabial fold.

Buccinator (2) – The principle muscle of the cheek, which compresses the cheeks and forms the lateral wall of the mouth.

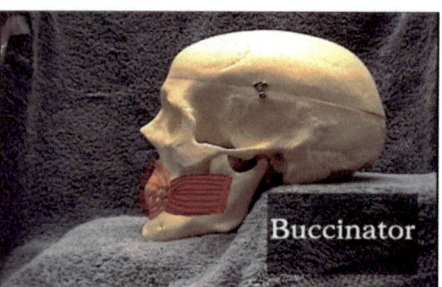

Important Information & Influence on Surface Form & Expression - Buccinator

- The buccinator is a thin, broad muscle that lines the cheek horizontally.
- This muscle compresses the cheek, retracts the angle of the mouth, and forms the lateral wall of the mouth. When contracted, the buccinator draws the corner of the mouth posteriorly.
- Resulting from the function of this muscle, it is also known as the "trumpeters muscle".
- The alveolar processes of the mandible and maxillary bones serve as the origination location for this muscle, and the muscle inserts into the orbicularis oris and the skin at the angle of the mouth.
- The buccinator also helps to form the angulus oris eminence, and the Bucco-facial Sulcus may form in this area.

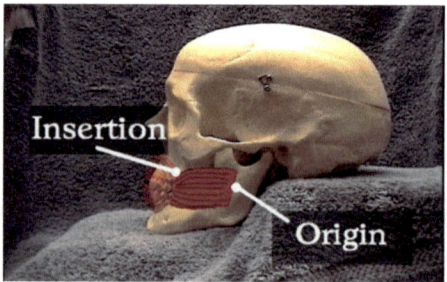

Depressor Anguli Oris (Triangularis) (2) – A muscle of facial expression which depresses the angle of the mouth.

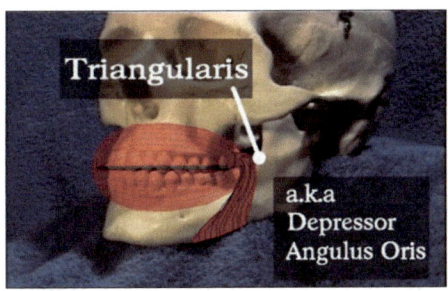

Important Information & Influence on Surface Form & Expression – Depressor Anguli Oris

- This muscle is located below the angle of the mouth. When contracted, the depressor anguli oris depresses the corner of the mouth.
- This muscle originates along the line of the jaw, and inserts into skin and muscles at the angle of the mouth.
- The depressor angulus oris helps to develop the angulus oris eminence.

Muscles of the Mouth and Anterior Cheek

Quadratus Labii Superioris (2) – In actuality, this is a multi-headed group of muscles that is constructed of the three following muscles: Levator Labii Superioris Alaeque Nasi, Levator Labii Superioris, and the Zygomaticus Minor. Here, we will look at the three muscles that compromise the entire group. The name quadratus is thus derived from the cumulative shape of the muscle group, not the number of muscles included.

> **Levator Labii Superioris Alaeque Nasi** – A muscle of facial expression that elevates the upper lip and dilates the nostril opening; the common elevator.
>
> **Levator Labii Superioris** – A muscle of facial expression which elevates and extends the upper lip.
>
> **Zygomaticus Minor** – Muscle of the face, which draw the superior lip superiorly and anteriorly.

Important Information & Influence on Surface Form & Expression – Quadratus Labii Superioris

- This muscle grouping, the Quadratus Labii Superioris, is below each eye along the cheek.
- The entire group serves to raise the upper lip.
- The grouping originates at the maxilla and zygomatic bones and inserts into the orbicularis oris muscle and the skin at the superior margin of the upper lip, between the wing of the nose and the corner of the mouth.
- This muscle grouping helps form the nasolabial sulcus.

Levator Anguli Oris - A muscle of facial expression that elevates the angle of the mouth.

Important Information & Influence on Surface Form & Expression – Levator Anguli Oris

- This muscle is located below the quadratus labii superioris, located in the region of the canine tooth.
- The levator anguli oris raises the corner of the mouth when contracted.
- This muscle originates at the canine fossa and inserts into the angle of the mouth where the muscle fibers intermingle with the other muscles in this region.
- This muscle contributes to the formation of the nasolabial fold and the angulus oris eminence.

Risorius - The narrow, superficial band of muscles, which pull the angle of the mouth laterally.

Important Information & Influence on Surface Form & Expression - Risorius

- This muscle is located on the anterior and lateral cheek.
- This narrow band of muscle draws the corners of the mouth laterally, "false smiling".
- This muscle originates in the fascia over the masseter muscle and inserts into the skin at the angle of the mouth.
- The risorius helps create the lateral cheek wall.

RESTORATIVE ART: FOUNDATION & PRACTICE: CHAPTER 5

Depressor Labii Inferioris - A muscle of facial expression that draws the lower lip inferiorly and slightly lateral.

Important Information & Influence on Surface Form & Expression – Depressor Labii Inferioris

- The depressor labii inferioris is also known as the quadratus muscle.
- This muscle, located below the corners of the mouth, when contracted, depresses the lower lip.
- The muscle originates at the base and side of the chin, and inserts into the skin of the lower lip.
- This muscle serves as a space filler, changes the form of the line of closure of the mouth, and causes the Angulus Oris Sulcus to assume an oblique form.

Mentalis - The muscle that elevates and protrudes the inferior lip and wrinkles the skin over the chin.

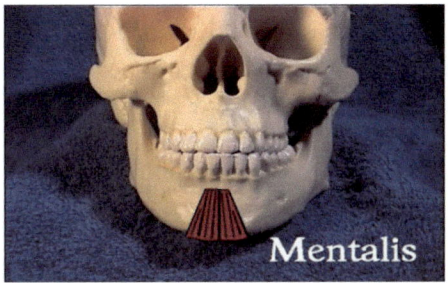

Important Information & Influence on Surface Form & Expression - Mentalis

- This muscle, located on the chin, serves to elevate and protrude the inferior lip, and wrinkle the skin over the chin.
- The mentalis muscle moves the chin superiorly.
- The muscle originates on top of the chin at the bone and inserts into the skin at the base of the chin.
- The mass of this muscle causes the chin to have a greater anterior projection.
- The external projection of the chin is called the "prominence of the chin".
- When some fibers of the mentalis muscle attach into, and hold down, the median plane of the chin, it forms either a dimple or a cleft in the external surface. If the cleft extends downward enough to separate the surface into two lobes, it is referred to as a bilobated chin.

Muscles of the Neck

Platysma – Thin layer of muscle covering the anterior aspect of the neck.

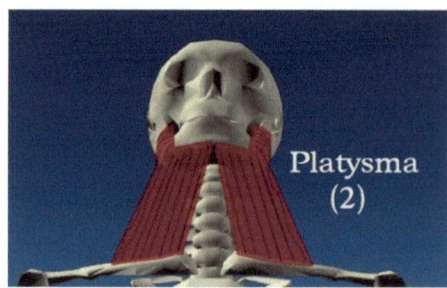

Important Information & Influence on Surface Form & Expression - Platysma

- This muscle is a thin, flat, and very large sheet of muscle that lines the skin on both sides of the anterior surface of the neck.
- The platysma wrinkles the skin of the neck and chest and depresses the mandible and inferior lip.
- The muscle originates at the collar bone and the muscle fibers extend upward and forward to the lower jaw. The muscle then inserts into skin of the lateral cheek, lower lip, and the corners of the mouth.
- As people age, the platysma loses muscle tone and the skin starts to sag. This loss of muscle tone contributes to the formation of several facial markings; these include the bucco-facial sulcus, mandibular sulcus, serrated jawline, and the platysmal sulci.

Sternocleidomastoid (SCM) - A muscle of the neck that is attached to the mastoid process of the temporal bone and by separate heads to the sternum and clavicle; marks the widest part of the neck.

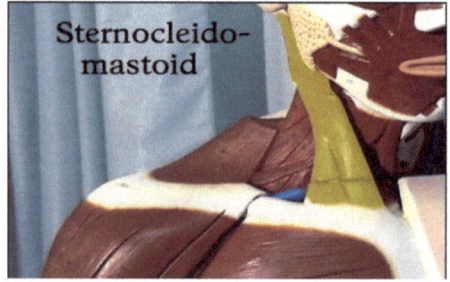

Restorative Art: Foundation & Practice: Chapter 5

Important Information & Influence on Surface Form & Expression - Sternocleidomastoid

- The SCM is a long, fleshy muscle that helps give form to the side of the neck and lowers the head.
- The muscle originates at the pit of the neck (sternum and clavicle) and inserts into the mastoid process of the temporal bone.
- The widest part of the neck is measured from one belly of the SCM to the other.
- Note: The right common carotid may be found medially and deep from the right SCM.

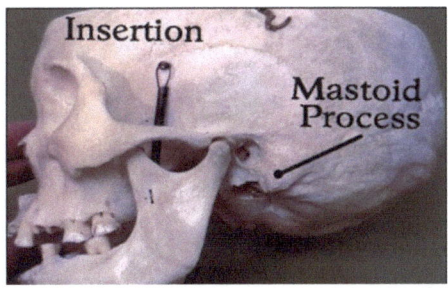

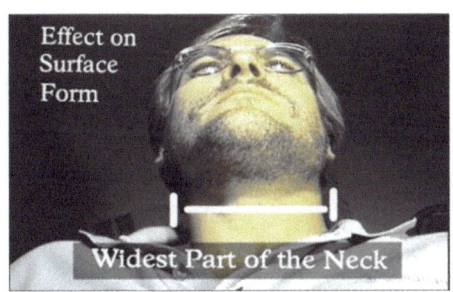

Restorative Art: Foundation & Practice: Chapter 5

Digastric – A double-bellied muscle that draws the hyoid bone superiorly.

Important Information & Influence on Surface Form & Expression - Digastric

- The digastric is located below the body of the mandible; it is a double-bellied muscle that draws the hyoid bone superiorly.
- This muscle helps to manipulate the tongue.
- The muscle originates behind and below the incisor teeth of the mandible and inserts into the hyoid bone.
- This muscle helps to form the cords of the neck.

Chapter Conclusion

The fundamental purpose of this chapter was to provide additional information regarding elements that impact personal appearance. This chapter presented a collection of muscles including those of the cranium, facial expression, as well as the mouth and anterior cheek. For each muscle, information was delivered that explained the function and the influence on surface form and expression. Also, the component parts of each muscle were presented, and the origin and insertion points for the collection of muscles were identified. The next chapter expands on the journey to discover elements that contribute to personal appearance; chapter six explores subcutaneous tissues, integument, and facial markings.

References

Professional Experience and Educational Presentations:
A great deal of the content of this book has been derived from years of professional experience as an embalmer, funeral director, and funeral service educator.

Drake, R. L., Vogl, W., Mitchell, A. W. M., & Gray, H. (2005). *Gray's anatomy for students.* Philadelphia: Elsevier/Churchhill Livingstone.

Klicker, R. (2002). *Restorative art and science.* Buffalo, NY: Thanos Institute.

Mayer, J. S. (1980). *Restorative art.* Dallas, TX: Professional Training Schools.

Mayer, R. G. (2012). *Embalming: History, theory, and practice* (5th ed.). New York, NY: McGraw-Hill.

Chapter Six

Subcutaneous Tissues, Integument, and Facial Markings

Chapter Learning Objectives

Upon completion of the study of this chapter students should:

- Be able to define various subcutaneous tissues including fascia, glands, and adipose
- Understand what is referred to as integument tissues, including derma and epidermis
- Be able to list the factors responsible for creating facial markings
- Be able to identify factors that contribute to the formation of facial markings
- Have knowledge related to the description of various facial markings
- Be able to describe the classifications of facial markings, both the nine natural facial markings and the eleven acquired facial markings

The previous two chapters presented elements of skeletal and muscular anatomy related to restorative art. The placement of these chapters was intentional; the central purpose has been to help the reader grasp elements related to individual appearance. The skills required to excel as a restorative artist are reliant upon an understanding of the elements that influence human appearance. In an effort to fully explore the connection between the bones, muscles, tissues, and surface appearance, we now explore tissues and identifying facial markings. Here, we identify subcutaneous tissues, integument, and then fully explore facial markings.

Subcutaneous Tissues Defined

Subcutaneous is defined as situated or occurring beneath the skin.

Fascia – Layer of areolar tissue covering the whole muscle trunk

Glands - a specialized cell, group of cells, or organ of endothelial origin that selectively removes materials from the blood, concentrates or alters them, and secretes them for further use in the body or for elimination from the body

Adipose – Loose connective tissue full of fat cells

RESTORATIVE ART: FOUNDATION & PRACTICE: CHAPTER 6

Integument Considered

Integument describes something that covers or encloses, especially an enveloping layer such as skin, membrane, or cuticle, of an organism or one of its parts.

Derma (dermis, skin) – The corium, or true skin

Epidermis – The outermost layer of skin; the cuticle or scarf skin

Facial Markings

As we consider **identifying facial markings**, the character lines of the face and neck: wrinkles, grooves, cords, and dimples, we need to state that these markings are caused by muscles and are classified as either natural or acquired. These markings are unique by nature, and numerous factors are responsible for the exact appearance of these markings. First, we will examine factors that impact the appearance of facial markings, and then we will consider each of the identifying facial markings, both the nine natural facial markings and the eleven acquired markings.

Factors Responsible for Facial Markings

Muscles create identifying facial markings through attachments and continual movement, but several items influence the significance or lack thereof of these markings. It is beneficial to the restorative artist to remain mindful that facial markings exhibit asymmetry (neither natural nor acquired facial markings that occur on both sides of the face are truly symmetrical), and that the termination of all facial markings is indefinite. Here, we consider these influential elements.

Heredity – The transmission of genetic characteristics from parents to offspring is one way of describing heredity, and this no doubt influences the appearance of facial markings. People tend to exhibit similar appearances as their parents, and this includes identifying facial markings.

Age – The influence of time. Facial muscles continually move facial tissues over the course of a lifetime. These repetitive motions initiate the creation of the acquired facial markings. Typically, as people age, the number of facial markings increase. It is also common for the appearance of these markings to intensify over time.

Environment – Central to influencing facial markings are dry climates that experience high levels of sunshine. When skin is exposed to significant levels of sunshine, it serves to dry the tissue, which will foster and accentuate facial markings. Individuals that are exposed to high levels of sunshine over time tend to have a heightened presentation of facial markings, a darker complexion with more markings; these markings tend to be well defined and firmly placed in the skin.

Muscle Striation and Action – The alignment of muscle fibers and the more we work our muscles impact facial markings. Muscle development, over time, can have various impacts on facial markings. Individuals with well-developed muscle mass may exhibit fewer markings initially, but when the muscle mass reduces over time, this may lead to sagging tissues, which would increase the number and intensity of facial markings.

Position of the Body – Note that during life (the body is in an erect position) the effect of gravity on sagging muscle and skin tissues draws them in an inferior direction. Over time, this appearance may become the "norm" appearance to family and friends. This is the appearance they are accustomed to when they see their loved one or friend.

When someone dies, and the body is in a supine position for embalming and/or for viewing, the gravitational pull on these tissues is in the posterior direction. This may impact the appearance of the individual; some have even claimed that these individuals look a little younger as the posterior pull on these tissues has caused the facial tissues to have a tighter appearance.

Condition of the Body – It is important to remain mindful that when people experience rapid weight loss, rapidly gain weight, take on water, or other conditions will impact the number and significance of facial markings. When people rapidly lose weight, the wrinkling and folding of the now excess tissues will impact appearance, many times making them appear older than reality. Consequently, bodies with large amounts of adipose tissue will exhibit fewer markings that appear less significant; they may appear to be younger than is the case. We also need to mention that many times we receive bodies that have been impacted by various pathological conditions or trauma. It is important that the restorative artist is vigilant to make sure that any markings that have been impacted by disease or trauma are appropriately reinstated through their restorative work.

Physiognomical Description of Facial Markings

Sulcus – A furrow, wrinkle, or groove

Furrow (wrinkle) – A crevice in the skin accompanied by adjacent elevations

Groove – An elongated depression in a relatively level plane or surface

RESTORATIVE ART: FOUNDATION & PRACTICE: CHAPTER 6

Fold – An elongated prominence adjoining a surface

Eminence – A prominence or projection

Classification of Facial Markings

Natural Facial Markings (9)

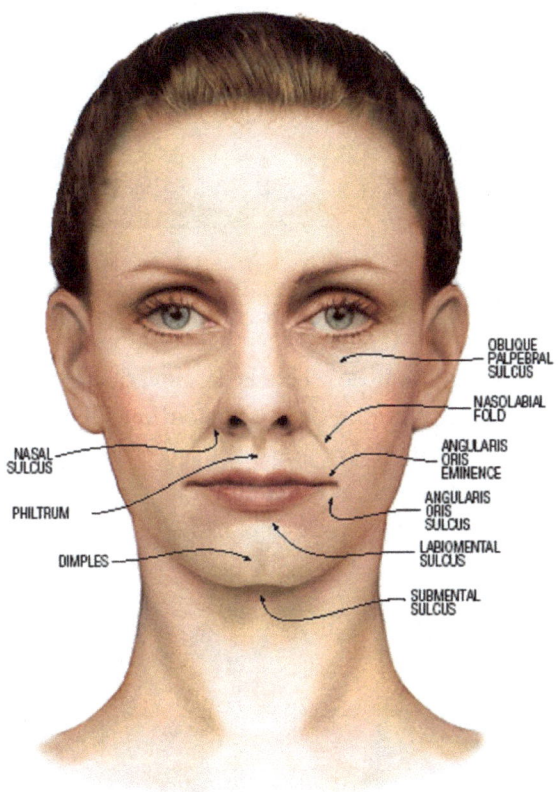

NATURAL FACIAL MARKINGS

NINE NATURAL FACIAL MARKINGS
- Oblique Palpebral Sulci
- Nasal Sulci
- Nasolabial Folds
- Philtrum
- Angularis Oris Eminence
- Angularis Oris Sulci
- Labiomental Sulcus
- Submental Sulcus

Image created and owned by Martha Cansler

The Natural Facial Markings (9)

Philtrum – This is the vertical groove located medially on the superior lip. The philtrum extends between the columna nasi and the margin of the red lip. The lateral margins are slightly raised as they form an unbalanced parenthetical curvature. The widest separation of the curvature of the lateral margins typically coincides with the location of the deepest part of the groove. Note: the philtrum may be obscured in extreme old age.

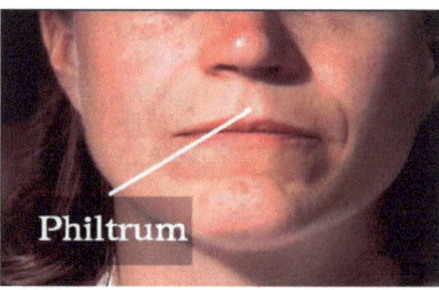

Nasolabial Fold – The anterior fold of the cheek which descends laterally along the upper lip from the wing of the nose. This is an elevation of the anterior cheek and typically exhibits a curved, straight, or sinuous outline. The degree of elevation varies in proportion to the amount of adipose tissue within the cheek. This marking is often associated with the creation of an individual's "norm" and therefore it is critical that restorative artists take time to recreate these markings if they have been distorted or damaged.

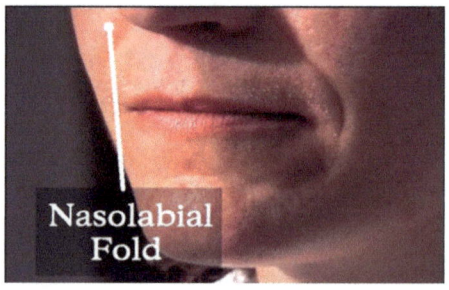

Nasal Sulcus – This is the angular area between the posterior margin of the wing of the nose and the nasolabial fold and sometimes described as an angular depression in the uppermost part of the upper lip. The corner of the angle is formed by the junction of the wing of the nose and the nasolabial fold.

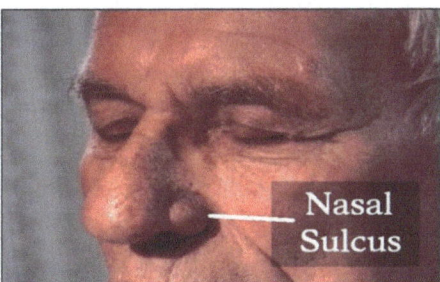

Oblique Palpebral Sulcus – This is a shallow, curved groove below the medial corner of the eyelids. It forms the common border for the medial portion of the infra-orbital area and the side of the nose. This marking typically originates immediately below the medial canthus and extends along the bony margin of the orbit, fading in depth, normally terminating near the middle of the eye.

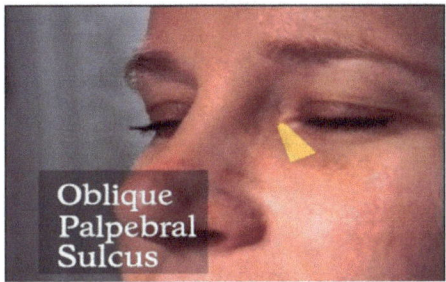

Angulus Oris Eminence – The small convex prominence found lateral to the end of the line of closure of the mouth. This elevation is located to the outer side and slightly above the corner of the mouth, and is formed by the combined insertions of the zygomatic, buccinator, and depressor anguli oris muscles.

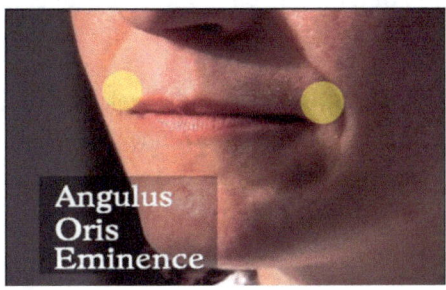

Angulus Oris Sulcus – The groove found at each end of the line of closure of the mouth, immediately below each end of the line of closure of the mouth. The corner of the angular depression corresponds with the corner of the mouth, and the lateral margins are directed downward and outward along the adjoining elevation of the angulus oris eminence, and the medial margin is relatively undefined as it merges into the inferior integumentary lip. The size and depth of this marking varies depending on the degree of prominence of the angulus oris eminence. In youth, this facial marking tends to exhibit a triangular depression formation.

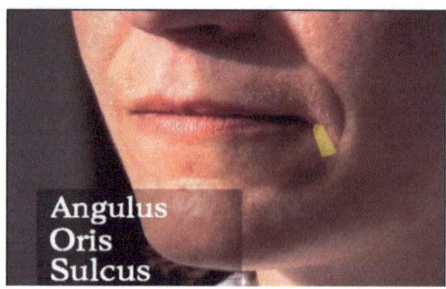

Labiomental Sulcus – This is the junction of the lower integumentary lip and the superior border of the chin, which may appear as a furrow. The linear form of this sulcus creates an arch with the uppermost part at the median line.

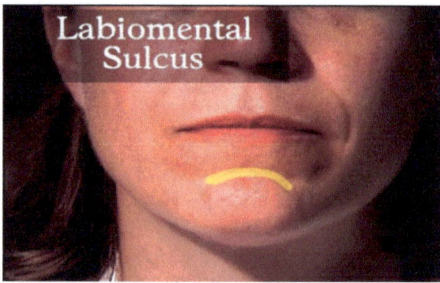

Submental Sulcus – This describes the junction of the base of the chin and the submandibular area, which may appear as a furrow. This furrow may help contribute to the formation of a double chin and is most perceptible in the profile view.

Dimples – Shallow depressions located on the cheek or chin in a rounded or vertical form. Cheek dimples appear on a transverse plane with the line of closure of the lips; the precise location varies from person to person. Chin dimples typically form on the median line. An elongated chin dimple is referred to as a cleft. If such a cleft extends enough to create two distinct lobes, this is referred to as a bilobated chin.

RESTORATIVE ART: FOUNDATION & PRACTICE: CHAPTER 6

Acquired facial Markings (11)

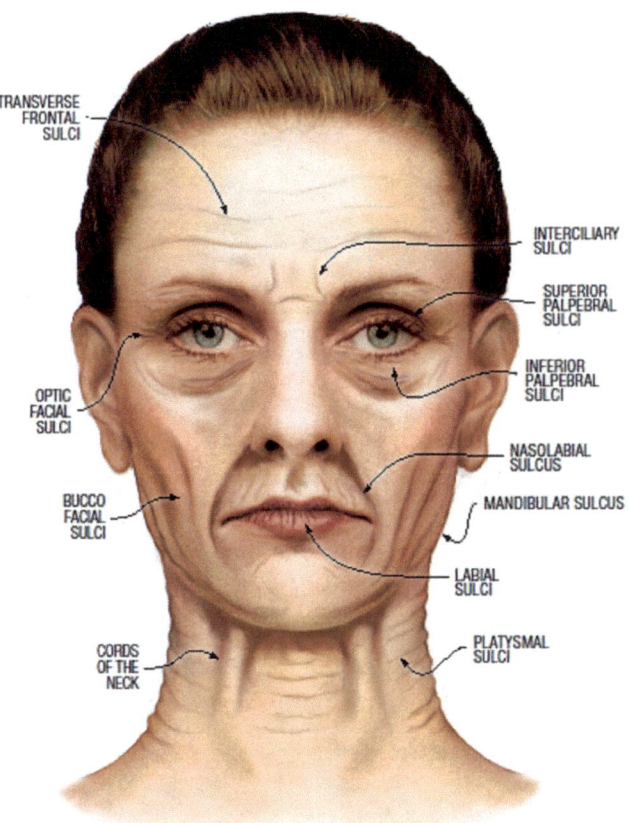

Image created and owned by Martha Cansler

The Acquired Facial Markings (11)

Nasolabial Sulcus – This furrow is medial and adjacent to the nasolabial fold. This marking originates with the nasolabial fold at the superior margin of the wing of the nose and may extend downward along the margin of the nasolabial fold.

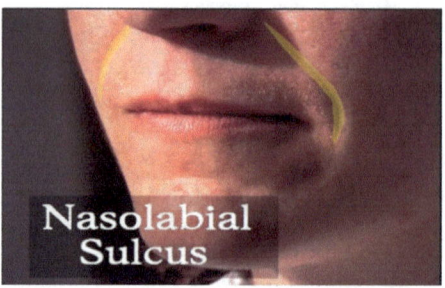

Transverse Frontal Sulci – These are the furrows which cross the forehead, also known as the horizontal furrows of the forehead. These sulci vary in width, depth, curvature, and inclination. They may be continuous across the forehead or be interrupted, and commonly, the depth of these lines diminishes as they taper towards the terminating ends. A common form exhibited by these sulci indicates a dip in curvature in the central plane of the forehead, and usually the markings closer to the eyebrows appear deeper than the more superior ones.

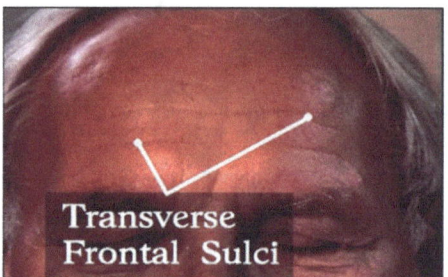

Interciliary Sulci – These sulci are the vertical or transverse furrows between the eyebrows. The vertical interciliary sulci have been further described as one or more vertical or slightly oblique furrows that extend from the root of the nose, superiorly, between the eyebrows to terminate indefinitely into the glabella. These markings are the result of the continual contraction of the corrugator muscle. The transverse interciliary sulci are specifically described as one or more horizontal or slightly oblique furrows located between the root of the nose and the dip at the bridge. These markings are created by the continual contraction of the procerus muscle.

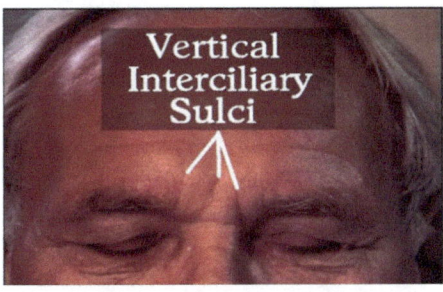

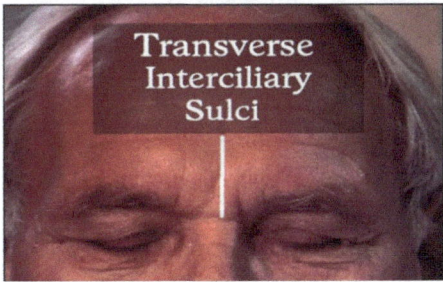

Optic Facial Sulci (Crow's feet) – These furrows radiate from the lateral corner of the eye. They develop from the contractions of the orbicularis oculi muscle. These are generally the first acquired facial markings to appear.

Superior Palpebral Sulcus – This is the furrow of the superior border of the upper eyelid. This furrow defines the upper border when present, as it is typically only obvious when there is an absence of fatty tissue in the supra-orbital area and when the superficial tissues are relatively firm. This sulcus may be partially obscured by sagging of the superficial tissues from the supraorbital area if the person has experienced a combination of loss of fatty tissue, muscle tone, and tissue elasticity.

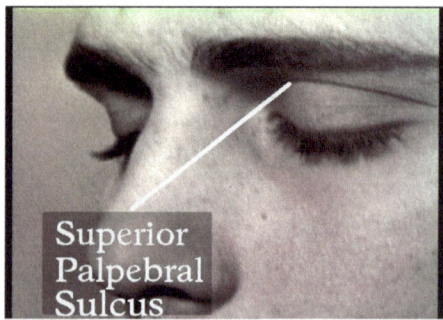

Inferior Palpebral Sulcus – This is the furrow of the lower attached border of the inferior palpebra. This sulcus is not always present, especially when tissues are firm. When visible, it appears as thin, shallow, arched sulci along the attached margin of the inferior eyelid.

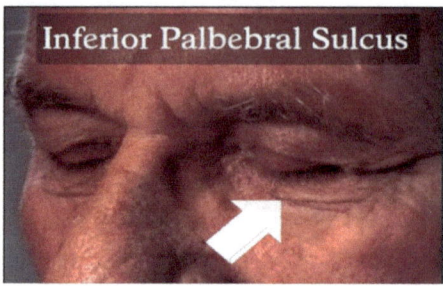

Bucco-Facial Sulcus – This is a vertical furrow of the cheek. This sulcus originates in the soft middle area of the lateral cheek and is caused by the contractions of the buccinator muscle. The bucco-facial sulcus may start as a short vertical furrow and throughout aging it may continue to mature and extend both in a superior and inferior direction. Superiorly it may curve under and in front of the cheekbone to merge with the oblique palpebral sulcus. Inferiorly, over time, it may merge with the mandibular sulcus. The extension of this sulcus into the anterior cheek and down the line of the jaw may be the result of the loss of adipose tissue, muscle tone, and tissue elasticity.

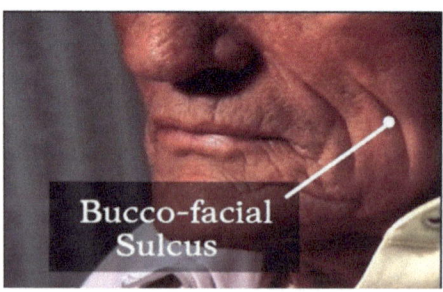

Mandibular Sulcus – This is the furrow beneath the jawline, which rises vertically on the cheek. If multiple formations of the sulci are present, it is referred to as a serrated jaw line. The term serrated is used as it describes the angular notches that separate the multiple folds of sagging skin.

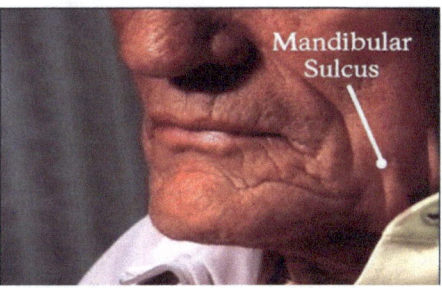

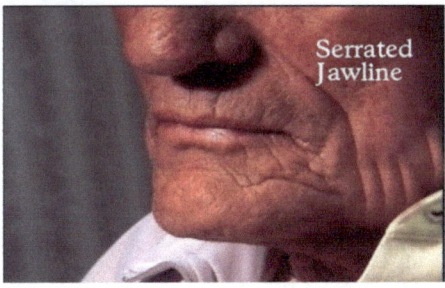

Labial Sulci (furrows of age) – The vertical furrows of each lip extending from within the mucous membranes into the integumentary lips. These commonly first occur in the upper lip. These sulci form as the lip begins to atrophy, and they extend from within the red lip into the integumentary lip.

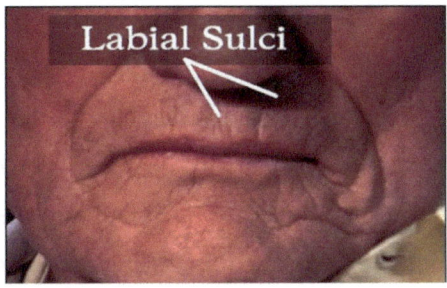

Platysmal Sulci – These sulci are the transverse, dipping furrows of the neck. They run across both the front and sides of the neck.

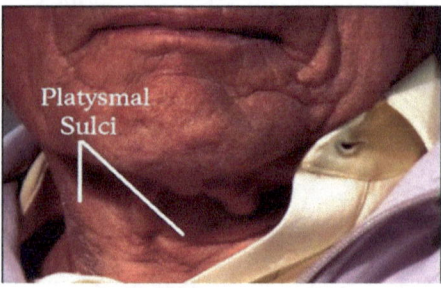

Cords of the Neck – These are the vertical prominences of the neck. On thin, emaciated individuals, the cords of the neck may run to the sternum.

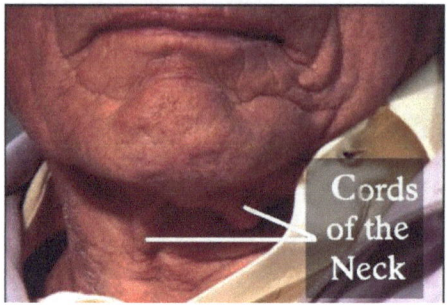

Chapter Conclusion

This chapter explored various classifications of tissues and then delved into an in-depth presentation of facial markings. The chapter started with information related to various subcutaneous tissues including fascia, glands, and adipose. Then integument was discussed, both derma and epidermis. Next, the reader was exposed to facial markings. Factors responsible for these markings as well as factors that contribute to markings were covered. The study of this chapter then turned to the actual classifications of the facial markings. Detailed information about the nine natural facial markings and the eleven acquired facial markings concluded the information covered in this chapter. The next chapter will explore the value and interpretation of photographs, facial proportions, facial profiles, facial shapes, and the bilateral appearance of facial features.

References

Professional Experience and Educational Presentations:
A great deal of the content of this book has been derived from years of professional experience as an embalmer, funeral director, and funeral service educator.

Klicker, R. (2002). *Restorative art and science*. Buffalo, NY: Thanos Institute.

Mayer, J. S. (1980). *Restorative art*. Dallas, TX: Professional Training Schools.

Mayer, R. G. (2012). *Embalming: History, theory, and practice* (5th ed.).

New York, NY: McGraw-Hill.

Prager, G. J. (1955). *Postmortem restorative art*. Amelia, OH: G. Joseph Prager.

Spriggs, A. O. (1964). *Champion restorative art* (6th ed.). Springfield, OH: The

Champion Company.

Chapter Seven

Value and Interpretation of Photographs, Facial Proportions, Facial Profiles, Facial Shapes, & the Bilateral Appearance of Facial Features

Chapter Learning Objectives

Upon completion of the study of this chapter students should:

- Understand the value of photographs to the restorative process and be able to appropriately interpret various photographs
- Comprehend the impact of facial proportions on restorative art and be able to apply this knowledge in practice
- Be able to categorize facial profiles, identify the characteristics associated with various profiles, and understand the most and least common profiles
- Understand and recognize the various facial shapes, and have knowledge related to the most and least common shapes
- Understand the bilateral appearance of facial features and comprehend the importance of this reality as it relates to restorative art

This chapter presents fundamental aspects associated with restorative art. In order to be a qualified restorative artist, one must grasp a general understanding of the value and interpretation of photographs, facial profiles, facial shapes, and the bilateral appearance of facial features. After we examine these topics, the following unit will explore specific features and associated restorative techniques, followed by general restorative techniques. The foundation established in this chapter will allow you to comprehend the full understanding of the restorative treatments that are explored in the next three chapters.

Value and Interpretation of Photographs

Obtaining recent, detailed photographs is central to delivering skilled, meaningful restorations. Photographs not only provide detail of the "norm" but also represent family expectations; they provide the restorative artist with a goal. As a general rule, it is best to try to secure photographs for general cosmetic work, hair preparation, and other restorations. It is advised to secure the most recent photo available, as facial characteristics may exhibit dramatic changes over time. Furthermore, utilizing mathematical computations, you can determine the size of a missing feature using photographs.

Mathematical Computations

As mentioned above, using mathematical computations you can determine the size of missing features with the aid of a photo. Here, we offer these two methods: the proportion method and the scale method.

The **proportion method** utilizes simple cross multiplication. In order to utilize this technique, you must have a quality, recent photograph and only be missing a certain part of the face or a feature. Here is the formula:

$$\frac{\text{Length of face or feature (PHOTO)}}{\text{Length of face or feature (BODY)}} = \frac{\text{Width of face or feature (PHOTO)}}{\text{Width of face or feature (BODY)}}$$

In order to calculate this equation, you must have three known items then solve for the one unknown. For example, if you have a body and you need to determine the actual width of the eye providing the length of the eye is known to be 20mm. You can then measure the length and width of the eye on the photo to isolate the single unknown. It is important to only use one photo to take the measurements, and always utilize the same unit of measurement; in our sample we utilize the millimeter as our unit of measurement. Given the information above, if the photo revealed a length or 10mm and a width of 5mm, here, we solve the equation to determine the width of the eye on the body.

$$\frac{10\text{mm}}{20\text{mm}} \times \frac{5\text{mm}}{\text{Unknown (X)}}$$

So, 10mm • X = 10Xmm and 5 • 20mm = 100mm

Therefore, 10Xmm = 100mm

Then, you must solve the equation to isolate X in order to determine the value. Set the equation up as:

$$\frac{10X\text{mm}}{10\text{mm}} = \frac{100\text{mm}}{10}$$

10Xmm divided by 10mm, the 10mm cancel each other out and leave you with an isolated X. 100 divided by 10 = 10mm. Therefore, X = 10mm. You have successfully determined the width of an eye to be 10mm utilizing cross multiplication, the proportion method.

The **scale method** works in the same way maps work to estimate "the actual distance" between two locations given the distance on a map, in essence a ratio. To use this method, the restorative artist needs to determine a "scale number" for the photograph that will be used to determine feature size on a body. Once this scale number is determined, you simply multiply the scale number with the length or width of a feature as measured in the photograph. Then, this information is used when working on the restoration. To determine the scale number, divide the width or length of a feature (BODY) by the width or length of a feature (PHOTO), here is the calculation:

$$\frac{\text{Width of feature (BODY)}}{\text{Width of feature (PHOTO)}}$$

RESTORATIVE ART: FOUNDATION & PRACTICE: CHAPTER 7

Here is an example. If you know that the width of the eye on the body is 30mm, and the width of the same eye on a photograph is 3mm, here is how you solve to determine a scale number:

$$\frac{30mm}{3mm} = 10mm$$

30mm divided by 3mm equals 10mm; therefore, the scale number for this situation is 10mm. This allows the restorative artist the ability to multiply any feature in this specific photograph by 10mm to determine the size of a missing feature. Note that this scale number is specific to this single photograph! Also, as with any mathematical computation to determine feature size, always be sure to use the same unit of measurement when completing and utilizing the calculations.

Considering various Images

It is well established that photographs are fundamental to the ability to deliver quality regarding the appearance of the deceased. It is best practice to obtain recent photos, as these will offer insight into the deceased's recent "norm". This is also crucial as facial features change throughout life, making recent photographs the most valuable to the restorative artist. Therefore, the best photographs for restorative purposes are recent, clear pictures that are not subjected to flat lighting, and it is best that these are not group pictures. At first consideration one may think any photo will do; this is far from the truth. Different types of pictures, perspectives, and age of photographs play a big role with respect to how valuable any particular photo will be in the restorative process. Here, we consider various images as well as photo perspectives.

A **Snapshot** is a casual photograph, typically taken quickly with a small personal handheld camera. As this is the age of the "smart phone", the most commonly taken snap shots are captured on personal phones. These images reveal details, natural imperfections, and they commonly expose the person in their "own" element. The best snapshots will be recent, clear photos that are not subjected to flat lighting and focused on the person of interest. In the past, funeral service professionals would indicate the importance of using a magnifying glass to enlarge photographs to detect detail. Contemporary funeral directors might ask what is a magnifying glass, as they are accustomed to enlarging digital images that were either sent via email to the funeral home or brought to the funeral home utilizing digital storage mediums. Be aware that people may bring snapshots that are group photographs, which may present a challenge to the restorative artist. Other considerations include bad lighting and things that might detract from the actual representation of the central figure of the arrangement. Items such as headwear, facial expressions (duck face, laughter or other silly facial expressions), sun glasses or other articles that might prevent the best representation of the person we are working to restore.

Professional portraits, a photograph of a person, especially of the face, taken by a professional photographer are often the images families select to bring into funeral homes when pictures of the deceased are requested. These photos no doubt have advantages, as they are often large, and focus on a single person, but they also have many disadvantages. The disadvantages include the possibility of enhanced studio lighting, to create ambiance or for corrective purposes. Furthermore, most professional pictures are airbrushed. They have been "touched up" so the image no longer reveals natural imperfections in order to enhance the person's appearance. As it is common practice to receive professional portraits from families, use these, as they offer insights into certain features, but also remember the disadvantages of these images, as they are often altered and do not fully reflect the current likeness of the deceased.

Digital images, by definition are a representation of a real image as a set of numbers that can be stored and handled by a digital computer. Typically, these produce high definition images that are easily modified and transferred via electronic medium. Most contemporary photographs are either originally shot using a digital device, or they are old images that have been modified to exist as digital images. As these images are inexpensive to store, most people now have quite a collection of digital images and are frequently documenting life experiences. Consequently funeral directors typically have more images made available to them when it comes time to prepare a body for visitation, viewing, or major restorations than in the past. Much like other photographs, the restorative artist must be sure the correct person is identified when a photo is of more than one person, and also be aware that even the novice photographer has access to cameras and many apps that can easily modify images. It is necessary to communicate with families to ascertain the exact likeness they desire when viewing the deceased.

Inversion of the photograph for detection of asymmetry has long been a suggested operation for embalmers and restorative artists. Why? This is a suggested technique because it closely resembles the view many embalmers have when operating from the standing above the head; an additional benefit is that this inverted view is less familiar to the restorative artist making it easier to detect asymmetrical forms that exist and may have been overlooked from the standard view.

Values of the **three-quarter view**, although not as beneficial as a profile image when considering anterior projection of the face and facial features, the three-quarter view is more commonly available to the restorative artist. The three-quarter view image suggests form of the profile and reveals the degree of fullness of the cheeks.

The **profile view** has the distinction of offering the most accurate displays of projections and recessions. Most families will not have a true profile photograph to provide to funeral directors, hence the significance of the three-quarter view.

The **frontal view**, common in photography, displays length and width relationships. These images serve to assist the restorative artist with respect to general hair and cosmetics as well as restorative treatments.

Considering Lighting

When considering various types of photographs and the possible advantages and disadvantages associated with these pictures related to restorative art, one must consider the impact of lighting. Lighting has a direct impact on the highlights and shadows that are present on individuals. Interpretation of highlights and shadows of a photograph and the proper relationship to the natural prominences, cavities, and depressions of the face influence the viability of various photographs. A **highlight,** a surface lying at right angles to the source of illumination, which reflects the maximum amount of light; the brighter part and a **shadow**, surfaces which do not lie at right angles to the source of illumination or are obscured by other surfaces and which reflect little or no light, these items are no doubt important to determine unique elements of individuals personal appearance. Here, we consider the impact on photographs of normal, directional, and flat lighting.

Normal lighting, a source of lighting from above the head allows the prominences that have the greatest projection to reflect the greatest amount of light and the deeper areas to reflect little light.

Directional lighting simply means lighting that travels in a specific direction. While general lighting provides even, overall illumination, directional lighting highlights a specific object. It is also usually provided by a stronger light source. When considering the human face, directional lighting may misrepresent normal light and dark areas. This will make it more difficult for restorative artists to determine the individual's real highlights and shadows associated with their face.

Flat light is defined as lighting that produces minimal contrast in the scene, which means there is very little contrast between the highlights and shadows. Photos with flat light can often lack depth, making these photographs of little value to the restorative artist.

Facial Proportions

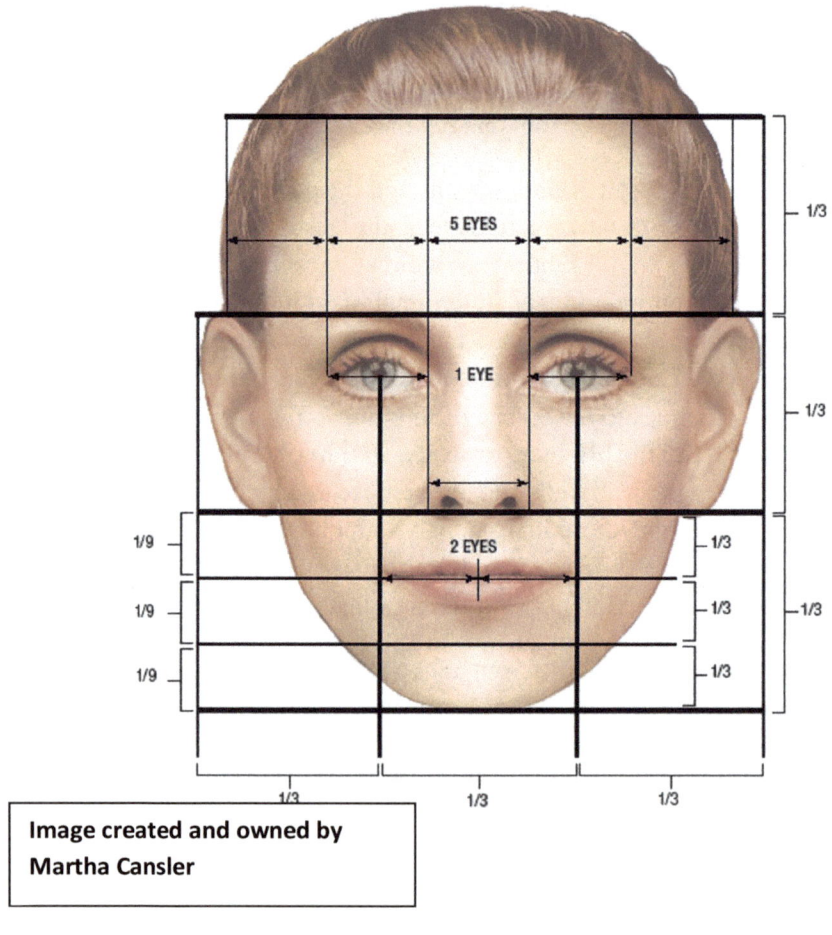

Image created and owned by Martha Cansler

Restorative Art: Foundation & Practice: Chapter 7

In addition to, or in the absence of available photographs, facial proportions can serve the restorative artist when modeling the face in order to achieve appropriate size, projection, and associated relationships with other features when performing this work. **Proportions** are defined as the relationships of the size of one feature as compared with another feature or with the width or length of the face. For obvious reasons, our main concern here is with facial proportions, or mathematical relationships of the facial features to one another and/or to the head and face, as these relationships can assist the embalmer in securing an appropriate presentation of the deceased. The study of these proportions allows funeral professionals the opportunity to detect similarities in the size of various features as well as to notice the differences in size relationships. These relationships more fully allow the restorative artist the ability to achieve appropriate size of features, as we know that even if you are able to achieve quality regarding the shape of a feature, if the size is incorrect, you will not be able to present the desired appearance to the family. When considering facial proportions, vertical measurements will be used to describe "length" and horizontal measurements will be used to describe "width", and make note that height will be described as the vertical measurement of a part of a feature.

Proportions Represented/Horizontal and Vertical Lines

A key element to understanding basic facial proportions is to establish an image that represents these basic facial proportions (see the image on the previous page). This is commonly accomplished by superimposing a series of horizontal and vertical lines over a facial image. This practice allows the restorative artist the ability to visualize these standard facial proportions. The horizontal lines that serve to separate the divisions of the face are as follows: across the normal hairline, across the eyebrow and top of the ears, through the line of closure of the eyes on adults, across the base of the nose and base of the earlobe, through the line of closure of the lips, across the superior border of the chin, and across the base of the chin. The standard vertical lines utilized include through the medial end of each eye, extension from the medial end of each eye to the wings of the nose, through the lateral corner of each eye, along each side of the face, and the extension from the middle of each eye to the corners of the mouth. See the image on the previous page for such representation. When examining the length of the face (using the horizontal lines) note that the lines establish three equal divisions, separating the face into equal thirds, and each 1/3 section is further divided into thirds, creating a total of 9/9 (see image on the previous page). The top 1/3 of the face is the distance between the normal hairline and the eyebrows. The middle third is represented by the distance from the eyebrow to the base of the nose, and the lower third is measured by the area between the base of the nose and the base of the chin. Note that the length of the ear equals the distance of 1/3 the length of the face; therefore one can say that the face is three ear lengths long. Also note that the length of the ear equals the length of the nose, making the length of the face also equal to the distance of three nose lengths. This allows you to estimate distances of length using these standard proportions. For example, using 1/9ths, what is the distance between the normal hairline and the line of closure of the lips? Looking at the image on page 124, it is simple to calculate this distance as 7/9ths. You can use this method to estimate the distance between various facial features. Other items to consider include that the length of the ear is equal to the length from the base of the nose to the base of the chin. Also, the length of the ear is also equal to the length from the outer corner of the eyelid to the ear passage. Other related lengths: the line of the closure of the lips lies halfway between the base of the nose and the top of the chin, and the eyes are located halfway between the vertex of the cranium and the base of the chin. When considering the width (using the vertical lines) on the face, notice that the widest part of the face is measured as being five eyes wide at the Zygomatic Arches. Also note that the distance of the base of the nose is equal to the distance of one eye; therefore, the widest part of the face can also be referred to as being five bases of the nose wide. When examining these proportions, notice that you can estimate many sizes using these measurements; simply calculate the distance between any locations using a standard proportion as the unit of measurement (for example the width of an eye, or the width of the base of the nose).

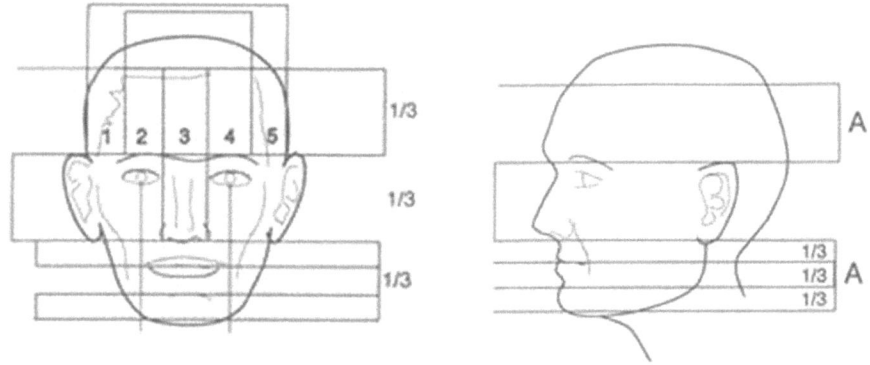

Proportional Relationships

As we consider the significance and use of these proportions, one might consider the origin of such references. These proportions date back to ancient Greek sculpture, which developed the Canon of Beauty. In the Canon of Beauty, the head is oval in outline; the upper portion is a little wider than the lower. The greatest width of the oval is approximately two-thirds of the length. The height of an adult can be measured in head-lengths; the average adult's height is approximately seven and one-half head-lengths while exceptionally tall adults may measure eight (Mayer, 1980).

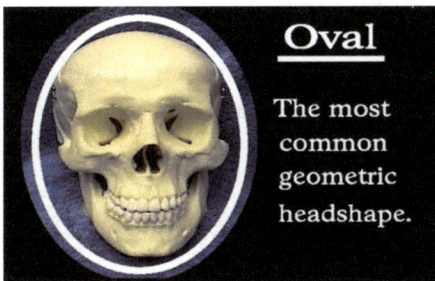
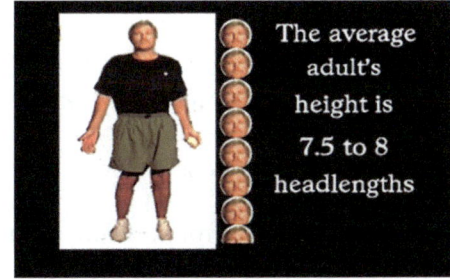

It is also important to note that the length of the head is measured between two parallel lines which extend across the vertex of the head and the base of the chin. Therefore, the middle of the length of the head extends horizontally across the eyes. Do not confuse this with the length of the face; physiognomy identifies this measurement as from the normal hairline to the base of the chin. Also note that anatomically, the face is measured from the eyes to the base of the chin. Considering the measurements of the head, it is also true that the dimension from the tip of the lobe of the nose to the greatest protrusion of the back of the head is equal to the size of the length of the head.

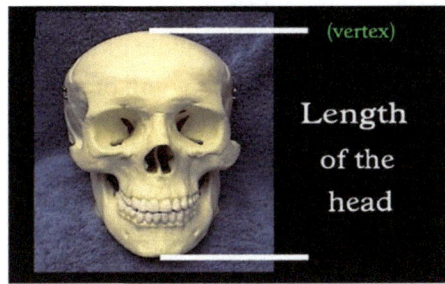
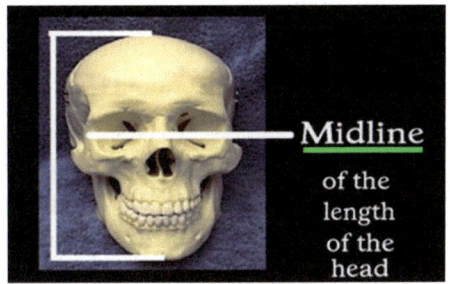

Additional Measurements and Supplemental Equalities

Here, we suggest additional measurements of interest that may be useful to the restorative artist. On many people, the following are equal to 2/3 of the length of the face:

- From the tip of thumb to tip of index finger
- From the ear passage to the tip of the nose
- From the eyebrow to the base of the chin
- From the hairline to the base of the nose
- From ear passage to ear passage (through the head)

It has also been suggested that when held parallel, the distance from the tip of the thumb to the tip of the index finger equals 1/3 the length of the face.

Other helpful proportions include:

- The distance from the root of the nose to the base of the wing of the nose is equal to the length of the first two joints of the index finger.
- The vertical distance on the median line of the lips (from the base of the nose) to the line of closure of the lips is equal to the length of the first joint of the index finger.
- The line of closure of the lips lies halfway between the base of the nose and the top of the chin.
- The eyes are located halfway between the vertex of the cranium and the base of the chin.
- The distance between the eyes is one eye width.
- The width across the base of the nose is the width of one eye.
- The distance between the outer corners of the eyes is the width of three eyes.
- The distance between the zygomatic arches is the width of five eyes.
- The corners of the mouth are vertically aligned with the middle of the eyes.
- The width of the mouth (from corner to corner) equals the width of two eyes.
- The width of the mouth is twice the width of the base of the nose. Since the face is five eyes wide, and the dimension between the outer canthi is the width of three eyes, the distance from the outer corner of one eye to the peak of the zygomatic arch on the other side of the face is four eyes wide.

Restorative Art: Foundation & Practice: Chapter 7

Ultimately, knowledge of various facial proportions can serve to expand the required skillset to perform restorative work. Although not sufficient to perform all work, these may serve as a necessary component in the complete collection of knowledge and skills required to serve in this capacity.

Facial Profiles

Individual personal appearance is created by a multitude of various elements. We have considered skeletal and muscular anatomy and surface facial markings as well as explored proportional measurements used by restorative artists. Just as length and width relationships impact the skull and overall head shapes, the degree of projection or depth of the parts of the face (along the anterior median line of the face) affect the profile appearance of the individual. In this section, we introduce facial profiles, the three basic linear forms as well as six additional combination forms. All classifications of profiles are based on the classic head of Ancient Greek sculpture, in which the forehead, upper lip, and chin form a vertical plane. The nose is not included in the description. The forehead is described by its direction from the eyebrow upward; and the chin is described by its relationship to the upper lip.

Basic Linear Forms

From the profile view, there are three basic forms; here, the three basic linear forms are identified.

Convex Profile (most common profile) describes a profile in which the forehead recedes posteriorly from the eyebrows and the chin recedes from the plane of the upper lip.

Concave Profile (least common profile) describes a profile in which the forehead protrudes beyond the eyebrows while the chin protrudes beyond the plane of the upper lip.

Vertical (perpendicular or balanced) Profile is one in which the forehead, upper lip, and chin project equally to an imaginary vertical line.

Additional Forms

In addition to the three basic linear forms, six additional classifications are determined by combining parts of the three basic profiles. When considering the additional profile forms, note the following: use a hyphen between the two combined parts, the first term refers to the forehead, and the second term refers to the chin. With the additional six forms, a total of nine facial linear profiles are identified. Here, the additional forms are identified.

Convex-concave profile (receding forehead and protruding chin) is a variation in which the forehead recedes from the eyebrows while the chin protrudes beyond the plane of the upper lip.

Concave-convex profile (protruding forehead and receding chin) is a profile variation in which the forehead protrudes beyond the eyebrows while the chin recedes from the plane of the upper lip.

Vertical-convex profile (balanced forehead and receding chin) is a profile in which the forehead and the eyebrows project equally to a vertical line and the chin recedes from the projection of the upper lip.

Vertical-concave profile (balanced forehead and protruding chin) is a profile in which the forehead and the eyebrows project equally to a vertical line and the chin protrudes more than the upper lip.

Convex-vertical profile (receding forehead and balanced chin) is a profile variation in which the forehead recedes from the eyebrows while the chin and upper lip project equally to an imaginary vertical line.

Concave-vertical profile (protruding forehead and balanced chin) is a profile variation in which the forehead protrudes beyond the eyebrows while the upper lip and chin project equally to an imaginary vertical line.

The three basic linear forms, in addition to the six combinations of the basic forms, make a total of nine linear profile forms. The most commonly observed linear profile form is the convex profile, while the least common formation is the concave profile. See the illustration on the following page for a graphic representation of both the basic and combined facial linear profiles.

RESTORATIVE ART: FOUNDATION & PRACTICE: CHAPTER 7

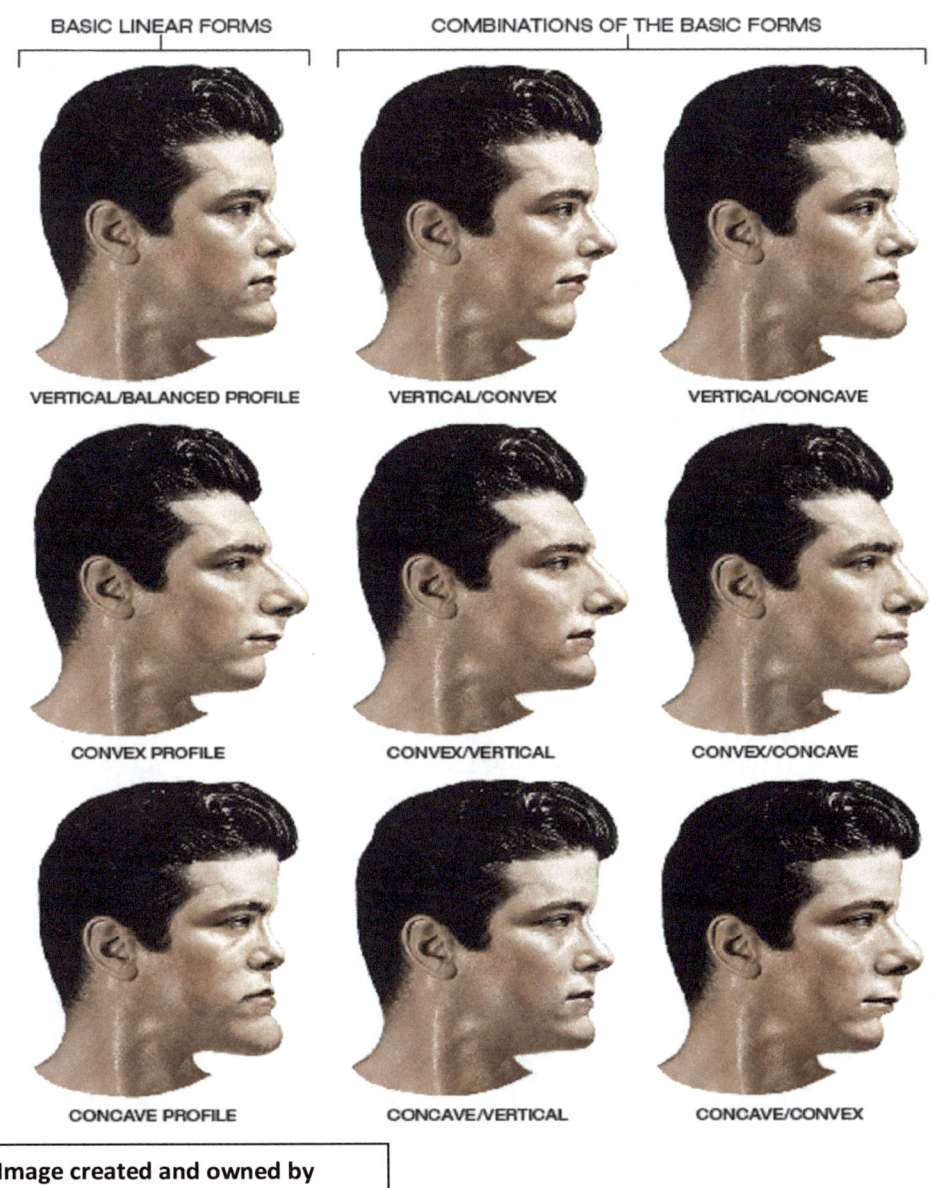

Image created and owned by Martha Cansler

RESTORATIVE ART: FOUNDATION & PRACTICE: CHAPTER 7

Facial Shapes

A great deal of the groundwork and study to prepare to become a restorative artist centers on understanding human form. Not only individual appearance, but also what has influenced this appearance. Here, we consider another element of recognizable form, geometric head forms from the fontal view. Why is it necessary to grasp this knowledge? Loss of form of the head through embalming, swelling, or wax restorations can lead to the loss of this identifiable shape; the people that knew the decedent best will no doubt be disappointed in such appearance.

Like so many features, the overall head form does not remain constant throughout life. All you need to do is observe a series of photographs of the same person over time. Therefore, restorations with an outdated photograph will not help achieve successful results.

Overall head shape is influenced by its bony structure. Head shape, as viewed from the front, is classified according to the geometric pattern made by its outline. This pattern is influenced by relative proportions of the head with respect to width. The three following areas of width, in conjunction with the length of the head impact overall head shape and are central to classifying head shapes. The three transverse dimensions of width are:

- Bi-parietal width – the widest part of the cranium
- Bi-zygomatic width – the widest part of the face
- Bi-mandibular width – across the angles of the jaw

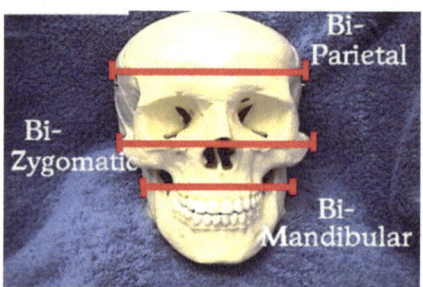 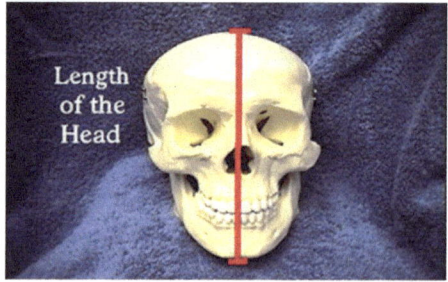

The length of the head is that dimension which occurs between two horizontal lines, assumed to extend, between the vertex of the head and the base of the chin.

Seven facial shapes from the frontal view are classified. Here are these shapes:

The **oval** facial shape is one with a rounded forehead, cheeks, and chin and is longer than it is wide. This frontal view is one in which the head is generally egg shaped, with the cranium slightly wider than the jaws. This is the most common geometric head form.

The **round (infantine)** facial shape is characterized as one that the vertical distance and the width between the cheekbones are equal and the cheeks and chin are rounded. This form has been noted to exhibit maximum curvature.

Square is a facial shape in which the vertical and horizontal measurements are equal, the hairline is straight, and the jaw is angled. This head form has been described as broad and exhibiting very little curvature. The forehead is wide and the angles of the mandible are usually low as well as wide; the overall form has been characterized as "strong".

Triangular is a facial shape in which the forehead is pointed, the sides widen inferiorly, and the jaw is the widest point. This frontal view exhibits a face that is wider between the angles of the mandible than it is at the forehead, representing a triangle in shape. This is the least common geometric head form.

Inverted Triangle is a facial shape with a wide angular forehead, angular jaw, and pointed chin. This shape has been described as a head which is wide at the forehead and narrow at the jaw.

Diamond is a facial shape in which the cheeks are the widest point accompanied by a narrowing forehead and chin. This geometric head shape is widest across the cheekbones, narrowing in width in both the forehead and the jaws.

Oblong is a facial shape in which the head is long and narrow throughout.

These seven facial shapes further assist the restorative art student in grasping a full understanding of human appearance. This is critical, as we are called to recreate natural form and color in order to provide families and friends with a peaceful, meaningful, viewing of the deceased. On the following page, an illustration is provided that graphically represents each of the facial shapes. This can further assist students in an overall understanding of various personal appearances.

RESTORATIVE ART: FOUNDATION & PRACTICE: CHAPTER 7

HEAD SHAPES
(FRONTAL VIEW)

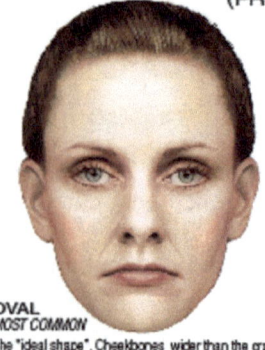

OVAL
MOST COMMON
The "ideal shape". Cheekbones wider than the cranium. Cranium slightly wider than lower jaw

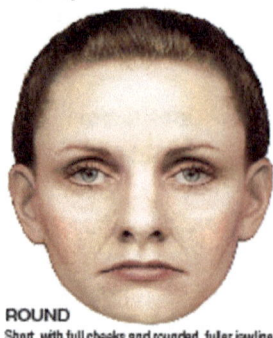

ROUND
Short, with full cheeks and rounded, fuller jawline. Rounded cranium.

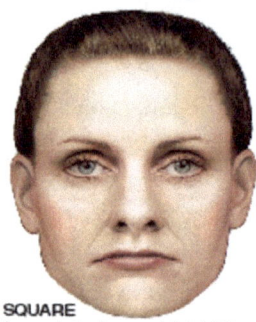

SQUARE
Appears short and composed of straight lines. Forehead, jawline and cheeks approximately the same width.

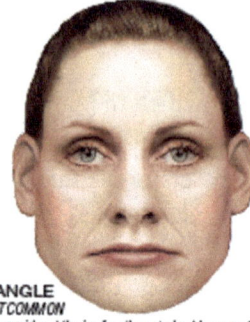

TRIANGLE
LEAST COMMON
Appears wider at the jawline than at cheekbone and forehead. Forehead is most narrow feature. Eyes close-set.

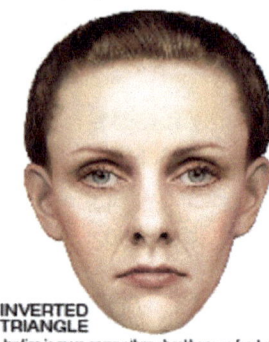

INVERTED TRIANGLE
Jawline is more narrow than cheekbone or forehead. Forehead is widest feature. Eyes wideset.

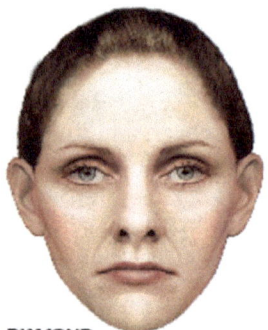

DIAMOND
Wide cheekbones. Narrow forehead and jawline. Greatest width is across cheekbone.

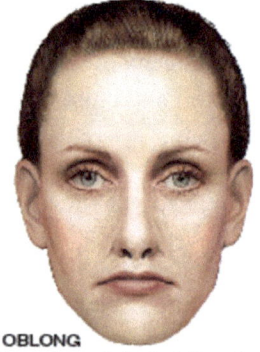

OBLONG
Long and narrow. Forehead and chin round or square. Nose usually long.

Image created and owned by Martha Cansler

RESTORATIVE ART: FOUNDATION & PRACTICE: CHAPTER 7

The Bilateral Appearance of facial Features

Thus far in this chapter, we have considered multiple items that may assist the restorative artist in identifying and recreating human form. We have deliberated facial proportions, facial profiles, facial shapes, and now we explore the bilateral appearance of facial features. The reality of human form is that most people exhibit **bilateral differences** (dissimilarities existing in the two sides or halves of an object) when considering facial features, although many features display similarities, generally speaking paired facial features reveal **asymmetry** (lack of symmetry, balance, or proportion). Here, we identify features that truly exhibit asymmetry followed by surfaces of the face that show more similarity.

Asymmetry of Features

The following facial features are typically asymmetric in nature:

- Eyelids and eyebrows
- Ears (exhibit the greatest differences in position, form, and size)
- Cheeks
- Nose
- Mouth

Surfaces exhibiting a similarity of bilateral curvature

The following surfaces typically exhibit similarity of bilateral curvature:

- Forehead
- Cheeks (considered keys to bilateral formation)
- Superior Integumentary lip
- Chin

RESTORATIVE ART: FOUNDATION & PRACTICE: CHAPTER 7

Chapter Conclusion

This chapter presented the importance of receiving photographs when preparing a body for viewing regardless if extensive restorative work is required or otherwise. Also, the reader explored how to interpret photographs to aid in the restorative process. After this instruction, the reader discovered several topics related to understanding and implementing restorative treatments. These included the examination of facial proportions, facial profiles, facial shapes, and the bilateral appearance of facial features. Collectively, this knowledge has advanced the educational requirements to excel as a restorative artist. The next chapter will start to implement the background provided thus far in the book as you will read about specific facial features (nose, mouth, eyes, and ears) and restorations associated with these features.

References

Professional Experience and Educational Presentations:
A great deal of the content of this book has been derived from years of professional experience as an embalmer, funeral director, and funeral service educator.

Klicker, R. (2002). *Restorative art and science*. Buffalo, NY: Thanos Institute.

Mayer, J. S. (1980). *Restorative art*. Dallas, TX: Professional Training Schools.

Mayer, R. G. (2012). *Embalming: History, theory, and practice* (5th ed.).

New York, NY: McGraw-Hill.

Prager, G. J. (1955). *Postmortem restorative art*. Amelia, OH: G. Joseph Prager.

Spriggs, A. O. (1964). *Champion restorative art* (6th ed.). Springfield, OH: The

Champion Company.

Unit 3

Understanding Specific Features and associated Restorative Techniques

- Chapter 8:

  Facial Features and Associated Restorations

- Chapter 9:

  Hair and Hair Restorations

Chapter Eight:

Facial Features and Associated Restorations

Chapter Author: Cody L. Lopasky, M.A.

Chapter Learning Objectives

Upon completion of the study of this chapter students should:

- Understand the general characteristics of the major facial features
- Know the parts and anatomy of each facial feature
- Comprehend the varied issues that require feature restoration
- Describe the techniques that are unique to restoring each facial feature

Introduction

The human face has a very distinctive form. Aside from geometric structure, much of the face's character comes from the combination of the individual facial features. Each has its own specific parts and variations. The combination and interaction of individual features often make a person's face much easier to remember than a name. Names are simply groupings of letters and can be very common. The face is a human identifying quality that is truly unique. In the words of philosopher Ludwig Wittgenstein, "The face is the soul of the body."

In this chapter, we will discuss the individual human facial features, the issues for each that may require restoration, and the associated restorative procedures and techniques. Specifically included will be the following: nose, mouth, chin, eyes, and ears.

NOSE

The nose is an unpaired facial feature that sits along the median line. Its internal and external structures comprise both the means by which humans smell and also the beginning portion of the respiratory system. As a facial feature, the nose provides the greatest anterior projection of the face and can be quite a distinguishing characteristic, especially from the profile.

RESTORATIVE ART: FOUNDATION & PRACTICE: CHAPTER 8

Classifications

There are two distinct ways by which to classify the nose. The **Nasal Index** (or Racial Index) and the **Profile Classification**. The Nasal Index is an anthropological classification using a ratio to compare the nasal width and length. Normally, this classification is used for noses seen in the frontal view. For the Profile Classification, the nose is viewed from the side and classified by its linear profile form. Each of the two classification systems contains three separate types explained in the tables below.

Nasal Index	
Leptorrhine	A nose that is long, narrow, and high-bridged; common to those of Western European ancestry.
Mesorrhine	A nose that is medium broad and medium-low bridged; common to those of Asian ancestry.
Platyrrhine	A nose that is short, broad, and has minimum projection; common to those of African ancestry.

Profile Classification	
Straight Nasal Profile (a.k.a. Grecian)	A nasal profile in which the dorsum exhibits a straight line from root to tip; most common nasal profile.
Convex Nasal Profile (a.k.a. Roman, Aquiline, or Hooked)	A nasal profile which exhibits an outward hump or bump in the bridge; may appear curved or hooked.
Concave Nasal Profile (a.k.a. Snub, Infantine, or Retrousse)	A nasal profile in which the bridge dips inward from root to tip; the tip may be turned upward as well.

Anatomy and Parts

The internal anatomy of the nose is comprised of bones, bony margins, and cartilage. The **nasal cavity** is the orifice in the skull whose margins are created by the nasal bones and the maxilla. Inferior to the glabella sit the **nasal bones**. Together, these small paired bones form a dome over the superior portion of the nasal cavity and aid in determining the nose's angle of inclination. On the inferior margin of the nasal cavity sits the **nasal spine of the maxilla**. This sharp, bony projection is located on the median line and helps to indicate the bony length of the nose. The **septum** is a vertical piece of cartilage that divides the nasal cavity into two separate chambers and is responsible for any asymmetry of the nose. With the cartilage, two bones are also included in the formation of the septum. The **vomer** forms the inferior and posterior portions of the septum, and the **perpendicular plate of the ethmoid bone** forms the superior portion of the septum. To differentiate from the cartilage, these bones are termed the bony nasal septum. In addition to the septum, cartilage is also used in the support and internal formation of the sides of the nose: the superior and inferior **lateral cartilages**.

Externally, the nose is made up of many different parts. The height of the nose is determined from root to base. The majority of this vertical length is known as the **dorsum**. The dorsum of the nose is the anterior, protruding ridge that contains the **root**, **bridge**, **protruding lobe**, and **tip**.

> Root – the apex (most superior point) of the nose which is normally formed by a concave dip just inferior to the forehead
>
> Bridge – the arched portion of the nose supported by the nasal bones
>
> Protruding Lobe – the rounded anterior projection of the inferior part of the dorsum
>
> Tip – the point of greatest projection of the lobe

On the inferior margin of the nose sit the **anterior nares**, or external nostril openings. Individually, these are termed the right anterior naris and the left anterior naris. Between the anterior nares is the **columna nasi**, which is the skin partition between the nostrils, and it is the most inferior part of the nose. Surrounding the outer margins of the nostrils are the lateral lobes of the nose known as the **wings of the nose**; the nose's widest point. The **arch of the wings** forms a distinctive arc shape around the nostrils. The lateral walls between the bridge and the wings are simply known as the **sides of the nose**.

Together, the combination of the anterior nares, the columna nasi, and the inferior margins of the wings are known as the **base of the nose**. This designation is important to the horizontal lines used in facial proportions.

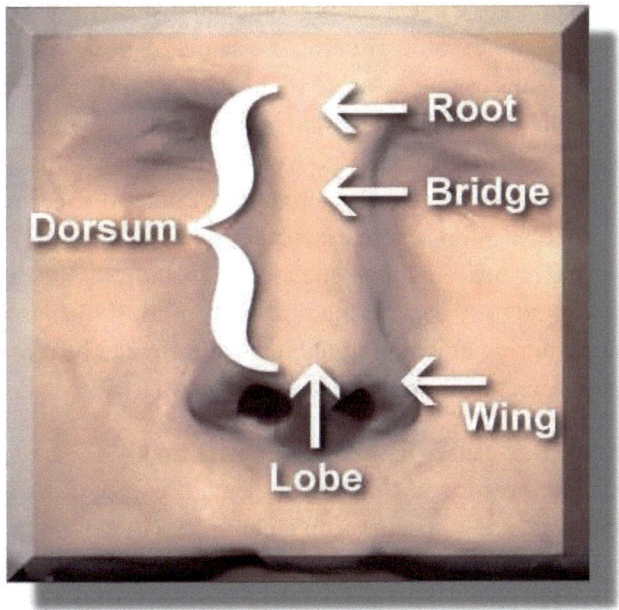

Restorations

Due to its prominent position on the face, it is paramount that the nose of a decedent appears natural. The nose can be prone to certain issues that may require restoration. The most common are tissue erosion and nasal distortion. The antemortem use of medical nasal tubes can cause both (Mayer, 2012).

In the case of tissue erosion, the restoration will depend on the extent of the damage and whether any tissue is missing. Ensure the area is firm, clean, and dry in all instances. For small abrasions, localized topical embalming or cauterizing may be necessary. After treatment, these areas can be cosmetized as any other discoloration. If nasal tissue is severely damaged, necrotic, or is missing, then wax will be needed to complete the restoration. Any necrotic tissue should be excised first. Then, any missing tissue should be modeled and reconstructed with wax; the use of photographs for accuracy is strongly encouraged. A medium or firm wax works best for these restorations due to its ability to maintain its modeled form. To colorize the restored area, cosmetics may be mixed with the wax before usage or applied on top of the wax after restoration is complete. Ensure that the edges of any waxed areas are feathered to properly reduce artificiality.

Nasal distortions normally result in the nose being flattened down toward the face or leaning to one side or the other. The causes of such distortions include: pathological conditions/disease, superficial pressure, and fracture/trauma.

Cancer is the main causative agent for pathological distortion of natural nasal form; though other diseases are capable of doing the same. A nose that has been distorted by cancer normally leans to one side due to the cancer's effect on the muscles and tissue surrounding the nose. On milder cases of distortion, pressure can be applied to the side of the nose during embalming to make it lean back toward the midline. This can be accomplished with a rolled-up towel or other device and is done during the embalming process. With severe cases, temporary sutures may need to be used. They are secured to the nose and then anchored to healthy tissue on whichever side of the face will pull the nose back in the right direction. If the nasal tissue firms in the correct position during embalming, then the sutures can be removed afterward. Otherwise, more discreet anchoring sutures and waxing will be necessary.

Superficial pressure that causes nasal distortions normally occurs postmortem. This often results from the position of the body at death (i.e. face down), body bags, cot covers, or poor storage and transportation techniques. In death, the tissue of the deceased lacks the ability to "spring back" as it does in life. Light massage during arterial injection may correct mild distortions. This is similar to the effect on mildly emaciated cases where the tissue is simply filled in by the process of arterial injection. With more severe distortions from external pressure, the anterior nares will need to be packed with mortuary putty, cotton, or other suitable materials. This will keep the nostrils artificially inflated during arterial injection and keep the recreated natural form and projection of the nose. These items can then be removed once the tissues have set-up and/or firmed after embalming.

Nasal distortions due to fracture or caused by trauma are restored in much the same way as those caused by external pressure. The main difference is whether the skin is broken or not. Normally, fractured nasal bones can be manually manipulated back into an acceptable position. The use of small rods or elongated instruments inserted in the nostrils can aid in correcting the fracture. Cosmetic brush handles work well for this task. Then, the anterior nares should be packed to ensure the correct form is maintained throughout arterial injection. If the skin is broken due to the fracture, then the area should be treated and either sutured or cemented/glued depending on severity. Wax will be required to hide the affected area if sutures are used.

MOUTH

The mouth is an unpaired facial feature located within the inferior third of the face. It is the center of expression for the deceased; the eyes having ceded this role after death. Embalmers and restorative artists should expect to encounter more issues with properly posing the mouth than with any other facial feature. With more problems possible, and its role in expression, greater time and effort should be spent on the mouth. Poor posing or restoration of this feature can void all of the time spent preparing a decedent if the family is unhappy with the mouth, and by default, the face and its expression.

Characteristics

The mouth is the beginning of the digestive tract, the place where mastication occurs, and the main vehicle for verbal communication. By laymen's standards, the mouth is simply the lips. In reality, the external boundaries of the mouth include much more. They consist of the base of the nose, the nasolabial folds, and the junction of the inferior integumentary lip and the superior border of the chin; the location of the labiomental sulcus. Everything within these boundaries is considered to be the mouth.

Generally, the mouth tends to exhibit some degree of asymmetry on each individual person. For example, the lips may be thicker on one side or the line of closure may curve differently from one side to the other. These differences from the norm should be noted by the restorative artist to ensure they are not changed during embalming and restoration.

In natural repose, the teeth of the superior and inferior jaws are slightly separated. Absent of extreme emotions or expressions, people do not clinch their teeth together. This natural small space between the upper and lower teeth, most evident with the incisors, is known as the **dime gap**. The name implies that the space is small enough for only a (flat) dime to fit between the teeth. This dime gap and the associated standards of the mouth may be violated if a decedent is toothless. Consult with the family to ensure the decedent looks as desired.

Prognathism

With the mouth, certain deviations from the norm are referred to as a type of **prognathism**; defined as a projection of the jaw or jaws beyond the upper part of the face (forehead); especially noticeable in the profile. There are five separate forms of prognathism that affect the external appearance of the mouth. Each is explained in the chart below.

Types of Prognathism	
Infranasal Prognathism	The base of the nasal cavity protrudes abnormally.
Maxillary Prognathism	The superior jaw protrudes.
Mandibular Prognathism	The inferior jaw protrudes.
Dental Prognathism	Oblique insertion of the teeth (a.k.a. Buck teeth)
Alveolar Prognathism	Abnormal protrusion of the alveolar processes

Anatomy and Parts

The underlying, bony structure of the mouth is made up of the maxilla and mandible which are covered at length in another chapter. On the surface, there are several parts within the previously stated boundaries of the mouth. The most recognizable are the **mucous membranes,** which are the visible red surfaces of the lips. The red coloring of the mucous membranes varies from person to person and also within a single mucous membrane. Superior and inferior to the mucous membranes are the skin portions of the lips, known as **integumentary lips**. The superior integumentary lip is located between the base of the nose and the superior mucous membrane. The inferior integumentary lip is located between the inferior mucous membrane and the superior margin of the chin.

The remaining external parts of the mouth are contained entirely within the mucous membranes themselves. Each mucous membrane (superior and inferior) has a **weather line**. This is the line of color change that marks the junction of the wet and dry portions of each mucous membrane. The wet portion is that which is more toward the inside of the mouth and normally unexposed. The dry portion is more superficial, tends to be lighter in color, and is normally exposed. On the midline of the superior mucous membrane sits a tiny prominence called the **medial lobe**.

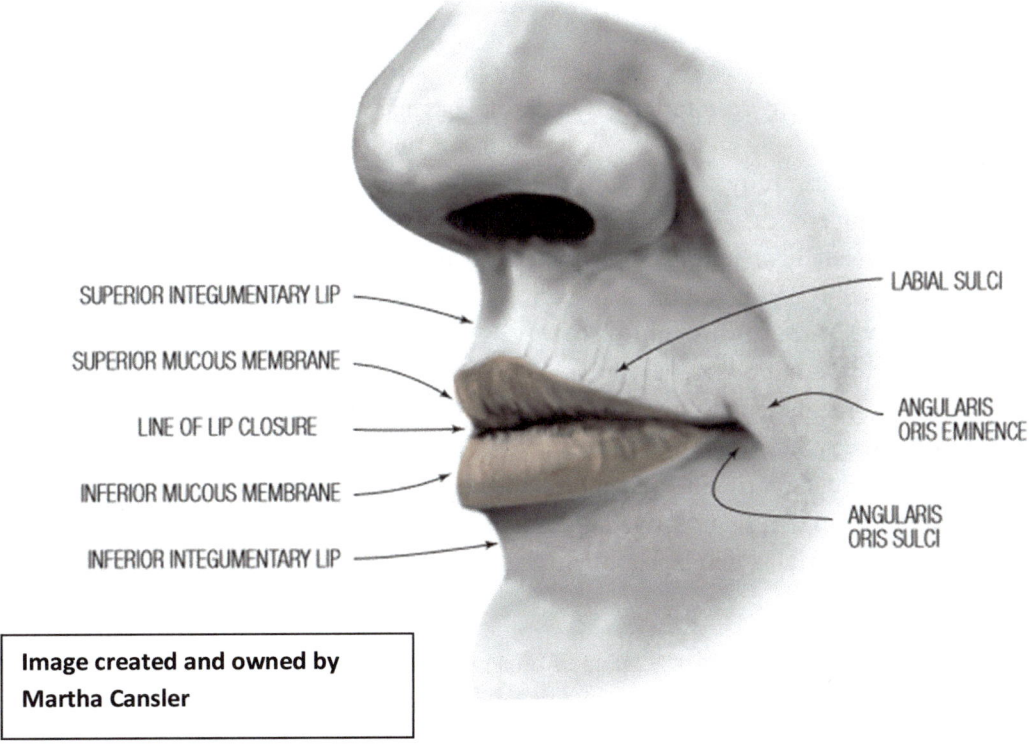

Image created and owned by Martha Cansler

Between the two mucous membranes, at the point where they contact each other, is the **line of closure of the mouth**. The term line of closure is used for both the mouth and the eyes, but the two are unique. The line of closure for the mouth has five natural arcs, or curved lines. On certain individuals, these five arcs combine to create the classic shape of a hunting bow or Cupid's bow. This hunting bow shape is also evident on the superior margin of the superior mucous membrane. On each mucous membrane, normally the dry portion, are small vertical sulci known as vertical lines. They are spaced randomly and do not follow a pattern. The vertical lines should be recreated if wax restorations are required for the mucous membranes.

Five arcs of the hunting bow:

Restorative Art: Foundation & Practice: Chapter 8

Restorations

For the mouth, expression is key. The restorative artist should keep this fact in mind when doing any restorations. On normal cases, restoration of the mouth will simply involve closing and posing it during the setting of features. Be mindful that the expression, carefully crafted during feature setting, can become changed during the embalming process. In all cases, ensure that the mouth is closed and the expression created is natural and pleasant. Closing the mouth is commonly done via a **needle injector** and wired brads or with a suturing method; **musculature suture, mandibular suture, sublingual suture** (Mayer, 2012). The expression can be manipulated by adding material under any or all of the following: mucous membranes, integumentary lips, and corners of the mouth. Materials can include mouth formers, cotton, and mortuary putty. Due to the effect of gravity on a body in the supine position (laying on a table), the corners of the mouth may be drawn posteriorly and present a negative appearance. Slightly elevating the corners of the mouth with material added beneath will lessen this effect and create a more pleasant expression.

The five types of prognathism can each present issues for the restorative artist, but dental prognathism tends to be the most troublesome. Restoring the mouth to natural form will depend on the severity of the prognathism. In milder cases, manual manipulation is often enough to bring the lips together. The lips may be cemented or glued to ensure they remain closed during embalming. Petroleum jelly can also work for this task and is less harsh, but it may not maintain closure for all cases. Also, the cotton sling method may be used. This involves narrow cotton strips being moistened and placed both superior and inferior to the mucous membranes (encircling them) to hold them together with pressure. A more invasive restorative procedure is to sever the frenulum, a small piece of skin that connect the lip and gum where the two meet. Doing so gives the restorative artist greater rage of movement in the lips. In the most extreme cases of dental prognathism, there are two options. First, with appropriate authorization, the teeth can be extracted and the contour of the mouth is then created using a mouth former and cotton (this book does not endorse this technique). Second, the visible teeth may be polished/cleaned and the lips left slightly open. These two methods for extreme prognathism should only be used as a last resort and with a family's explicit authorization.

Lip closure and correcting lip separation can utilize several options. During feature setting, lip closure is often done naturally through the process of posing the lips. For troublesome lips, an adhesive lip cream, petroleum jelly, or the cotton sling method (described previously) can be used to hold the lips together during embalming. Some embalmers prefer to glue/cement parted lips prior to embalming, although this is not advised as it seals a pathway for the evacuation of fluids during the embalming procedure, and others prefer to do this post-embalming. The latter option allows the lips a chance to fill in during arterial injection to a point where they expand and come in contact. Lip separation after embalming is very common and is due to several factors, often the simple dehydration of tissues. This can easily be corrected by cementing or gluing the lips. First, ensure that the lips are dry and free of debris. Then, apply adhesive behind the weather line on one or both lips. Finally, bring the two lips together carefully and hold for a short period. After drying, any visible excess adhesive should be removed with solvent, being careful not to disrupt the adhesive holding the lips together. In extreme cases where adhesives fail to correct separated lips, the restorative artist can use lip wax to fill in the gap between the two mucous membranes. The wax can then be shaped to correct the natural contours, and a new line of closure can be created with a spatula. As with other wax restorations, lip wax can be mixed with cosmetics before use or cosmetized after application and shaping.

It is common for decedents to be missing some or all of their natural teeth. Some will have dentures and others will not. If dentures are present, then ensure that they are firmly in place, aligned correctly, and used as the decedent did in life. This applies to complete dentures, partial dentures, plates, etc. When teeth are missing and dentures are not present, use cotton or mortuary putty to fill in the space of the missing teeth after securing the jaws. Then use a mouth former to recreate the natural contour of the closed mouth. Mouth formers should be cut to size in order to avoid an artificial appearance. If dentures are not provided until after embalming (during arrangements or when clothing is delivered), then do not attempt to reopen the mouth and utilize them. The dentures can simply be placed (in a container) under the pillow of the casket or in the foot end, discarded, or returned to the family with a general explanation. In all instances, follow the firm's policy on dentures received after embalming.

Moisture content of the lips can also present issues for the restorative artist. Both extremes of moisture content require attention: dehydrated lips and swollen lips. Emaciated cases and those with dehydrated lips may be corrected during embalming itself where the lips naturally "plump up" during arterial injection. When this fails to occur, a cotton compress soaked in a humectant chemical may solve the problem if time permits. Additionally, the lips can be hypodermically injected with tissue builder. Always coat dehydrated lips with massage cream after embalming, regardless of restorative treatment. For swollen lips, restoration is done with methods similar to treating other instances of localized swelling. Edematous cases with swollen lips may have the issue resolved with the use of edema corrective chemicals during arterial injection; though effects may not be immediately apparent. A number of options exist if the problem remains after embalming. First, external pressure or an electric spatula may reduce the swelling, but use massage cream as a barrier to prevent damage to the tissue. Next, **channeling** and incising (creating a passageway via puncture or incision and encourage the removal of watery fluids and gasses) may allow excess moisture to vacate the lips. Another option is to hypodermically inject an astringent or cauterizing chemical into the lips. In doing so, care should be taken to avoid over-inflation. Finally, surgical reduction (the actual removal of tissues, fluids and gasses via excision) can be used, but this should be viewed as a last resort due to the excess mutilation and additional restoration involved.

CHIN

The most inferior portion of the human face is the chin. Per the facial proportions, the length of the face is divided into thirds, and the inferior third is further subdivided into thirds. The chin comprises the inferior third of this inferior third of the face; in other words, a ninth of the face. Due to its requisite inclusion in facial length, the chin and its structure are quite important.

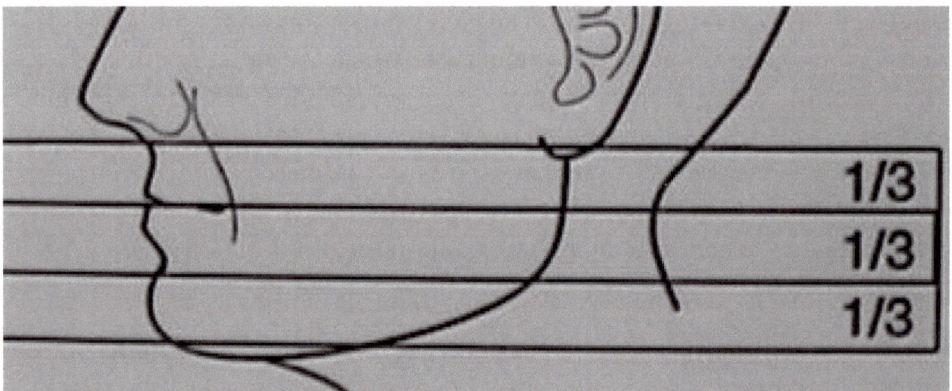

Characteristics

The chin area is known as the mental region. Anatomically, the term *mental* should not be confused with the brain and intelligence, recall that mentum is Latin for chin. The shape of the chin aids in facial recognition, both from the frontal view as well as the profile. Variations of chin shape influence the various geometric head forms. Also, the projection or recession of the chin is instrumental in determining which of the nine facial profiles an individual exhibits.

RESTORATIVE ART: FOUNDATION & PRACTICE: CHAPTER 8

Anatomy and Parts

The chin is made of bone, muscle, and skin tissue. Forming the base for all chin structure is the mandible; specifically the **mental eminence** of the body of the mandible. This is the anterior portion of the mandible that creates the projection of the chin. Covering the mental eminence is the **mentalis muscle**. The muscle itself is thick and flat, which adds bulk to the prominence and anterior projection of the chin. Tissue and skin comprise the outer surface of the chin.

The superior margin of the chin is defined by the labiomental sulcus which is a furrow at the junction of the inferior integumentary lip and the superior tissue of the chin. Dimples are a common external feature of the chin. These form through actions of the mentalis muscle and appear as a single shallow depression on the chin located on the median line. Variations can lead to elongated chin dimples and create a cleft chin. The inferior margin of the chin is sometimes defined by the submental furrow or submental sulcus. This is the junction of the base of the chin and the submandibular area, more commonly visible on individuals with excess adipose tissue.

Restorations

On most cases, the chin will rarely need restoration. Simple issues requiring attention will be lacerations and abrasions. These are corrected as they would be on other parts of the body. On males, restoration of any facial hair on the chin may be required in some instances. These hair restorations are covered in a separate chapter.

More significant restorations of the chin are often the result of trauma where all or significant portions of the chin structure are missing. For these cases, wax restoration is needed to correct the natural shape and prominence of the chin. Like any restoration involving wax, ensure the affected area is firm, dry, and clean. Apply a generous amount of wax and form it into the desired shape. The use of photographs from several angles is strongly encouraged for accuracy. Measurement is key to correctly recreating the chin. The restorative artist should rely on the facial proportions and all available means of measurement. A common mistake is to simply cover the affected area without rebuilding the projection of the chin. This highlights artificiality and does not restore a decedent to natural form. Since the chin is a ninth of the facial length, care should be taken to ensure facial proportions and the chin projection are correct. Upon completion, feather the wax into the surrounding area and cosmetize like any other wax restoration.

RESTORATIVE ART: FOUNDATION & PRACTICE: CHAPTER 8

EYES

The eyes are a paired facial feature located at the halfway point of the length of the head. In life, they enable a person to see and are the center of expression. In death, they should be closed in natural repose showing only the lids. The closed eyelids do not contribute much to a decedent's facial expression, simply form and static details (Mayer, 1980).

Characteristics

From the frontal view, the closed eye appears almond-shaped. Its vertical dimension is thicker toward the medial end and tapers to the lateral end. The greatest height is medially offset from the center of the closed eye. Due to the presence and position of the cornea, the point of greatest anterior projection for the closed eye is also offset medially from the center. In profile, the superior eyelid has slightly more anterior projection than the inferior eyelid. Each closed eye forms a rounded convexity. Because of this, the medial end of the eye is not visible in the profile view.

Anatomy and Parts

The foundational structure of the eye is the orbital cavity, or eye socket, and its bony margins. The orbital cavity contains the eyeball itself and is protected by its bony margins. These margins are created by the Maxilla, Frontal Bone, and the Zygomatic Bones. The superior rim is termed the **Supraorbital Margin** and is formed by the frontal bone. Of all four margins, the superior margin provides the most protection for the eye. This is due to its greater anterior projection than any other rim, often quite prominent on certain individuals. The lateral margin is called the **Zygomaticofrontal Process**. It is created by extensions of both the Zygomatic Bone and the Frontal Bone, and it forms a slight concave dip between the forehead and cheekbone. The medial rim of the orbital cavity is created by the frontal process of the maxilla and is situated more anteriorly than the lateral margin. The fourth rim is the inferior margin of the orbital cavity. This margin is formed by the zygomatic bone and the maxilla. From the frontal view, this margin forms a concave dip toward the lateral margin, and bilaterally, it forms a sigmoid "S" curve (Mayer, 1980).

In terms of size, the eye socket is slightly larger than the eyeball itself which is about one inch in diameter. This can be slightly smaller in females. The cornea, a transparent structure, sits on the anterior portion of the eyeball. Located behind the cornea is the iris, which surrounds the pupil.

RESTORATIVE ART: FOUNDATION & PRACTICE: CHAPTER 8

Externally, the closed eye is represented by the superior and inferior eyelids, or **palpebrae**. The **superior palpebra** is much larger in surface area than the inferior and also hugs the eyeball more closely. It extends from the uppermost portion of the eyeball to the bottom of the iris. The superior margin of the upper eyelid is the attached margin (attached to the tissue immediately superior to the eyeball), and its inferior margin is the free or unattached margin. The **inferior palpebra** is much smaller, has less anterior projection, and has less convexity than the superior palpebra. Its attached margin is at the inferior part of the eyeball, and its free or unattached margin rises to meet the superior palpebra. Between the two palpebrae is the **line of the closure of the eye**.

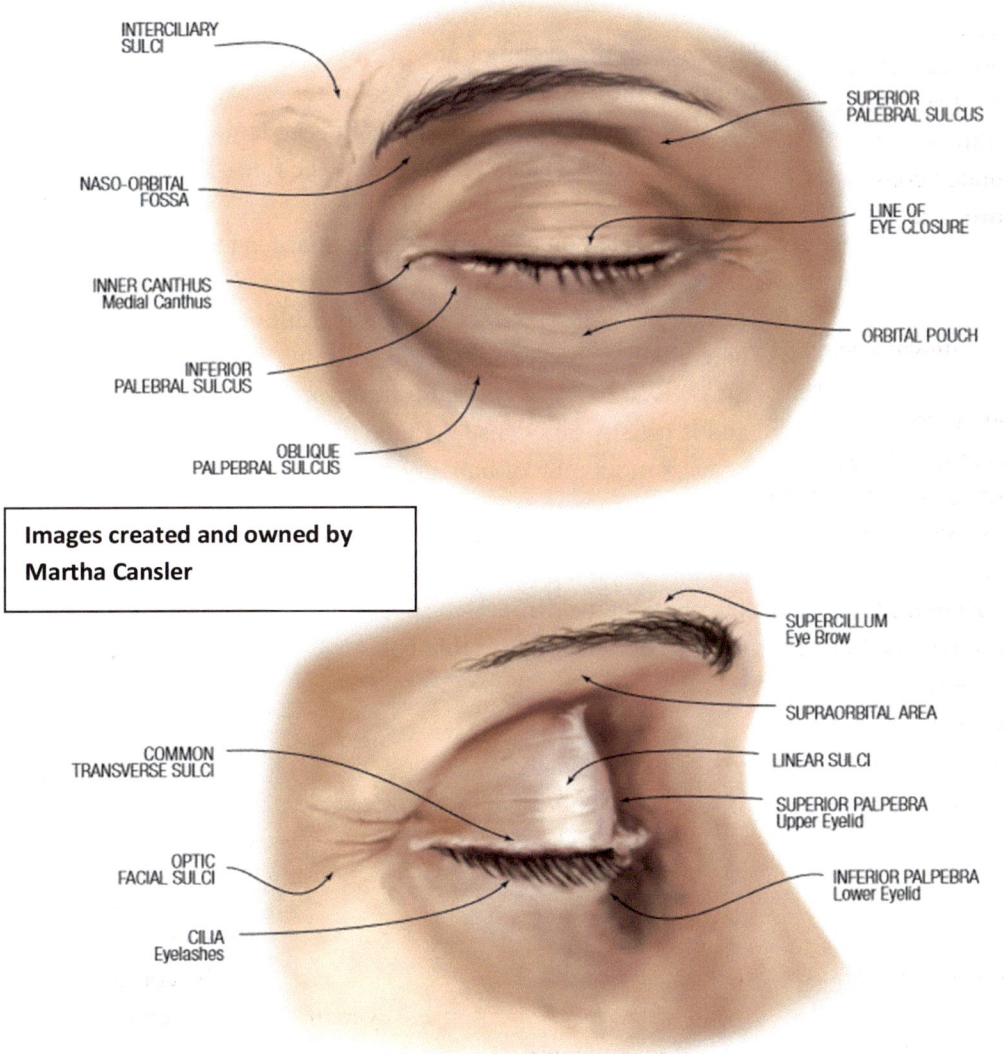

Images created and owned by Martha Cansler

The line of closure forms across the lower third of the eye socket. Specifically, the two eyelids abut at the line of closure but do not overlap. Due to the bilateral curvature of the face, the lateral end of the line of closure is both inferior and posterior to the medial end. Located at this medial end is the medial corner of the eye known as the **medial canthus** or inner canthus. The medial canthus forms a small elevation over the tear duct. The lateral corner of the eye is known as the **lateral canthus**. Immediately superior to the closed eye are the **naso-orbital fossa** and the **supraorbital area**. The former is a triangular concavity located between the root of the nose and the superior palpebra, directly inferior to the head of the eyebrow. The latter is simply the region between the attached margin of the superior palpebra and the eyebrow.

Two distinct types of hair occur on the eyelid or near the eye. First are the fringes of hair along the free margins of the eyelids known as **cilia**, or eyelashes. Cilia are irregular in abundance, spacing, and length. They arrange in random clusters, sometimes forming inverted triangles. The extreme ends of the line of closure contain no cilia, and on the inferior palpebra, cilia are quite sparse. The second type of hair in the area of the eye is located on each supraorbital margin and is known as the **supercilium**, or eyebrow. Hair is thickest at the medial end of the eyebrow and diminishes as it continues laterally. Hair growth for the supercilium is obliquely upward and outward. There are three parts of each supercilium: the head, body, and tail. The head contains the densest hair growth and is at the medial end. The body is located in the middle and is usually less dense than the head. The tail is the lateral end, it contains the sparsest amount of hair, and generally points to the ear passage.

There are numerous natural and acquired facial markings that occur on or about the eye, which can greatly contribute to the distinctive appearance of the eye on each individual. These markings are detailed in the table below.

Facial Markings of the Eye	
Superior Palpebral Sulcus	A curved transverse furrow along the attached margin of the superior palpebrae
Inferior Palpebral Sulcus	A thin curved furrow along the attached margin of the inferior palpebrae
Optic Facial Sulci "Crow's Feet"	Furrows radiating from the lateral corners of the eyes
Oblique Palpebral Sulcus	A shallow curving furrow that originates below the medial canthus; extends along the inferior margin of the orbit
Orbital Pouch "Bags under the eyes"	A fullness between the inferior palpebral sulcus and the oblique palpebral sulcus
Common Transverse Sulcus	A transverse furrow on the superior palpebrae located just above the cilia
Linear Sulci	Short broken furrows that fan out from opposite corners of the eye towards each other; normally more visible on the superior palpebrae

Restorations

The eyes can be affected by numerous issues that require restoration. A common problem is sunken eyes, which occur either as a natural change after death or from pathological antemortem conditions. The simplest corrective measure for mildly sunken eyes is to use an eyecap; trim the eyecap to size if necessary. If this does not adequately correct the appearance, then cotton may be placed between the eyeball and the eyecap to create more bulk, and therefore greater projection, behind the eyelid. For more severe cases of sunken eyes, tissue builder should be hypodermically injected into the tissue behind the eyeball. Using either the medial or lateral canthus, guide the needle along the body margin until it reaches the posterior part of the orbital cavity (Mayer, 2012). Inject the tissue builder slowly until the desired projection is achieved; too much will cause the eyes to protrude abnormally. When the restorative artist is dealing with collapsed eyes, the preferred treatment is to inject tissue builder directly into the eyeball itself but avoid the iris. However, be aware that this technique may create additional leakage concerns.

While sunken eyes are common, the opposite is also possible. Swelling or protrusion of the eye may be caused by the eyeball or the tissue around the eye (palpebra, orbital pouch, etc.). For some cases, external pressure may be enough to reduce the swelling. When this is not effective for the tissues surrounding the eye, a compress with or injection of an astringent chemical may be necessary. Additionally, channeling may be used to drain fluids and gas from the area. When the eyeball itself is the problem, either cranial aspiration (inserting an infant trocar or hypodermic needle into either nasal passage and through the cribriform plate of the ethmoid bone and remove gasses or liquids) or aspiration of the eyeball may relieve pressure and allow the protruding eyeball to sink back into the orbital cavity. For the most severe cases, removal of the eyeball may be required, with authorization. In these instances, the eyeball and its projection must be recreated.

Discolorations in the area of the closed eye are often the result of trauma; "black eye" is the common vernacular (Klicker, 2002). Treating discolorations in the area of the eye is similar to doing so on the rest of the body. Corrective options include the use of bleaching agents (on a compress or injected hypodermically) and using opaque cream cosmetics to cover the discoloration.

On some cases, wrinkling of the eyelids and dehydration may occur. This can be either natural or the result of treatments used to reduce swelling (i.e. chemical compresses or hypodermic injection). On mild cases, massage cream or a small compress soaked with humectant can be applied to the affected area. Also, an electric spatula can be used to reduce wrinkling, but the eyelids should first be covered in massage cream to eliminate damage to the skin. For severe dehydration or wrinkling, wax may be used. The wrinkled portion of the eyelid can be removed and recreated with wax, or the entire area can be waxed over and reconstructed to produce the correct form. Similarly, the medial canthus on each eye can become dehydrated and form a small opening or depression; often discolored. To correct this, the area can be filled with a small amount of lip wax or soft wax. Some practitioners prefer to cement the opening of the medial canthus first (Klicker, 2002).

Lacerations, abrasions, and other trauma can occur on the palpebrae or in the area of the eye. These can be corrected as they would be on other areas. Small lacerations may be cemented. Larger lacerations will require wax, and in some cases, areas of tissue may require excision. This can involve a portion of or the entire affected palpebra. When possible, it is beneficial to retain the unattached margin(s) in order to keep the natural cilia, thus requiring less restoration and reducing artificiality.

RESTORATIVE ART: FOUNDATION & PRACTICE: CHAPTER 8

A common restoration problem is separation of the eyelids, even on normal cases. If an eyecap was not used during feature setting, then introducing one post-embalming may fix the issue. However, tissues firmed after embalming may not provide enough elasticity to properly insert an eyecap. The corrective measure often employed is simply applying an adhesive to keep the two eyelids together. Care must be taken to correctly place the line of closure and reduce the risk of excess adhesive running down the inferior palpebra. In addition to adhesives, the lids may be stretched and manipulated using an aneurysm hook or needle, providing greater range of movement that may allow proper closure. In extreme cases, the levator palpebrae superioris muscle may be severed, and this will allow the superior palpebra to move more freely. The muscle itself is located above the eyeball and can be accessed by guiding a severing instrument under the superior eyelid between the eyeball and superior bony margin of the orbit. It is recommended that this task be done with blunt-blunt or blunt-sharp scissors.

The growth in donation has led to an increase in cases requiring restoration following complete eye removal, or **enucleation**. In these cases, restoration will begin during arterial injection. First, remove any temporary packing placed in the orbital cavity by the harvesting organization. Open and gently stretch the palpebrae, and then dry each eye socket. Care should be taken to avoid swelling and discolorations because these are more common due to the trauma already experienced by the tissue in the area. After drying, the orbital cavities should be packed with cotton soaked with a cauterizing chemical. An eyecap should then be placed over the cotton to keep the proper form during injection. Do not use pre-injection, and consider the use of a restricted cervical injection; in all cases, a lower than normal rate of flow and pressure setting should be used. This will reduce the likelihood of swelling. After embalming, remove the temporary packing and dry the eye sockets again. Using wax or mortuary putty, recreate the form of the eyeball, and set into each empty cavity. Then, place an eyecap on top, and close the palpebrae using an adhesive if necessary (Klicker, 2002).

EARS

The ears are a paired facial feature located on each side of the head. Although included in discussions of the face and important for viewing purposes, the ears are not a part of the face by definition. The ear is the organ of hearing, and its visible, external part is known as the auricle (Rizzo, 2001). This external portion is the focus of restoration. Since the bones of the ear (incus, stapes, malleus) are internal, they have no bearing on restoration.

Characteristics

No two ears are the same, even on the same individual. A person's ears can be as unique as a fingerprint, and they change less in a lifetime than any other facial feature (Mayer, 1980). Normally, one ear is situated slightly more superior than the other, and each will exhibit differences in form. The ear itself is made of cartilage, except for the lobe which is comprised of connective tissue. The ear is one-third the length of the face, which is also the length of the nose. This makes the ear very important for facial proportions.

Anatomy and Parts

The ear is composed of numerous parts. These parts are divided into two separate categories: depressions/cavities and elevations/ridges. Descriptions of the parts within each category are included in the tables below.

Depressions & Cavities of the Ear	
External Auditory Meatus (Ear Passage)	The opening or passageway of the ear canal, not visible from the frontal or profile views
Concha	The concave shell of the ear; the deepest depression of the ear
Triangular Fossa	The depression between the Crura of the Antihelix; the second deepest depression of the ear
Scapha	The fossa between the inner and outer rims of the ear; the shallowest depression of the ear
Intertragic Notch	The notch or opening between the Tragus and Antitragus; the spillway of the ear

RESTORATIVE ART: FOUNDATION & PRACTICE: CHAPTER 8

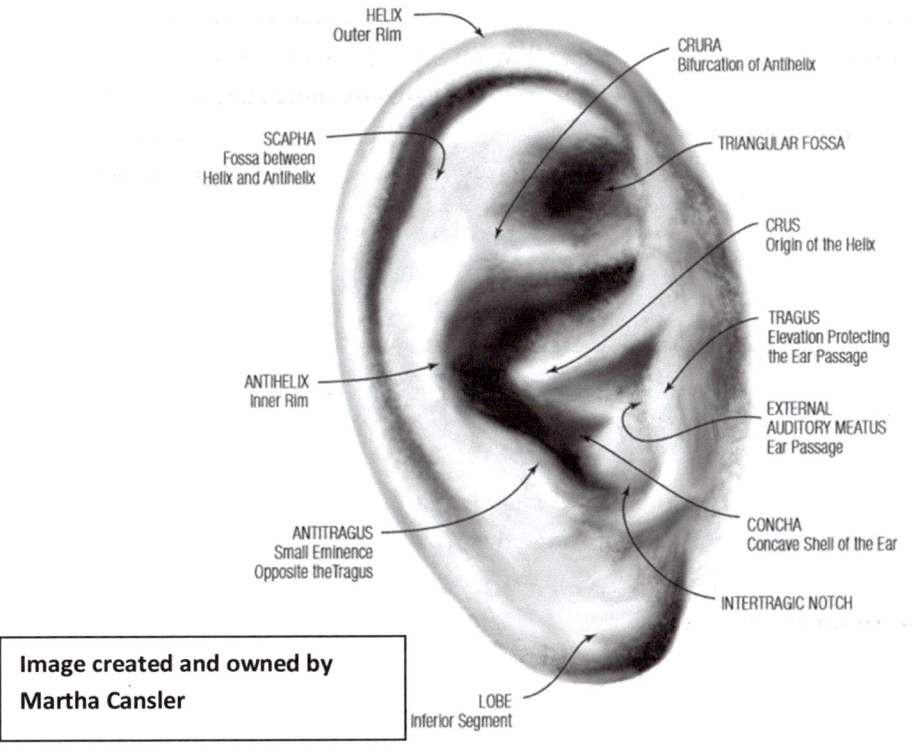

Image created and owned by Martha Cansler

Elevations & Ridges of the Ear	
Helix	The outer rim of the ear; has the general shape of a question mark
Crus of the Helix	The origin of the Helix which is flattened in the Concha
Antihelix	The inner rim of the ear; bifurcates superiorly
Crura of the Antihelix (Superior Crus & Anterior Crus)	The bifurcating branches of the Antihelix; formed by the Superior Crus and the Anterior Crus

Tragus	The projection protecting the ear passage; arises from the posterior margin of the lateral cheek
Antitragus	The small eminence obliquely opposite the Tragus; helps to form the Intertragic Notch
Lobe	The inferior third of the ear; its anterior margin can be attached or detached

Restorations

In general, the ear will present fewer restorative issues than other facial features. Problems requiring restoration normally include: discolorations, abrasions, damaged ears/missing parts, and completely missing ears.

Discolorations and abrasions can be treated the same as with any other part of the body. Some abrasions will require surface embalming to ensure adequate treatment. For discolorations, a bleaching agent and/or chemical compress works well, but care must be taken to keep the compress in place due to the location of the ear. In any case, cosmetics should be applied to finalize the concealment of any abrasions or discolorations. During cosmetizing, it should be noted that the ears are also considered to be a warm color area of the face.

For damaged or missing ears, first ensure that the area itself, and any remaining tissue or ear structure, are properly treated and thoroughly dried. These cases will require wax reconstruction of the ear or any missing parts. Excise any tissue that will hinder the process. With missing ear parts, recreate them from wax, attach, and feather into the surrounding ear structure. Cosmetics can be applied over the wax after completion or mixed with the wax before application to the area. For missing ears, recreate them from wax based on recent photographs; rely heavily on the applicable facial proportions and measurements. For attachment, utilize the four structures of the Temporal Bone that help to locate the correct position of the modeled ear: **external auditory meatus**, **mastoid process**, **zygomatic arch**, and **mandibular fossa**. Once the ear is in the correct location, the angle of inclination must be determined. Essentially, the ear passage on the modeled ear is aligned with the ear passage on the head. Then, the modeled ear is pivoted until the anterior edge is parallel with an imaginary line running from the eyebrow to the upper lip. An incorrect angle of inclination will give the appearance of artificiality, regardless of the skill in recreating the form of the ear.

Chapter Conclusion

In this chapter, the basics of each facial feature were discussed. The nose, mouth, chin, eyes, and ears were all examined to determine their specific anatomy, parts, and characteristics. When applicable, additional information regarding a feature was included, as with the two nasal classifications. The restorative treatments for each individual feature were also explored in detail. These treatments should be used as a preliminary guide, since each individual case will present its own unique issues, often a combination of those discussed in this chapter.

References

Professional Experience and Educational Presentations:
A great deal of the content of this book has been derived from years of professional experience as an embalmer, funeral director, and funeral service educator.

Klicker, R. (2002). *Restorative art and science.* Buffalo, NY: Thanos Institute.

Mayer, J. S. (1980). *Restorative art.* Dallas, TX: Professional Training Schools.

Mayer, R. G. (2012). *Embalming: History, theory, and practice* (5th ed.).

    New York, NY: McGraw-Hill.

Rizzo, D. (2001). *Delmar's fundamentals of anatomy & physiology.*

    Stamford, CT: Thomson Learning.

Chapter Nine: Hair and Hair Restorations

Chapter Author: Cody L. Lopasky, M.A.

Chapter Learning Objectives

Upon completion of this chapter, students should be able to:

- Distinguish the different types of applicable human hair
- Know the characteristics of each hair type
- Locate alternate sources of hair for restoration
- Describe the restorations that are unique to each type of hair

Introduction

The majority of the human body is covered in hair. It comes in many forms and varieties. Regardless of type, hair is mostly composed of keratin, and color is provided by the pigment **melanin**. Differing amounts and shades of melanin create the vast array of hair colors. Below the surface of the skin is the hair follicle and the root, where each hair develops. Above the surface of the skin is the visible part of the hair known as the shaft (Cohen & Taylor, 2009). From outermost to innermost, each individual hair has three layers; the cuticle, cortex, and medulla (Rizzo, 2001). Part of restoring a decedent to a natural appearance is care and preparation of all visible hair, including restorations of that hair when necessary.

In normal cases, hair treatment and restoration will simply entail washing and styling. Sometimes, it is necessary to use artificial color on the hair of a decedent at the request of the family. In these instances, it is important to use the exact same color and brand as directed (Klicker, 2012). Follow the instructions of the designated product for best results.

Greater detail is required for major hair restorations, which are the focus of this chapter. Included are the following types of hair and their associated restorations: head hair, cilia, supercilia, and facial hair. It should be noted that major hair restorations normally require missing hair to be recreated on the deceased. The sources of this hair can be numerous and will often depend on the type, color, or style of the hair to be restored, some natural and others artificial. Sources of hair for restoration are described in the table below. In all cases, hair restoration should be done post-embalming.

Hair Restoration Sources	
Decedent's Body	Hair can be taken from non-viewed parts of the decedent's body; e.g. the back of the head. This is often done for head hair since it is a match for color and type.
Wigs, Toupees, Hairpieces, Extensions, etc. (Artificial Hair)	It is recommended that all restorative artists keep on hand artificial hairpieces of differing color, length, and hairstyle. Pieces can be trimmed for use on many cases. *NOTE: Fake eyelashes can also be included in this category.*
Barber Shops and Salons	These locations are an excellent source of specific hair types, trimmed from the hair of customers.
Cosmetic Brushes	If the required hair for restoration matches that of a cosmetic brush, then the brush can be trimmed and its hair used for that purpose.

Head Hair

Characteristics

Of all hair types, head hair generally requires the most attention. This is true for both the living and the deceased. Everyone's hair is unique, and genetics play a large role. Head hair generally presents itself as straight, curly, or kinky/tightly curled. These differing textures are the result of the keratin and resulting elasticity of each hair (Rizzo, 2001).

In addition to texture, color is another identifying characteristic of head hair. As stated earlier, hair color is a product of the pigment melanin. More pigment creates darker hair colors, and the reverse is true for less pigment. Varying shades combine with a specific amount of melanin to create a wide range of natural human hair colors. As humans age, less pigment is produced, and hair begins to turn gray. White hair is the result of an absence of pigment as well as air bubbles in the shaft of the hair. The age at which humans go gray or white depends on many factors and varies considerably. While genetics are a major contributing factor, stress and traumatic events have also been shown to produce gray or white hair (Rizzo, 2001).

Head hair length is dependent on both personal style and genetics. Some people keep their hair long. Others keep it short to medium length, and some have no hair at all. Baldness can be a personal choice as well as the result of hereditary traits. Hair growth and loss is cyclical and occurs naturally. Genetic baldness, though, occurs when both hair and hair follicles are lost (Rizzo, 2001). In this situation, hair is unable to regrow in a normal cycle which produces baldness. It must also be noted that certain medical treatments like chemotherapy may also cause a person to go bald. However, according to the National Cancer Institute (2017) hair will normally grow back after the termination of treatments, sometimes in a different color or texture.

Restorations

Head hair restorations involve either portions of the hair or the entire head of hair. When the entirety of the hair is missing, two options exist: restore the hair or use an artificial covering. This can be a scarf, hat, or wig/hairpiece. If any of these artificial coverings were used by the decedent in life, then they should be used in death to ensure the correct appearance. When using artificial hair (wigs, toupees, etc.), it may require styling once placed on the decedent. It is rare that an entire head of hair will be restored versus simply using a covering. However, a full restoration can be done and is simply an expanded version of restoring a patch of missing head hair.

For a small to medium patch of missing hair, the area should first be cleaned to remove any debris and then dried. Hair should be placed onto the head in small sections or groups, one at a time. Depending on the length of hair and the size of the area to be restored, hair can be either attached with adhesive or embedded in a small layer of wax. Adhesive/glue is more secure, but wax provides a more natural appearance (Mayer, 1980). Adhesives can be applied to the head or applied to the attached end of the hair itself before placement on the head. When using wax, only the attached ends of the hair should be embedded, not the entire length of hair. Regardless of method, hair should be applied first to the most inferior area of restoration. With each successive section/group, apply slightly superior to the last. This will allow each layer to overlay that below it, giving a more natural appearance.

In cases where the entire head of hair must be recreated (in lieu of a wig, hat, etc.), the above steps for restoring a patch of hair should be followed. Start at the edges and work toward the crown. The reverse will be true for decedents that styled their hair in a combed-back or pulled-back direction. Focus on the edges that will be visible. These include the normal hairline on the forehead, temples, sideburns, and around the ears. Focus on accurate recreation of the part in the hair (if present) and the shape of the hairline (rounded, straight, widow's peak, etc.). Less attention can be paid to the posterior margins of the hair. These will be on the pillow and not a part of the visible area of the deceased.

Using photographs, ensure that the natural direction of hair growth or styling is accurately followed. Hair should be of the correct texture and color before application to the head. However, hair can be trimmed in length and lightly styled, if needed, after being applied. When doing so, care should be taken to ensure hair is not loosened or detached.

NOTE: A combination of hair restoration and covering may be used for the whole head. For instance, the front and side margins of the hair can be recreated and then used in conjunction with a hat, bandana, or other covering.

Cilia

Characteristics

The **cilia**, or eyelashes, are located on both the superior and inferior palpebrae, and they tend to be thicker than head hair. These fringes of hair exist on the free, or unattached, rims of each palpebra. They are irregular in spacing, length, and abundance. When the eye is closed, the eyelashes of the two palpebrae do not interlace; they simply meet (Mayer, 1980).

Cilia normally grow in small, uneven clusters. Sometimes these clusters form inverted triangles. However, no cilia exist on the extreme ends of the line of closure of the eye. On the upper eyelid, cilia curve upward, and on the lower eyelid, they curve downward. Due to the curvature of the eyeball and subsequent curvature of the palpebrae, the cilia tend to fan out. In other words, cilia on the medial end project medially. They become more anterior in projection toward the middle of the eye, and they project laterally on the lateral end. Cilia tend to be sparser on the inferior eyelid than on the superior. Older individuals may have scarce or almost non-existent cilia (Mayer, 1980).

Restorations

A common issue requiring restoration is missing cilia. Two main restorative options exist: application of fake/false eyelashes or recreation using individual hairs. It may be possible to recreate the eyelashes by simply working on the superior palpebra alone, since more cilia exist here. Many restorative artists find it unnecessary to recreate both the upper and lower eyelashes when the upper alone will suffice.

When using fake eyelashes, know that they are generally produced to look enhanced and uniform. This appearance is contrary to that of normal cilia for the average decedent. Ensure a natural look by "roughing up" the lashes a bit. Next, trim and shape the lashes with scissors to eliminate any equidistant spacing or obvious pattern. It is best to trim the lashes with scissors in line (or parallel) with the hairs versus across them perpendicularly (Mayer, 1980). The latter will create lashes of equal length.

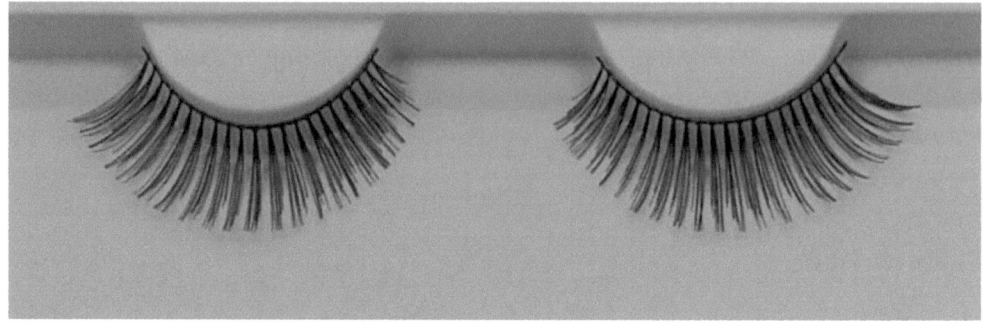

Product differences exist, but most fake eyelashes come affixed to a strip for ease of application. This strip may come with adhesive pre-attached or it may be required to add adhesive. In either case, a small amount of adhesive may be beneficial for ensuring the lashes do not detach later. Remember that fake eyelashes and their adhesive are not specifically produced for non-living tissue. Start at the medial end of the eyelid for attachment, and finish at the lateral end (Klicker, 2002). Some practitioners may prefer to adhere the strip to the immediate underside of the superior palpebral, on the line of closure itself. This second option will hide the strip, when needed, to reduce artificiality. If needed, repeat for the inferior cilia.

When attaching individual hair(s) to recreate the cilia, ensure the sourced hairs are of equal color and texture to that of the deceased. Affix in place using a small amount of adhesive on one end. In lieu of adhesive, a small area of wax can be applied to the anterior margin of the superior eyelid and hairs embedded into it. Hairs can be attached individually or in small groups. Using groups may be more efficient and also help to recreate the inverted triangles often seen with natural lashes. When restoration is done using individual hairs or clusters, ensure that the lashes are curled, when necessary using an eyelash curler, and that the angle of projection is correct.

Supercilia

Characteristics

The eyebrows, or **supercilia**, are located on the supraorbital margins. Generally, the eyebrows of a female are situated more superiorly than they are on a male. Males tend to have thicker, bushier, and less defined eyebrows (Flood, 2010). Eyebrows will differ from person to person, and some people pluck and/or trim their eyebrows to produce a specific shape or style.

An imaginary line running vertically from the lateral boundary of the wing of the nose marks the medial margin of the eyebrow. The termination, or lateral margin, of each supercilium is denoted by an imaginary line extending from the same point outside the wing of the nose and running through the lateral canthus of the eye (Flood, 2010).

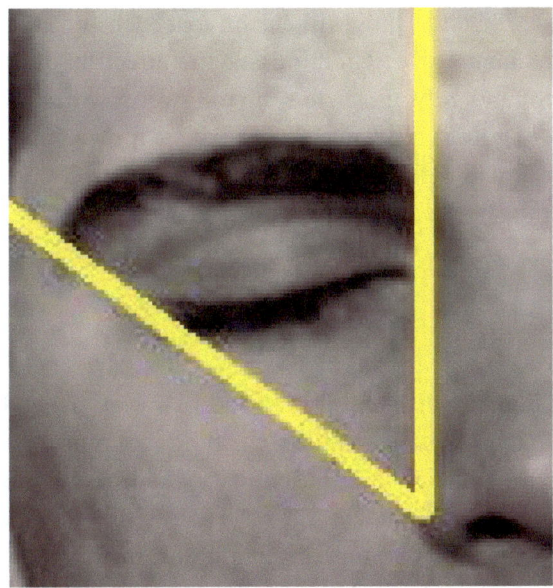

Each supercilium forms a slight upward arc and contains three parts: **head, body**, and **tail**. The head encompasses the medial end of the eyebrow and has the densest concentration of hair. The body is the middle portion and contains less hair than the head. The tail contains the sparsest amount of hair and is the lateral end of the eyebrow. Additionally (and of note for restorations), the tail points toward the ear passage.

Restorations

Restorations of the supercilium will normally involve recreating a missing part or the entire eyebrow. For small areas with missing hair or even less dense hair, an eyebrow pencil can be used to fill in as desired. Care should be taken to choose the correct color and avoid adding too much color. Additionally, small missing portions can be filled in with hair by using adhesive on one end of the hair and affixing to the eyebrow with forceps. Ensure that the added hair is situated in the correct direction of growth.

When the entire supercilium needs to be restored, a wax foundation should be used. A thin layer of wax, colored to match the surrounding skin tone, is first applied to the eyebrow area. This should be made just larger than the actual eyebrow. For reference, be sure to mark the correct points of origin and termination; either physically or mentally. Recreated supercilia that are either too short or too long will look unnatural. The color and texture of hair used in the restoration should match that of the decedent. Hair from the back of the decedent's head may be ideal for this task. Beginning at the lateral end of the eyebrow, embed hairs into the wax and work toward the medial end. This will ensure that each successive layer of hair will overlap those more lateral. Keep in mind that the direction of hair growth for the supercilia is upward and outward. After the full eyebrow has been recreated, lightly trim to the correct length, if needed. NOTE: Age and personal grooming may affect the shape and "bushiness" of the eyebrows - always consult current photographs to confirm the authenticity of restorations.

Facial Hair

Characteristics

Facial hair comes in many different forms, and its variations go by different names. Popular culture often creates nicknames and additional monikers for the many versions of each type of facial hair. Individuals wear these in differing styles and lengths. The goatee of one decedent, for instance, will not be the exact same as another decedent. Facial hair texture, direction of growth, abundance, and personal preference all play a role in this. Although others exist and variations abound, the three most commonly encountered types of facial hair are mustache, beard, and goatee.

RESTORATIVE ART: FOUNDATION & PRACTICE: CHAPTER 9

Mustache: A mustache consists of facial hair grown on the superior integumentary lip; though it can also extend into the cheeks and/or inferior integumentary lip. Styles vary widely and include variations such as the handlebar, pencil, Fu Manchu, etc. Mustaches can be kept neatly trimmed or left bushy. The general direction of hair growth is downward and outward. However, larger mustache examples may exhibit multiple hair growth directions based on the differing locations on the face.

Beard: Beards come in many shapes, forms, and lengths. A full beard is facial hair growth that connects each sideburn by covering a large portion of the lower part of the face. Hair extends down from each sideburn, encompasses an area of the cheek, runs along the jawline and portions of the neck, covers the chin, and generally includes a mustache. While a full beard normally includes all of these, variations of a full beard will drop or add certain facial areas based on style. The upper part of the sideburn may resemble head hair in texture, but below this, the texture will change to that of facial hair, which tends to be coarser. The direction of hair growth will depend on the section of the beard and the part of the face upon which it grows. Generally, hair growth is downward. It tends to grow in a more posterior direction as the beard goes more laterally. However, hair growth on individuals will vary, especially on the chin and neck regions. Like mustaches, beards may be short and neatly trimmed or kept bushy and/or lengthy.

Goatee: A goatee is essentially a smaller version of a beard only encompassing the central part of the lower third of the face. Variants may or may not include a mustache. With a mustache, facial hair growth encircles the mouth and covers the chin. Often, a goatee is contained between the nasolabial folds and extends downward onto the chin. However, certain individuals may grow a goatee past these margins and include portions of the cheeks and neck. Like a beard, the direction of hair growth will depend on the section of the goatee, but it is generally in a downward pointing direction.

Restorations

Each individual type of facial hair will require its own distinct restoration. The key aspects for any restoration are hair color, texture, and direction of growth. These specifics must be matched, using photographs, in order to achieve an accurate recreation. It must be noted that faux facial hair can be purchased for use from costume/theatrical suppliers. However, due to time constraints and availability, facial hair restorations are most often accomplished with wax and sourced hair.

Restoring a part or all of a mustache can be the simplest of facial hair restorations; especially in terms of surface area. To recreate the entire mustache, a small layer of wax (just larger than the mustache itself) should be applied to the area. In other words, the superior integumentary lip. This process is similar to that of restoring a complete eyebrow. Small clusters of hair are added one at a time, and each is embedded into the layer of wax. As with head hair restorations, each layer should slightly overlap the one that preceded it. Start at the lateral ends of the mustache, and work toward the midline. Make certain that the hairs are angled in the correct direction of growth. Also, pay close attention to the linear outline of the mustache. It is common to see a "V" shape below the columna nasi or an inverted "V" shape above the central arc of the superior mucous membrane, which contains no hair (Mayer, 1980). If needed, trim the hairs after completion. For smaller patches of hair missing from a mustache, use the above technique on the localized area. Ensure that the embedded hairs are feathered into the surrounding natural hair.

Beard and goatee restorations will follow a similar patten as the restoration of a mustache. The main differences are direction of hair growth (which varies widely based on many factors) and the size of the area to be restored. Often, only a part of the beard or goatee will be missing. In these instances, recreate the affected area much like other hair restorations. First, apply a thin layer of wax. Next, embed hair into the wax in the direction of growth, and trim to the correct length. For very small patches of missing hair, adhesive can be used in lieu of wax. Again, make sure that the restored hair is feathered into the surrounding beard or goatee. Since a myriad of styles exist, current close-up photographs are essential.

Acquiring sourced hair for beard and goatee restorations may be slightly difficult. This hair is normally coarser and may not match that of a hairpiece or cosmetic brush. Barbershops and salons can be an excellent source. Also, decedents with a larger bearded area can provide the hair for their own restorations; especially when only a small area is missing. For these cases, it is possible to use hair from the underside of the beard. Removing hair from this region will not affect the decedent's appearance since this area is hidden under the bulk of the beard when lying in a casket.

NOTE: This section admittedly discusses only the simplest forms of facial hair and omits numerous deviations from these standard options. Restorations of any and all variants should utilize the aforementioned processes and adapt them on a case-by-case basis.

Chapter Conclusion

In this chapter, the different types of human hair and their restorations were explored. Head hair, eyelashes, eyebrows, and facial hair were each examined to determine their characteristics and the restorative treatments that are unique to that type of hair. With facial hair, three main variations were discussed, though many forms and styles do exist as versions of those three. Also included were the anatomy of hair itself and the possible sources of hair for use in restorations.

References

Professional Experience and Educational Presentations:
A great deal of the content of this book has been derived from years of professional experience as an embalmer, funeral director, and funeral service educator.

Cohen, B., & Taylor, J. (2009). *Memmler's structure and function of the human body* (9th ed.). Baltimore, MD: Lippincott Williams & Wilkins.

Flood, J. (2010). *Facial reconstruction for artists*. Springfield, MO:
WindSongBooks.

Klicker, R. (2002). *Restorative art and science*. Buffalo, NY: Thanos Institute.

Mayer, J. S. (1980). *Restorative art*. Dallas, TX: Professional Training Schools.

National Cancer Institute. (2017). Hair loss (alopecia) and cancer treatment.
Retrieved from https://www.cancer.gov/about-cancer/treatment/side-effects/hair-loss

Rizzo, D. (2001). *Delmar's fundamentals of anatomy & physiology*.
Stamford, CT: Thomson Learning.

Unit 4

General Restorative Treatments

•

Chapter 10:

General Restorative Treatments

•

Chapter 11:

Sutures

Chapter Ten

General Restorative Treatments

Images in this chapter courtesy of: Anthony Fleege, MBA, & Sydney Baumeister

Chapter Learning Objectives

Upon completion of the study of this chapter students should:

- Recall the classifications of cases that require restorative treatments
- Understand the timeframes and order of treatments associated with restorative work
- Comprehend the connection between setting features and the restorative process
- Understand general restorative treatments and have a foundation to replicate each treatment

In many respects, the content in this chapter is exactly what this text has been preparing for from the start, actual techniques utilized when restoring human remains to natural form and color. Before we engage in this presentation it is important to acknowledge that these are considered "general" restorative techniques; therefore the information contained provides a baseline for various techniques. They provide readers with procedures commonly utilized when performing specific restorations and suggestions for various challenges the embalmer may encounter. This is done with the knowledge that many techniques exist to perform various restorative treatments. The best technique for any specific case is the one that is authorized, ethical, moral, within legal parameters, and ultimately provides the best results. Before we offer these general restorative treatments, it is helpful to offer classifications of remains requiring restoration as well as discuss timeframes when certain restorations should take place.

Classification of Cases Requiring Treatment

Information is power. Understanding that bodies that require restoration have experienced some pathway to this reality can be helpful. Furthermore, the successful restorative artist will benefit from identifying the specific pathway, as this information can assist in selecting the best professional technique to execute in order to achieve the best results. Generally speaking causes for restorations fall within four classifications: injury, disease, post-mortem tissue changes, and natural age progression processes.

Injury

Common classifications for cases that require restorative work are those that have endured some type of injury. Regardless if resulting from a motor vehicle accident, house fire, homicidal action, or suicidal act the resulting realities are injuries. It would be impossible to try to list all possible causes of injuries; just remain cognizant of the fact that many times cases require restorative work as a result of injuries.

Disease

Another classification for cases requiring restorative work are those that necessitate restoration due to damage resulting from disease processes. Consistent with injuries, it would be impossible to adequately list all of the potential diseases that may cause problems resulting in a need for restorative work, but just consider any disease that leads to emaciation, edema, discolorations, or amputations. Consider the complications of cancer, AIDS, hepatitis, or any wasting disease. Ultimately, it is important for the restorative artist to grasp the connection between disease processes and the need for restorative work, as this may assist in selecting the best treatment for a successful restoration.

Post-mortem tissue changes

Three distinct timeframes exist when considering post-mortem tissue changes. These include before treatment (embalming or refrigeration), during the embalming procedure (providing the body is embalmed), and after embalming or other treatment. Here, we introduce a few items typically associated with these timeframes.

- Before embalming (or other treatment) – decomposition, emaciation/dehydration, edema
- During embalming – swelling/distention of facial features
- After embalming (treatment) - decomposition, tissues gas, decomposition gas, distention, discoloration associated with purge, and dehydration

Natural age progression

The reality of the natural aging process is that often, it will present issues that may require restorative treatments. Over time, as the years add up, general reduction in muscle mass may lead to new skin tones and facial markings, or the once brown-haired individual may turn gray. Regardless of the impact, it is common for embalmers to address various conditions that resulted from natural age progression.

Order of Restorative Treatments

An important item to consider is the specific timeframe when various restorative treatments are suggested to take place. Although it is possible for some of the treatments to take place in more than one timeframe, generally, specific restorative treatments are best conducted at a specific time. Here, we consider such treatments with the note that these timeframes are associated with the embalming process but acknowledge that most restorative treatments are still viable even if the family decides against the embalming procedure.

- Pre-embalming – Initial bathing of the remains including washing the hair. This allows the removal of surface stains, dirt, and other debris that may be on the body or in the hair. This practice provides the embalmer better knowledge of the exact condition of the body. Setting the facial features is also a pre-embalming treatment as the embalming process will fixate tissues. This is also the appropriate time to employ temporary sutures if necessary, again the embalming process will fixate tissues. This is also a time when some embalmers prefer to shave remains as it is usually easier to shave unembalmed remains due to the elasticity of tissues. Although this is generally true, the embalmer should only shave remains when they are certain this is the family's desire, regardless of gender.
- Concurrent – Applications during the embalming procedure include any treatment that becomes necessary as a result of a specific body's reaction to the embalming procedure. This list is not exhaustive, as each embalming is unique, and the embalmer must utilize appropriate treatments that address specific concerns given any particular case. Common treatments employed

concurrently with the embalming procedure include removal of gasses or fluids from the abdominal, peritoneal, or thoracic cavity as these will cause distention as well as serve as a source of extravascular resistance to our embalming solution. Embalmers also commonly utilize manual pressure or wet cotton slings to apply pressure to areas of the body to reduce or prevent swelling. Another treatment that may be utilized during the embalming procedure is bleaching discolorations located in viewable areas. Although many embalmers prefer to wait until after embalming to bleach tissues, this practice is also often started during injection. Additionally, internal color changes due to adding active dyes to the embalming solution as well as the removal of intravascular discolorations are restorative treatments that take place during the embalming procedure.

- Post-embalming – Although no aspect of overall restorative treatments are more important than others, the bulk of restorative work is completed after the embalming procedure. Examples include but are not limited to the following: final bathing, washing of the hair and hairstyling, suturing and the concealment of sutures, excising tumors if necessary and authorized, hypodermic tissue building when necessary, any necessary reduction of swelling and modification of tissues, any necessary wax restorations, and final cosmetic application.

Feature Setting

The practice of setting features is a fundamental aspect of both the embalming procedure and restorative treatments. The final appearance of remains necessitates that the embalmer utilizes professional standards and take great care when setting the features. An error during this stage will create extra work later during the restoration. Therefore, we briefly outline elements associated with setting features (adapted from Mayer, 2012) immediately prior to examining general restorative treatments.

- Positioning Remains
  - Place remains in a comfortable and restful position.
  - The body should be in a supine position, with the head tilted to the right approximately 15 degrees, less for the obese case.
  - Custom may dictate hand placement; otherwise, work to achieve a comfortable position for the hands – Left hand over right is common to highlight a wedding band.
  - The embalmer should also consider appropriate placement of the legs. Typically, the feet should be as close together as possible. Also note

- Mouth and lip closure
  - Relieve any rigor mortis that may be present.
  - Disinfect the mouth.
  - If necessary disinfect dentures.
  - Close the mouth to observe natural closure.
  - Secure the mandible using an appropriate technique (needle injector, muscular suture, mandibular suture, dental tie, sublingual suture).
  - Place the lips in a desired position.
- Modeling the mouth
  - The curvature across the mouth and lips is described as horseshoe shaped.
  - If present, natural teeth will assist in the presentation of the natural form of the mouth. If absent, the embalmer may use dentures, if they are still appropriately sized for the remains, or use a mouth former, cotton, or mortuary putty to make sure the mouth has natural form.
  - Emaciated cases may require additional mortuary putty and/or cotton to aid in general appearance. Ultimately, these cases may require the injection of tissue builder before viewing.
- Positioning and closing the lips
  - It is essential that the embalmer secure a true line of closure when preparing remains for viewing. The mouth is convex in curvature from corner to corner. It is necessary to secure a closure that considers the weather lines when positioning the lips to achieve a natural appearance.
  - The line of closure is along the inferior margin of the upper teeth.
  - To help maintain the line of closure, it is common to use various adhesives, petroleum jelly, or massage cream.
- Eye closure
  - The line of closure is located in the inferior one-third of the orbit of the eye.
  - To help establish the appropriate anterior projecting of the eye, it is common to place eye caps or a piece of cotton under the eyelids.
  - Most embalmers find it beneficial to apply an adhesive prior to viewing to help maintain the line of closure for an extended period of time.
  - When it is difficult to achieve and maintain the line of closure, it is important to remember that the lids should abut, not overlap, and always work to maintain the line of closure in the appropriate inferior

third. Sometimes it is necessary to utilize wax to present the desired line of closure.

Restorative Treatments

Abrasions, Lacerations, Incisions, and Razor Burn Treatment

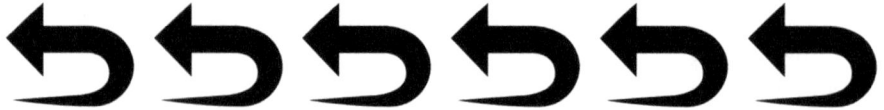

Abrasions

Abrasion, an antemortem and/or postmortem injury resulting from friction of the skin against a firm object resulting in the removal of the epidermis, is a common problem faced by restorative artists. As with any injury, the embalmer must take great care to examine the area prior to treatment. The depth and overall range of an abrasion will determine the amount of scabbing involved and the postmortem interval will impact the level of discoloration and level of dehydrated tissue associated with the problem area. Dehydrated tissue will turn dark and scabs (dried blood) will be a deep red; in most cases, both problems will need to be removed. Typically, these injuries can be easily restored, and when the appropriate steps are taken, these will no longer be visible nor will they present a leakage problem. As with most restorations, general recommendations include steps that should be taken before, during, or after the embalming procedure. It is important to state that most restorations are still possible regardless of a family's decision to select embalming or otherwise. This is a simple note to inform readers of the fact that a step indicating a timeframe related to the embalming process does not mean embalming is required to perform any specific treatment, just that if embalming is performed, these would be the recommended time frames.

When addressing abrasions, the embalmer needs to apply massage cream around the abraded area. This will help to prevent dehydration and discoloration of the tissue around the abrasion that may result from the leakage of embalming fluid. It is important that the massage cream is not applied directly to the abraded area, as this might prevent the area from becoming firm and dry, the goals of the embalming process. Once the abrasion is clean, firm, and dry it is necessary to remove scabs from the area, as scabs will challenge the restorative artist when attempting to create natural skin texture. Simply remove the scabs utilizing a scalpel or forceps, and it is also recommended to remove dehydrated tissue that resulted from the injury at this time. Once this treatment is concluded, the area should be dried with cotton and treated with a cauterizing agent to further address any concern of leakage. Now, the restoration can move into the next phase. At this point, it is necessary to secure the wound/injury closed. Most abrasions should not require sutures (see chapter 11 for the presentation of related sutures) but will necessitate cauterizing agents and adhesives followed by wax application. Remember the goal of a natural appearance, therefore we always apply appropriate skin texture and markings when completing a wax restoration. Once the area is restored, the restorative artist can move into the cosmetic phase of the restoration. As will be noted in the chapter on mortuary cosmetology, various types of products are available, and depending on the cosmetic utilized, it may be appropriate to apply the cosmetic with or on top of the wax. Each embalmer will develop personal preferences regarding what will work best given any specific case.

Prior to the image presentation regarding abrasions, it is prudent to mention razor burn. **Razor burn** is a darkened, air-dried area on the skin resulting from the removal of the epidermis while shaving. We have added this here, as it mirrors the definition of an abrasion regarding the removal of the epidermis. We acknowledge that this problem may also be classified as a discoloration, but it is included with abrasions, as it is this friction that would lead to the discoloration. This can usually be avoided if the embalmer uses care, appropriate shaving lotion, and new blades while shaving remains. Regardless of the care taken, razor burn may occur when preparing remains. As with other abrasions, the embalmer must take great care to treat razor burn, addressing not only the discoloration associated with the area but also removing scabs where necessary to allow for appropriate surface contour.

Abrasion treatments

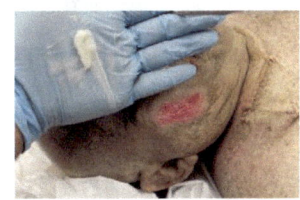  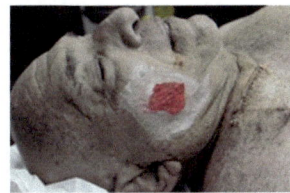

Application of massage cream around the abraded area followed by scab removal, note the application of massage cream to the scab after the abraded area is firm and dry, this may assist with scab removal

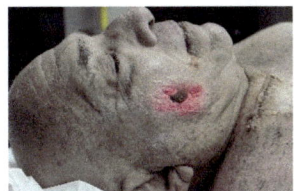 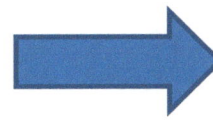 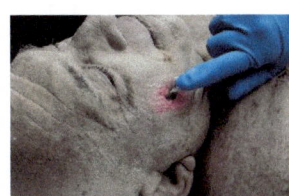

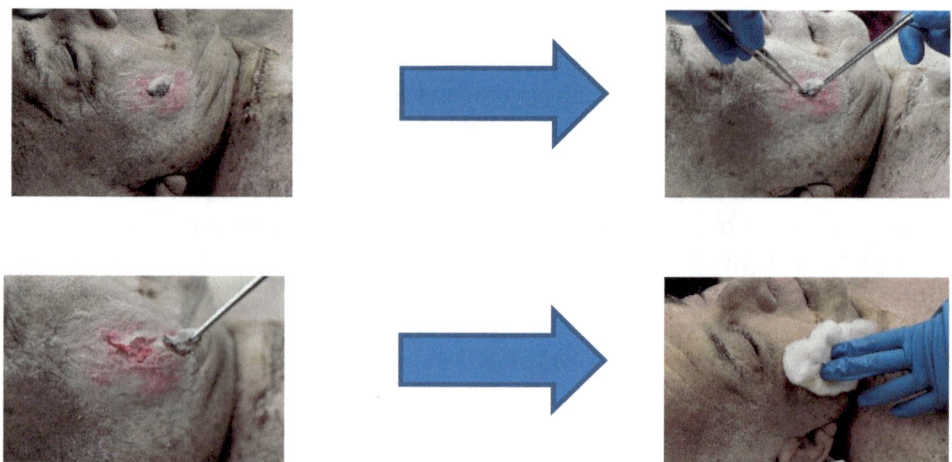

Application of a cauterizing agent with cotton followed by wax and cosmetic treatments

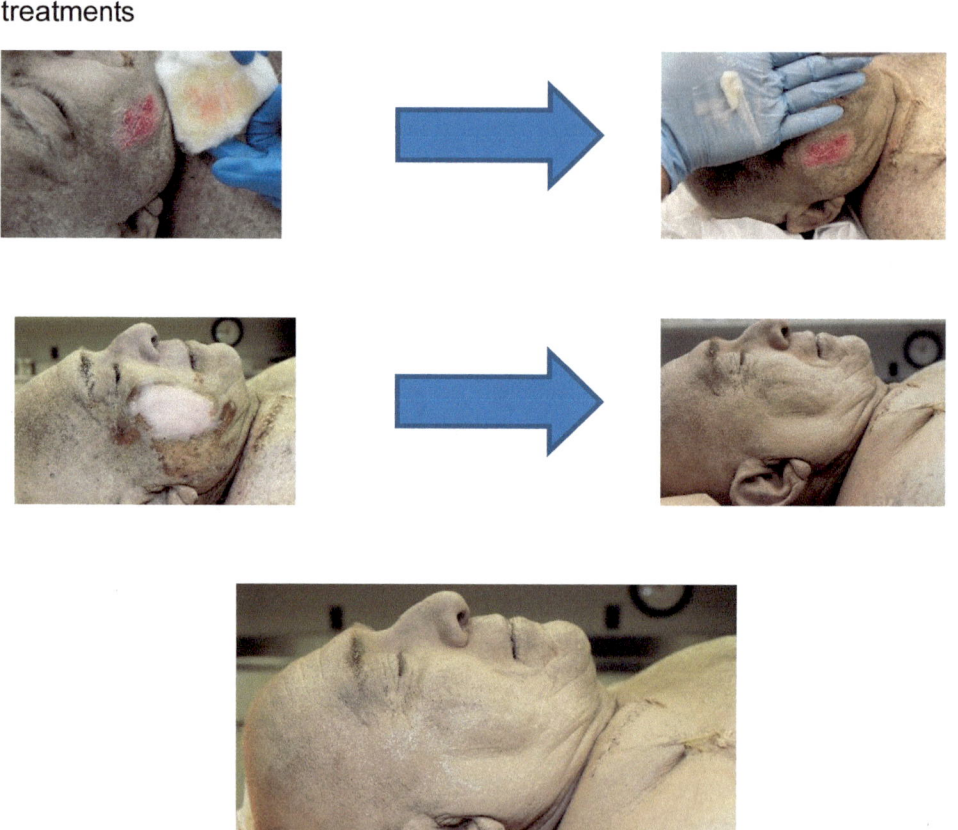

RESTORATIVE ART: FOUNDATION & PRACTICE: CHAPTER 10

Lacerations & Incisions

A **laceration** is an irregularly torn or jagged wound, while an **incision** is defined as a clean cut into tissue or skin. These two distinctly different wounds or cuts are presented here, together, as the common treatments to restore these are quite similar. As with any restoration, the embalmer must take great care to examine the nature and extent of the injury. Typically, lacerations are the result of a blunt force trauma injury and incisions the consequence of a sharp blade, scalpel, or knife perhaps.

As indicated above, the treatment of both lacerations and incisions are similar. Regardless of location, the site must be disinfected, dried, packed, sealed, and sutured closed. Any significant difference between addressing these two involves what steps may be required to make sure the surface level of the site meshes well with the adjoining tissue and maintains natural contour. The irregular nature of lacerations may also necessitate creative suturing.

If the embalming procedure will be performed, it may be necessary to utilize temporary sutures. This is the case if excess flaps of skin exist that should be fixated in an appropriate position; an important step in maintaining natural form and contour. These sutures, as temporary, will be removed after embalming and prior to additional restoration.

Here, we present the general step-by-step procedure for addressing a laceration or incision. The interior of the wound must be dried as well as possible with a cauterizing agent, this process will help prevent leakage in the area. It is valuable to apply massage cream around the area to minimize dehydration resulting from the application of the cauterizing pack. Once the wound is adequately dried, the embalmer should once again pat dry with cotton, pack with incision sealer or mortuary putty, then if necessary, trim dehydrated tissue that will prevent achieving clean margins when suturing the area. At this time, the restorative artist must select and perform the most appropriate suture (see chapter 11 for information performing various sutures and their recommended use) to achieve not only the closure of the site but also to maintain natural contour of the skin surface. Some practitioners prefer to use dental floss to suture small lacerations in viewable areas. Note that certain wounds/incisions may allow for the use of adhesives for closure, but sutures are typically the most secure method. Once the site is secured closed, the embalmer may proceed with appropriate wax and cosmetic application as required.

Discolorations and Stains

Discolorations and stains are commonly encountered when working to restore human remains. A **discoloration** is simply any abnormal color in or on the human body. These may be removed via arterial injection (when the discolorations are intravascular, i.e., livor mortis), if embalming is selected, or they require surface treatments if the discolorations are extravascular or if the discolorations are surface in nature. Common examples of discolorations that will require treatment beyond arterial injection include post-mortem stain, bruising that occurred antemortem, as well as any discolorations that may result from pathological conditions or traumatic events. When embalming is selected, the embalmer may observe the removal or lightening of these discolorations. If embalming is not selected, and when discolorations in viewable areas are not removed via arterial injection, then additional treatment is required to conceal the problematic areas. It is common practice to address these discolorations utilizing bleaching agents and/or cosmetic application.

Bleaching is the act of lightening a discoloration by hypodermic means or by surface compress. This treatment is common prior to cosmetic application. This practice can have a significant impact on the amount of cosmetic application required to conceal the area. Common agents used to bleach problem areas include cavity fluid, phenol and alcohol, preservative gels, and special bleaching fluids. This practice can lighten the area but may also lighten the tissue around the discoloration that was not stained, resulting in the need for additional cosmetic work. Also remember that these products may cause dehydration and fixation of the tissues impacted by the bleaching agents, and if a phenol based product is utilized, then once the degree of lightening is achieved the embalmer needs to neutralize the area with isopropyl alcohol or the bleaching agent will continue to lighten the area.

The two methods for bleaching application are the surface compress (see images below) and hypodermic injection. The surface compress is the simple application of a bleaching agent using a swatch of cotton. Prior to the application of the compress, you need to apply massage cream around the area that will be bleached to minimize the bleaching and dehydration of the surrounding areas. Once the bleaching surface compress is placed on the stain, it is best practice to cover the compress with plastic to diminish the vapors associated with the bleaching agent. During the time the compress is on the tissue, the embalmer needs to check the progress of the compress at regular intervals to make sure the compress is indeed working and also to make sure the compress is removed when the tissue color has been satisfactorily modified by the process.

It is also possible to bleach problem areas using hypodermic injection of the bleaching agent selected. It may prove difficult to inject only the specific stained area when using this method, because the embalmer must try to make sure the entire stained area receives the treatment. Similar to the surface compress, this technique may result in the dehydration or excessive bleaching of various areas, leaving the surface with various levels of color change which will require additional cosmetic treatment. When this method is used, the embalmer needs to try to inject the entire area that requires bleaching, but avoid the margins of the area that do not require the treatment. The embalmer must remember this is a treatment to impact the surface, so there is no need to inject deep tissues, and when the treatment is finished, the injection site(s) must be sealed closed with a small amount of tissue adhesive.

Surface compress bleaching treatments

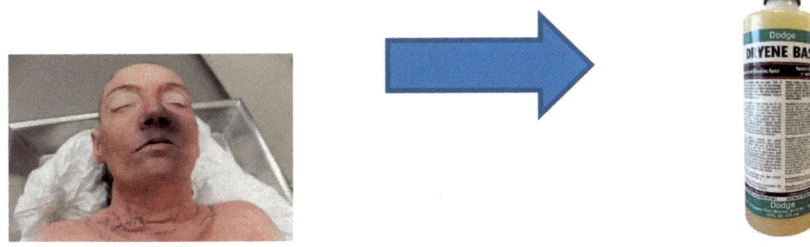

Application of appropriate bleaching agent utilizing a surface compress lightens the discolored area improving the surface for cosmetic work.

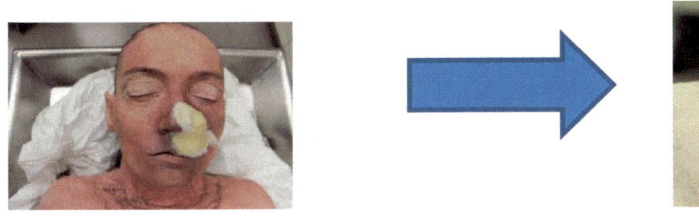

A **stain** is to discolor with foreign matter, which will require external surface treatments even if embalming is selected. By definition, a stain is on the surface of the tissue and will not be removed when the arterial embalming is performed. Note that internal stains are extravascular, versus an internal discoloration that is intravascular. An important step when working with human remains is the initial bathing of the body. This process will remove many surface discolorations and allow the embalmer a better idea of the exact nature of various discolorations/stains, which will assist in the appropriate treatment of these areas. It is important to take care to ensure that the friction created during surface stain removal does not damage the skin, especially on older decedents. Although it would be impossible to identify all possible surface stains an embalmer may encounter, it is possible to identify common surface stains and recommended agents for the removal of the stain.

Klicker (2002) identified **surface stain removers** associated with various stains:

Surface Stain	Suggested Stain Remover
Adhesive tape	Rubbing alcohol, ether
Blood	Cold water, ammonia
Paint	Turpentine, paint thinner
Nicotine	Lemon juice, household bleach
Tar/varnish	Acetone, commercial remover, liquid shampoo
Iodine	Alcohol
Mercurochrome	Household bleach
Grease	Ether, acetone, gasoline, liquid shampoo
Oil	Ether, kerosene, gasoline, carbon tetrachloride
Wax	Ether
Urine	Ammonia
Ink	Lemon juice, petroleum jelly
Glue	White vinegar, glue solvent
Lipstick	Dry cleaning solvent

Burns

Burns of various degrees are also common injuries the embalmer must treat. A **burn** is a tissue reaction or injury resulting from the application of heat, extreme cold, caustic material, radiation, friction, or electricity. Burns may be accompanied by foul odors, which arise from smoke, burnt tissue, infection, or the buildup of nitrogenous waste due to kidney failure. Here we categorize burns, provide characteristics, and present concerns and possible treatments related to restorative work.

A **first degree burn** is an injury caused by heat, which produces redness of the skin. Typically, the redness associated with a first degree burn will not require any special treatment, as the tissue is unbroken without destruction. The embalmer might increase the strength of solution if the case is embalmed to help fend off possible skin slip as well as apply massage cream before, during, and after embalming to help reduce dehydration and possible skin slip. Otherwise, one would predict positive results related to embalming and viewing of the remains.

A **second degree burn** is an injury that results in acute inflammation of the skin, blistering, and superficial destruction of dermis with edema and hyperemia of the tissues beneath the burn. Although special treatment will be required in these cases, there is no charring or major destruction of the tissues, but hair in these areas may be singed and require hair restoration (refer back to chapter 8 for hair restoration treatments).

When the embalmer encounters a second degree burn, it is important to relieve the pressure associated with the blisters by puncturing. If embalming is selected, this should be done prior to arterial injection, but if the blisters refill during embalming then they should once again be opened and drained. Consistent with the treatment of first degree burns, it is advisable to increase the strength of solution to assist in controlling skin slip and to secure the preservation of the area. After puncturing and draining, the blistered areas should be treated with a surface compress soaked in a cauterizing agent either concurrent with the embalming procedure or after the conclusion of the embalming. The embalmer will also need to remove any loose skin resulting in the blistered area, and then make sure the area is dried and sealed prior to final treatment. If the burn is in a viewable area, then after sealing, utilize wax restorations and cosmetics to complete the restoration. If the burn is located in a non-viewable area, once the sealing chemical has been applied, secure the area with appropriate plastic garments.

A **third degree burn** is an injury that results in the destruction of cutaneous and subcutaneous tissues. The tissue is seared or charred, and these injuries will require advanced treatments both regarding preservation if embalming is selected and also with general restorative treatments associated with preparing the body for viewing.

If embalming is selected, case analysis will determine the strength of solution. It is suggested to increase the strength of solution in order to adequately preserve the remains. Also, utilize supplemental embalming techniques (hypodermic injection or surface packs with cavity fluid or a cauterant) on any areas not receiving adequate arterial solution. It is also necessary to excise loose, damaged tissue. It may be necessary to pack deep wounds with cotton or appropriate mortuary mastic once the area has been cauterized. Exposed tissue should be treated with surface compresses to preserve and cauterize. Once fully dried, viewable areas should be restored with wax and cosmetics following the suggested treatments in this book. When working in non-viewable areas, once the area is fully dried, the embalmer should use appropriate plastic garments to guard against the possibility of leakage. If any of these areas require sutures, then select the most appropriate suture, and follow suggested protocol for the suture presented in the following chapter.

Although it is common for bodies that have experienced third degree burns to be able to be restored and viewed, it is also possible that the burns may be too extreme and not candidates for restoration or viewing.

Fourth degree burns are described as the total evacuation (absence) of tissue and are not considered appropriate for restorative treatments. Viewing is generally not an option unless the burn is localized to non-viewed areas such as the lower extremities.

Excising Tissue including Tumor Removal, Abscesses, and Neoplasms

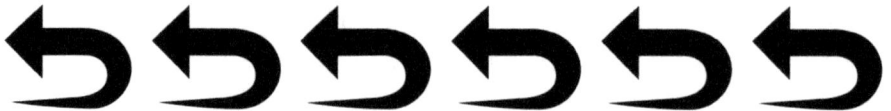

Embalmers may encounter bodies which have had tissue that has been excised antemortem, and it is also possible that restorative protocol will require the embalmer to excise tissue during embalming or restoration. Regardless of the source, it will be necessary for the embalmer to apply appropriate restorative treatments. In cases when the embalmer must excise tissue (a tumor or other mass), it is imperative that professional techniques are understood and applied. Regardless of the origin, the embalmer must disinfect, seal to prevent leakage, and restore the area when it is in a viewable area. Excising tissue is a common practice required for many restorative treatments. This practice has been linked to timeframes associated with the embalming process. This is important information to know, but in the current environment, it is necessary to acknowledge the reality that embalming is not always requested or authorized, yet restorative work may be performed, provided the necessary authorization is received from the next-of-kin/authorizing agent. Here, you will read many timeframes related to the embalming process. Do not confuse this to mean embalming is necessary to pursue these restorative treatments.

A **tumor** is an abnormal mass of tissue not normally found in a particular area. When an embalmer must excise a tumor or other mass, it is critical to first secure appropriate authorization and proceed with suggested professional protocol. Tumors in non-viewed areas may be left intact, provided they receive adequate embalming solution and as long as they do not distort the appearance of the body beneath their clothing. Tumors in viewable areas of the body may require excision. Bodies with tumors should be embalmed prior to removal of the tumor unless the mass impedes fluid distribution or distorts facial features. If it is necessary to remove the mass prior to embalming, the use of temporary sutures (interrupted or bridge suture) will be necessary. This suture is applied prior to embalming to hold surface areas in place during the embalming process. These sutures are intended to be removed post-embalming. These are single or multiple stitches, knotted on the surface to hold the skin in place (see chapter 11 for the presentation of this suture).

Post-embalming the embalmer should excise the mass with a scalpel. Mayer (1980) further describes the advantage of undercutting the edges of the excision. **Undercut**, the angled cut of the borders of an excision, made so that the skin surface will overhang the deeper tissues. He suggests that this technique will prevent the need of making the basket-weave suture intradermally. Also note that if the area is superficial (i.e. not too deep), the basket-weave may not be required. Further, this technique will help lock wax in position, and the slight dehydration of the tissues will not open a line of demarcation between the skin and the wax. Following the removal of the mass, cauterize exposed tissue and seal with an appropriate sealing chemical. Use a basket-weave suture (see chapter 11 for the presentation of this suture) to secure the margins of the excision and note that if this is a deep excision, you may need to first fill the recession with a firm wound-filler wax almost to the surface. Once the suture is secured, fill the excision with a wax (cosmetics may be added when appropriate) of medium firmness and restore normal contour and texture. When the area has the desired contour and skin texture, proceed with the correct cosmetic application.

An **abscess** is a localized accumulation of pus and usually requires the embalmer to drain the area. If embalming is authorized, then it is best to drain the area prior to arterial embalming, as this accumulation may serve as a source of extravascular resistance to the injection of the fluid. To drain the pus, insert a hypodermic needle and withdraw the pus with a syringe or lance the area, if necessary, to remove the pus. If during the embalming procedure the area fills with fluid or more pus then remove it as it appears. Next, it is necessary to again clean, disinfect, re-drain if necessary, and secure the area with a sealing chemical to prevent leakage prior to dressing for viewing. If in a nonviewable area, then seal the area, apply plastic garments, and proceed with dressing the body. If the abscess was in a viewable area then once the area has been sealed, use appropriate techniques presented in this book to restore the area to an acceptable appearance, including wax restorations with the application of skin texture, markings, and cosmetics. An abscess should not require the same invasive treatments required of tumor removal, but receiving authorization is best practice.

A **neoplasm** is a new and abnormal formation of tissue, as a tumor or growth. The embalmer should use techniques discussed above regarding tumor removal when a neoplasm is discovered, and the family authorizes the removal of the mass.

Restorative Art: Foundation & Practice: Chapter 10

Decapitation and Severed, Missing or Twisted Limbs and Bones

Decapitation

Although the restoration of a decapitated body is not common, it is possible that such a case will come across the embalmer's table. The professional restorative artist must understand the specific treatments suggested in such cases and be prepared to deliver positive results. Here, we identify three classifications of decapitation followed by specific treatments employed when working with a body that has experienced decapitation.

Classification

- Complete decapitation, or **decapitation**, is the separation of the head from the body.
- Orthopedic (**internal**) **decapitation**, trauma that occurs when the skull base separates from the spine.
- Partial decapitation is when a body has experienced significant trauma, but the head has not been completely separated from the body.

Treatments

When considering treatments for bodies that have experienced decapitation, we first consider orthopedic (internal) decapitation and partial decapitation.

When a person suffers an internal decapitation, the surface damage may be quite minimal. It is true that if this body is embalmed, problems associated with damaged vessels will most likely be a prime concern. Ultimately, the actual surface restorations required may be minimal with the main concern being that the head is stable for viewing. If the body is embalmed, then the fixation of the tissues will assist in this process, and then creating a depression in the pillow to further limit potential movement of the head may be all that is required. Any additional injuries that may accompany the internal injury should be addressed utilizing professional protocol described for various injuries and restorations in this book.

When the injury is described as a partial decapitation, the embalmer should proceed with necessary treatments using techniques presented in this book. By definition, this injury is more consistent with multiple treatments presented in this book; this is not technically a decapitation, as the head has not been separated from the body.

Appropriate techniques to utilize for these situations may be those related to abrasions, lacerations, fractures, severed, missing, twisted limbs and bones, or other wounds. The restoration of a body that has experienced partial decapitation is best described as a collection of various treatments that will provide the most desired results for viewing as opposed to attempting to outline a specific treatment for this injury.

When the embalmer encounters an actual complete decapitation, specific protocol is beneficial and advisable. Here we consider such treatments.

If embalming is authorized then the embalmer will need to embalm the head and trunk separately. One predicts injecting the head will offer additional challenges, as the injury will most likely damage arteries used for injection and may require not only arterial injection via appropriate, available, and intact arteries (common carotid, external carotid, internal carotid), but also hypodermic and surface embalming treatments. Keep in mind that, unlike most cases, an assistant will be required to hold the head while the embalmer sets features, prepares for injection, and during the actual injection. Consistent with treatment of the head, when embalming the torso it is also true that much damage may have been done to arteries used for injection. The embalmer must search for available arteries to inject (common carotid or axillary would be preferred), but again, it may be required to raise additional vessels in the arms and legs as well as utilize both hypodermic and surface embalming techniques in order to make sure the body is well-preserved.

Once the embalming is concluded, the embalmer may move forward with the reattachment and other restorative treatments.

Reattachment and stability

- Use PVC or wood dowels of appropriate length and sharp on both ends. Klicker (2002) suggests approximately 8-12 inches long but, it may be necessary to modify the length during the restoration to make sure the head and torso fit together appropriately. Insert one end into the spinal column of the vertebrae and the other end into the head passing through the foramen magnum of the occipital bone.
- The head may be placed in proper position by using two additional dowels inserted into the anterior part of the neck; into the deep muscular tissues (Mayer, 1980).
- The deep muscular tissue should be sutured around the neck and appropriate sealing and cauterizing agents are applied.
- Throughout the suturing process, the embalmer should pay strict attention to the contour that is being established. It may be necessary to apply cotton or mortuary mastic in order to achieve a natural appearance.
- The application of surface sutures is the next step. It is critical to secure the area closed with a durable suture, and if the area is viewable, then it may be

advised to utilize the intradermal suture (see chapter 11 for suture information).
- Proceed with appropriate wax restoration making sure to achieve appropriate contour, skin texture, and facial markings.
- Cosmetize the restored area as necessary.

Severed, missing or twisted limbs and bones

Unfortunately, many times embalmers encounter bodies that have experienced severed, twisted limbs or bones, or that are missing certain extremities altogether. Sometimes this is the result of traumatic accidents, violence, or medical management for a specific condition, for example, when an amputation is required as part of a medical treatment. Regardless of the origin of the condition the embalmer must address this restoration on a case-by-case basis. First, is the area viewable or not? Often, when a leg is severed, damaged, or missing the embalmer only needs to ensure the area is cleaned, disinfected, and preserved (provided embalming has been authorized), and take measures to prevent leakage (drying and cauterizing agents as well as plastic garments are suggested) followed by building the area with appropriate elements such as plastic pipe, wood dowels, and cottons to make sure the area has a natural size underneath the pants, dress, or other garment. If the damaged area is viewable, then more extreme measures will be required to secure a natural, desirable appearance

A **severed limb** is when body parts have been cut or broken apart or disjoined. This will necessitate embalming the disjoined limb separately from the rest of the body. As with decapitation, if the vascular system is intact, the embalmer may be able to inject the severed limb via arterial injection, but it is common that the damage associated with this injury will cause enough damage to the vascular system to prevent arterial injection; in these cases, the embalmer must utilize surface and hypodermic embalming applications. Also remember that even if you are able to inject the limb, it also might be required to use both surface and hypodermic techniques to make sure the area is well preserved. Post-embalming it is critical that all vessels visible are ligated and the entire area is treated with a cauterizing agent and sealed. Then, it is necessary to suture the deep muscle back together followed by the surface skin. At this point, it is wise to once again apply a surface sealing agent to further protect against leakage. Throughout the process, it is important to keep an eye on the length of the limb being reattached, as the length may be shortened as a result of the injury or loss of bone and tissue. If necessary, create a splint using wood dowels, metal rods, or plastic piping to assist in achieving a natural length of the limb prior to final sutures. It is also valuable to wrap the dowels, rods, or piping with sheets or rolled cotton to add bulk to the area and soften the area to the touch. Once the embalmer achieves an appropriate length, secure the area with body tape to keep it in the correct position before final sutures are applied. If additional treatments are required for final viewing, use applications outlined in this book regarding various restorative treatments to achieve the most pleasant memory picture for the family.

It is also common for embalmers to encounter bodies that are **missing limbs.** It is usually quite obvious if the missing limb is a relatively new development, or if the deceased had actually been missing the limb for an extended period of time. This is significant, because it is quite possible that the family and friends had become accustomed to the missing limb; it was the "norm." It is also true that in these cases, it very well may be possible the deceased had a prosthetic limb that the family may want to include with the person for viewing. In these cases, no restoration will be required, but the funeral director must communicate with the family to ascertain their wishes regarding the missing limb. Another possibility is that the deceased is missing a limb, and it is the result of a recent accident or surgery. In these cases, the funeral director must communicate with the family to determine what they prefer regarding the missing limb: clean, disinfect, seal and suture, or replace prior to viewing. Referring to this restoration as "replacement" may be deceptive, as we are typically only able to find suitable materials to fill and mimic the missing limb. If an arm and hand are missing, then a plastic sleeve or the sleeve of the shirt or dress can be stuffed with a soft material and a glove can also be stuffed to represent the hand. The wrist end of the glove must be attached (pinned or sutured) to the inside of the sleeve followed by appropriate positioning of the arm and hand. It also may be possible to attempt to recreate the hand using mortuary mastic and covering the mastic with wax, but this is a difficult restoration and is not common because it creates an artistic interpretation of the decedent's hand. Appropriate skin texture and markings can be added to the wax and artificial fingernails can replace the natural nails. This hand must also be attached to the sleeve and then positioned for viewing. If only one hand requires restoration, place the modeled hand under the natural hand when preparing for viewing (Klicker, 2002). A missing leg can be reproduced in a similar fashion stuffing thermal underwear, leggings, or plastic pants and placing these inside pants or under a dress. Then, stuff socks and attach inside the pant leg or dress to prevent them from separating from the leg.

The embalmer may also come across **twisted limbs.** This abnormality may create several difficulties for the embalmer. These include positioning and general distribution issues if the body will be embalmed. The cause of the problem will dictate the challenge(s) that the embalmer will encounter. These situations may arise due to arthritis or be the result of trauma. Regardless of the origin, if the body will be embalmed then prior to injection, the limb must be placed in a position appropriate for viewing. Klicker (2002) indicates that it may be necessary to sever ligaments, and Mayer (1980) states this may require cutting tendons after embalming to relieve the condition. Please know these are invasive, major restorations that require appropriate authorization. It is also true that many times the limb impacted by the problem may never be able to be fully placed in a favorable position. This will require the restorative artist to adjust the bedding and interior lining of the casket and use positioning blocks to provide the most positive viewing experience for the family.

Distension/Swelling

Embalmers frequently encounter swelling that may lead to the **distension** (a state of stretching out or becoming inflated) of tissues and features. Although the extent of the swelling may have great variability, it is always necessary to address these concerns and provide professional techniques to reduce or eliminate the swelling and minimize any distortion of tissues that may have developed as a result. In this section we consider some of the possible contributing factors that may result in swelling and distension followed by suggested methods to reduce the swelling in order to achieve an acceptable appearance. The term "distension" often has a negative connotation, but it can be beneficial; e.g. superficial vessels showing distribution or sunken tissues filling out on an emaciated case.

Contributing factors that may result in swelling and distention

Swelling results from the accumulation of liquids, gasses, solids, or semi-solids that are not normally present in that quantity. This can occur before or after death and before or during the embalming procedure. Here are some possible contributing factors when considering swelling and distention:

- Trauma, pathological realities, tumors, or other unique medical conditions and treatments specific to a body can lead to the formation of swelling and distention prior to death.
- The various types of decomposition can result in swelling and distention after death.
- Swelling and distention may also develop during the embalming of remains. The embalmer can cause swelling by injecting too much fluid relative to drainage, by creating an inappropriate concentration for the specific body conditions, or by too much manipulation of the body by massaging, flexing, and extending in an attempt to promote adequate distribution. It is also true that certain bodies will be more prone to distention and swelling during the embalming process such as decomposing or edematous bodies. The bottom line is that the embalmer must keep an eye on the face and neck and stop and re-analyze if swelling occurs.

RESTORATIVE ART: FOUNDATION & PRACTICE: CHAPTER 10

Methods of reduction
Regardless of the source, the embalmer must address swelling and distention when present. As with most restorations it is usually best to attempt the least invasive treatment first and get progressively more invasive as is necessary to secure a positive result. Here are some possible treatments when swelling and distention are encountered:

- **External pressure,** weight applied to a surface, may be used during or after the embalming and is often the first step taken in an attempt to reduce/eliminate swelling and distention. This technique may be as simple as a cotton compress saturated with water, manual digital pressure, or the application of a pneumatic or water collar. Another technique that utilizes external pressure is the electric spatula. In addition to pressure, this device adds heat to the equation. When using an electric spatula, it is essential to apply a very liberal amount of massage cream to the area and keep the spatula moving during use to make sure you do not burn the tissue. This device can have very positive results as the heat, pressure, and motion will assist in the reduction of the tissues.
- A **chemical compress** may also be applied to further reduce the swelling and possible distention. For example, a compress saturated with a concentrated cavity fluid will draw out moisture because of the hypertonic nature of the fluid. Cauterants may be used but be aware of their bleaching effect.
- **Constricting or astringent chemical injection** is another technique that may be helpful as a moisture reducer. As opposed to applying the chemical to the surface to draw moisture out as indicated above, here, you actually inject a reducing agent into the tissue to attempt to draw out more moisture.
- **Aspiration**, to draw out liquids or gasses by means of suction, is another useful treatment. This is the process of using a hypodermic needle and syringe or a small trocar to physically draw moisture out of the tissue.
Channeling, creation of dermal and subdermal passageways, through a single entry point in the tissue in order to allow for the removal of watery fluids and gasses, is performed in conjunction with aspiration to further aid in the removal of fluid and reduce the tissue.
- **Surgical reduction (excision, incision/lancing)**, the restoration to a normal position or level through surgical excision. This is when the restorative artist uses a scalpel to remove tissue and follows the reduction with the application of a cauterizing agent and secures with an appropriate suture.
- **Incisions/wicking** is when an area is given the opportunity to drain via an incision made by the embalmer. This technique can also include wicking, the placement of absorbent cotton in the incision to draw out fluids.

Desquamation (skin slip)

Desquamation (skin slip), the separation of the **epidermis** (the outermost layer of skin) from the **dermis** (the corium, or true skin) is a result of putrefaction. It is also true that skin can tear and require the attention of the restorative artist, but these tears are not caused by decomposition. Skin can tear either antemortem or postmortem. Antemortem tears may result from injuries, disease (kidney failure), compromised nature of the skin in advanced age, edema, exposure to excessive heat or cold, radioactive agents, or caustic chemicals. Postmortem true desquamation (skin slip) is the result of decomposition, specifically putrefaction and autolysis, and is often present on a body with other signs of decomposition (Mayer, 1980; Mayer, 2012; Klicker, 2002). It is also possible for skin slip to develop as a result of inadequate embalming, either too weak of a solution for the given case or a lack of securing adequate distribution of fluid. When the epidermis is sloughed off, the exposed dermis often undergoes drying and darkening, similar to an abrasion. Skin slip may also weep and drain similar to an abrasion, so the treatments are comparable.

Although it may be necessary to re-embalm remains that start to exhibit skin slip post–embalming, this is an extreme measure. When the problem is detected prior to embalming, puncture any blisters, and apply a cauterizing agent (cover the surface pack with plastic to minimize fumes) during or after embalming, if embalming is authorized. The embalmer will then remove any loose or jagged skin to secure the most favorable condition for the final restoration. If the embalming procedure is performed, then use an appropriate strength of solution based on case analysis, but if the body is exhibiting true desquamation, then this is a sign of decomposition, and this suggests using a stronger than normal concentration. If the tissue around the area impacted by the desquamation does not receive adequate preservative treatment and is not dry, then the embalmer will want to hypodermically inject this area with a preservative or cauterizing agent. It is important to dry and seal these areas and use suitable plastic garments in unviewed areas. If the affected area will be viewed, then use a liquid sealer, perform wax restorations including the addition of skin pores and associated skin markings, and then cosmetic applications in final preparation for viewing. Note that some embalmers prefer to attempt to salvage the existing flaps of skin. This treatment involves treating the undersurface with a drying agent and then attaching the flap of skin back in place using an adhesive. This technique will likely require small amounts of wax to feather the margins into the surrounding skin and then the application of appropriate cosmetics to fully blend this area into the adjoining tissue.

Fractures

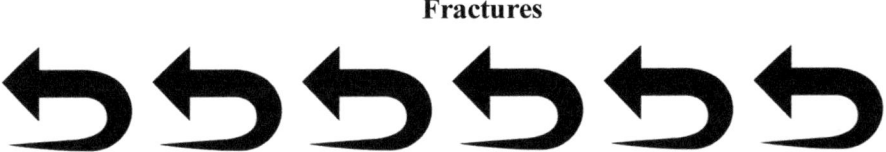

A fracture is simply a broken bone. Broken bones occur in different forms depending on whether they are partial or complete, and if they are simple or compound. Here, we operationalize two specific classifications of fractures: simple and compound. A **simple fracture** is a fractured bone that does not pierce the skin. A **compound fracture** is a broken bone that pierces the skin. Depending on location and severity, it is possible a simple fracture will not require any restorative work, but it is also possible that a simple fracture may result in embalming challenges if vascular disturbances are revealed and if the break is severe and impacts viewable areas. On the other hand, compound fractures will always require attention, as the embalmer will be required to address the tissue that was pierced by the bone at the minimum.

As is common when discussing restorative treatments, many timeframes are presented related to the embalming procedure. Although embalming will assist in the restoration, if embalming is not authorized it is still possible to perform many restorations, including work related to fractures. Here, we discuss treatments and consider timeframes as they are related to embalming, but please remember that if embalming is not authorized, it is still necessary to address fractures prior to final viewing.

Pre-embalming treatments are only required if the fracture distorts the shape and contour of the body or occludes fluid distribution.
- Depressions in viewable areas resulting from broken bones should be modified by surgically raising the bone or packing cotton under the skin to make sure the body has normal contour once tissues are fixated.
- Broken limbs should be straightened if necessary so that the fixation of tissues resulting from the embalming process will provide a natural and pleasant appearance.

Post-embalming procedures will allow the restorative artist the opportunity to perform advanced treatments on bodies that have experienced significant fractures.
- Crushed bones can be wired together to restore contour, and if adequate amounts of bone are not available, the embalmer may elect to supplement the existing bone structure with plastic, wood, or metal piping.
- Initial treatments performed prior to embalming to address contour problems should be removed and replaced with new permanent packing.
- Any incisions or other areas that the skin has been pierced must be secured closed with an appropriate suture and adhesive.
- Splints may be used to keep bones straight.

- Cauterizing, sealing, and the use of plastic garments should all be employed as necessary to preserve tissue and stop leakage.
- As required, the embalmer can perform wax restorations including the addition of skin pores and markings as well as cosmetic applications to prepare the body for viewing.

Hypodermic Tissue Building

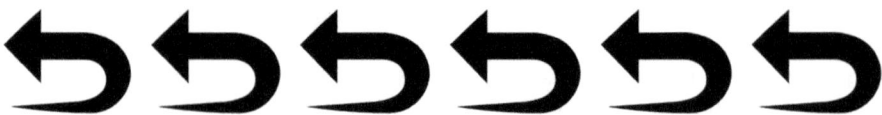

Hypodermic tissue building, the injection of special creams or liquids into the tissues through the use of a syringe and needle to restore natural contour, is a treatment commonly used by restorative artists. Hypodermic tissue building is performed after embalming (if embalming is selected and authorized). This technique is used to restore areas that have become emaciated due to dehydration or other wasting diseases. These degenerative processes can take place ante- or postmortem. Antemortem issues that may lead to conditions that require this treatment include side effects related to various diseases or the general deteriorating of tissues that often accompany advanced age. Postmortem realties such as extensive refrigeration or exposure to heat and sun light in an arid climate may promote general dehydration. Hypodermic tissue building can have a profound impact on the appearance of the deceased, restoring a more natural form. Yet, it is critical to remain mindful that the restoration of normal contour may not always be advised, as families may have become accustomed to the emaciation. Therefore, it is necessary to receive authorization prior to performing hypodermic tissue building.

As indicated above, this treatment is suggested to take place after embalming, if embalming is selected. This is in part because the embalming process has restorative elements that many times will provide the natural contour desired without having to employ hypodermic tissue building. If the decision is to perform tissue building, then the embalmer will need tissue building chemical, associated solvent, hypodermic needles, and syringes. It is best to have a variety of sizes and lengths of needles to best perform any specific treatment. Also, chemical companies offer both regular and firming feature builder; the firming version contains preservative chemicals (typically formaldehyde) to assist with firming the tissue injected. When performing hypodermic tissue building, the point of entry of the hypodermic needle should be in a hidden area such as regions of the hairline, in the nostrils, the corners of the mouth, in a fold of tissue, or in a recessed area to avoid detection after the treatment is concluded as the injection site often exhibits a dehydration mark (turns dark when exposed to air). The needle (prior to using any needle, make sure it is long enough to reach the area to be treated) is inserted in a hidden site and advances to the distal point of the injection (relatively superficial) and then the fluid is gradually injected as the needle is fanned (to make the buildup more even and natural) and withdrawn. Throughout the process, the embalmer may apply light pressure to impact the appearance of the contour being created by the tissue builder. Once the injection is completed, use tissue solvent to clean out the needle and syringe to prevent the coagulation of the material in these instruments.

Common Areas Treated with Hypodermic Tissue Building and Associated Hidden Injection Sites:

Temples – Suggested hidden points for injection:
Eyebrow – sideburn – hairline – behind the top of the ear – behind the anterior part of the helix

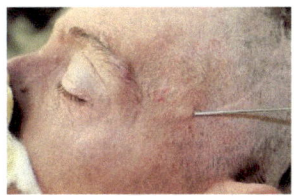
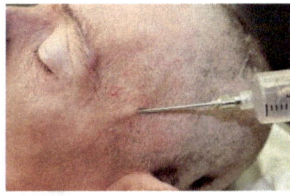
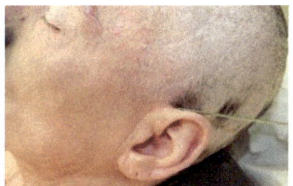

Eyes – Suggested hidden points for injection:
To project sunken eyes inject tissue builder behind the eyeball. Insert the needle between the eyelids at the medial end or inner canthus. For collapsed eyes, insert the needle directly into the eyeball, but avoid the iris.

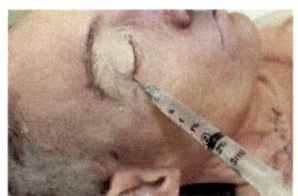
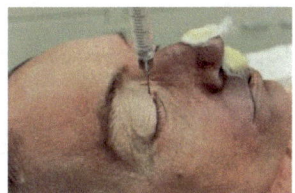

Cheeks– Suggested hidden points for injection:
Nostril, behind the wing of the nose, corners of the mouth, behind the lobe of the ear, behind the tragus of the ear, behind the upper part of the jawline, angle of the jaw

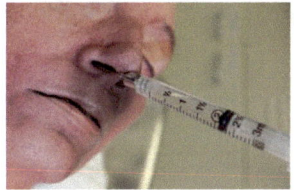
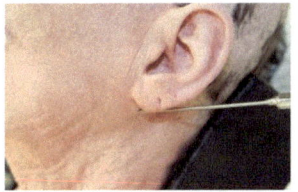
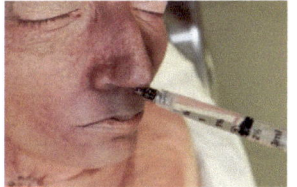

RESTORATIVE ART: FOUNDATION & PRACTICE: CHAPTER 10

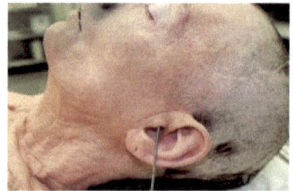 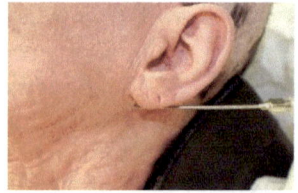 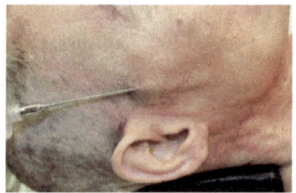

Lips– Suggested hidden points for injection:
Lateral corners at the termination of the line of closure. The embalmer should insert the needle to the central lobe of the lip requiring treatment and withdraw the needle as injecting the tissue building fluid. Then, perform the same treatment on the other side of the mouth. If both the superior and inferior lips require treatment, it will require four injections, two upper and two lower, each time inserting the needle to the medial lobe of the lips. The embalmer should use the same entry point at the angles of the mouth (both upper and lower) to reduce the number of entry points.

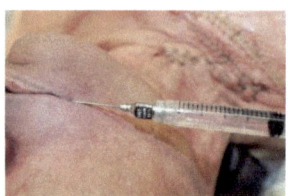 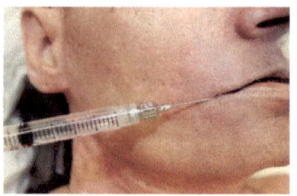

Hands– Suggested hidden points for injection:
Sides of fingers, between the knuckles, wrists, between thumb and index finger, baby finger at knuckle

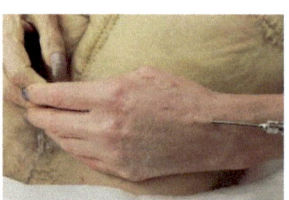 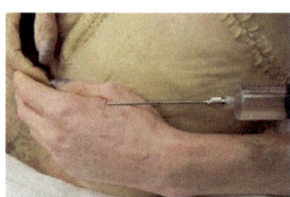 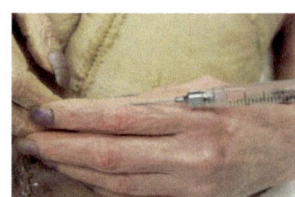

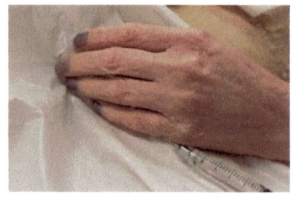 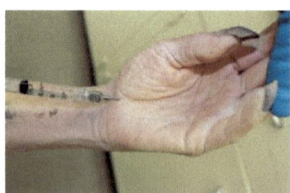 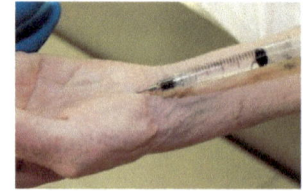

RESTORATIVE ART: FOUNDATION & PRACTICE: CHAPTER 10

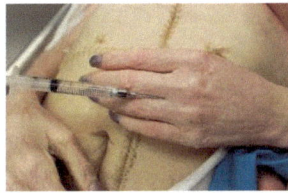 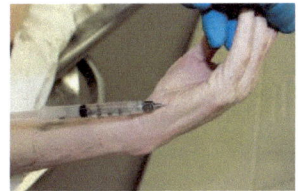 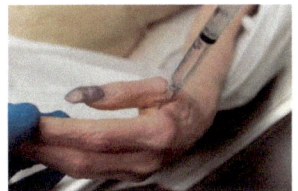

Neck– Suggested hidden points for injection:
Inside the ear, angle of the jaw

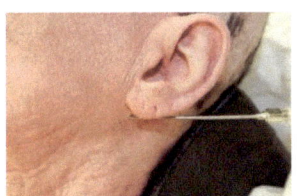 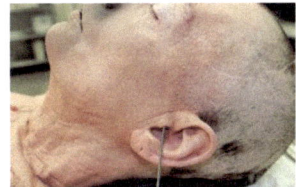

Forehead– Suggested hidden points for injection:
In the eyebrow, the hair

Chin– Suggested hidden points for injection:
Behind the earlobe, lower center of the chin

Supraorbital area– Suggested hidden points for injection:
Eyebrows

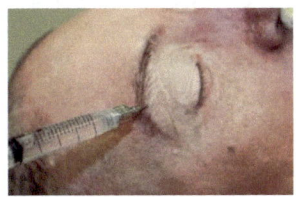 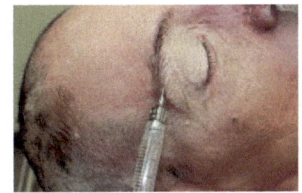

Wounds

Wounds come in a variety of shapes, sizes, and complexities and are the result of countless sources. Here, we present information about dealing with penetrating wounds as well as a discussion about contusions, hematomas, and injuries of a crushing and blunt force nature.

A **penetrating wound** is one that causes a puncture of the skin, a cavity, or an organ. These wounds are caused by a number of traumatic forces including bullets, knives, arrows, other flying objects, or car parts, as well as wounds that result from medical treatments such as arterial catheter lines and feeding tubes to mention but a few. The resulting wound can vary as much as the possible sources of these injuries. These wounds may be quite small and require minimal attention or quite large and necessitate a significant restoration. Keep in mind that these cases are often autopsied, therefore requiring additional treatment in that regard. Also remember that penetrating wounds may disturb circulation when the circulatory system is damaged and may also break bones, damage facial features, or other possible problems, which will all require the attention of the embalmer. No single treatment application can adequately cover the procedures that may be needed when dealing with penetrating wounds. The shrewd embalmer realizes that when addressing penetrating wounds, he or she will likely use a collection of the various techniques presented in this book, to make sure the wound is clean, dry, sealed, and appropriately treated. Like many of the applications in this book, it has become common to associate treatment timelines with the embalming procedure. Much of this restorative work can be accomplished without embalming, but this procedure will certainly provide the best scenario for achieving positive results. Therefore, here, you will read certain timeframes as related to embalming.

Pre-embalming
- Following the application of disinfectant droplet spray, perform an initial bathing of the remains in order to ascertain exact injuries as well as the extent of any wounds.
- Employ necessary treatments to properly position the body, including temporary sutures, when required.
- Apply massage cream around any wound.
- Prepare fluids based on case analysis.

Concurrent with embalming
- Leave wounds open (unless temporary sutures are required) to allow for drainage that may help minimize swelling in these areas. This will also

allow the embalmer the opportunity to detect distribution of fluid in these areas.
- Inject and utilize additional embalming techniques (surface compresses, hypodermic injections) to make sure the body is adequately preserved.
- Keep a keen eye on the body to detect any swelling that may occur, and then address any swelling that is detected (see the swelling and distention section in this text).

Post-embalming
- Excise dehydrated tissues around the margins of the wound.
- Cauterize the area with a sealing chemical.
- If it is a deep wound, use techniques such as those suggested in the section on excising tissue and tumor removal.
- Using an appropriate suture and sealing powder, secure the wound closed.
- Use liquid sealer if necessary.
- Apply plastic garments if in a non-viewable area.
- When necessary, perform hair restorations.
- When necessary perform necessary wax restorations employing skin texture, pores, contour and markings, as required.
- Cosmetic applications as necessary.

Klicker (2002) also identifies specifics related to pistol and rifle wounds. He states that a rifle is high velocity and a pistol is low velocity. He further indicates that wounds from close range are more severe than those from a distance. Furthermore, he indicates that a wound near the temple will likely result in swollen and/or discolored eyes. Klicker also provides classifications of types of pistol and rifle wounds. These classifications are:

Grazing – Marginal abrasion
Lacerating – Irregular tears in the cutaneous tissue
Penetrating – Bullet enters and stays in a cavity or organ
Perforating – Bullet enters and exits a cavity or organ
High velocity projectile – Bones may be shattered

Three other issues that are commonly encountered by the embalmer are **contusions**; (a bruise often accompanied with distension), hematomas, and injuries resulting from blunt force.

A contusion will necessitate additional preservation work (if embalming is authorized), as this area may not receive good distribution since the vascular system has been damaged in that area. It is also true that this area is a swelling concern indicated by possible distention and damage sustained by the vascular system. Utilize aspects of restorations dealing with discolorations, stains, swelling, and distention to adequately treat contusions.

A hematoma is a solid swelling of clotted blood within the tissues. This type of injury will require the embalmer to utilize a collection of treatments from the sections on swelling/distention, discolorations, and possibly excising tissues. The location of the hematoma will drive a lot of the decisions regarding treatment when dealing with hematomas. When in non-viewable areas, the embalmer must make sure the area is well-preserved (if embalming is authorized), and then secure the area to prevent any leakage. If in a viewable area, beyond making sure the area is preserved, the embalmer must again use the collection of techniques mentioned above to treat the area, including wax restorations and cosmetic applications when appropriate.

Injuries resulting from blunt force trauma are a common cause of death; therefore the embalmer will see these cases quite frequently. Blunt force trauma is physical trauma to a body part, either by impact, injury, or physical attack, and can also result from high-velocity impact. When a body experiences such trauma, the end results will vary. When working with bodies exhibiting blunt force trauma, consistent with other treatments and when embalming is authorized, make sure that the body receives good distribution and is well preserved. Then, it will be necessary to use a collection of the restorative techniques discussed in this book; each case will be unique. Regardless of the case, make sure to take measures to clean, disinfect, cauterize, and seal the area to prevent leakage. Then, if the injury is in a non-viewable area, use plastic garments, and make sure the remains have natural contour. If in a viewable area, then beyond securing the area clean, dry, and sealed, the embalmer must use various techniques presented in this book to restore the area back to natural form and color in preparation for viewing.

Cranial Autopsy Treatments

Specific treatments associated with embalming are most appropriate in an embalming textbook, but sometimes identifying restorative treatments related to certain embalming techniques is appropriate and solid information to include in a book about restorative art. Here, we discuss treatments associated with a cranial autopsy. Mayer (2012) identified a nine step restoration process when discussing restoring a cranial autopsy, he presented:

- After arterial embalming, dry out the base of the cranial cavity.
- Paint the inside of the cavity with a preservative gel.
- Pack the foramen magnum and the base of the cavity with autopsy compound and cotton to absorb any leakage.

- Attach the calvarium using a skull clamp and an adhesive or other appropriate attachment method.
- Fill the temple areas with mortuary mastic (or soft surface restorer wax) to remove the depression formed, if the temporalis muscles have been severed or removed.
- Paint the outside of the calvarium with an autopsy gel.
- Place mortuary mastic or incision seal powder along the inside of the scalp as the suturing proceeds.
- Suture closed using a worm (inversion) suture, beginning on the right side of the head and ending on the left because the origin of the suture will be less visible than the conclusion site.
- The inversion suture, properly done, leaves only a thin line on the scalp surface, which is easily waxed.

This step-by-step presentation offers a guide that allows the embalmer to properly restore the cranial cavity after an autopsy has been performed. It is essential that the cavity is dry and sealed, prior to securing the calvarium cap and suturing the scalp in place.

Nail Care and Restoration

On all cases, it is necessary to clean the fingernails, and this can be done prior to, concurrent with, or after the embalming procedure. Even if embalming has not been selected, it is important to clean the nails in preparation for the final viewing. Sometimes, fingernails require more than cleaning; often, they need to be trimmed, shaped, and even restored. It is common for the treatment to consist only of cleaning, trimming, and painting (when the family indicates a desire for painted nails) as this reestablishes a natural appearance for the deceased's hands. Other times, the nails may have been damaged, or due to the dying process the deceased has not been able to make it to the salon for a manicure and nail polish. Regardless of the source necessitating some type of nail restoration, it is our professional responsibility to recreate a positive memory picture for the family, and details matter; this includes fingernails. If the nail damage is minimal, good results may be obtained by cleaning, trimming, shaping, and applying nail polish, if the family indicates this preference. Other times, the damage may be extensive and require the application of false nails, followed by appropriate shaping and painting of the nails if desired. The same restoration would be appropriate for the deceased person that normally had longer, shaped, and colored nails while alive. The goal is always to achieve the most positive memory for the family.

Organ and Tissue Recovery

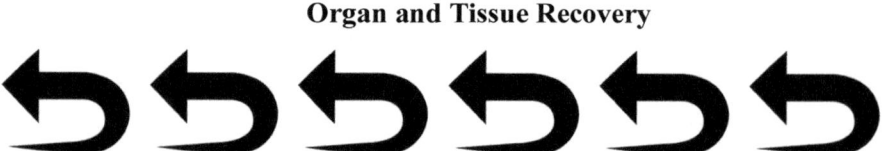

It is now commonplace for people to make the decision to donate organs and tissues for medical and research purposes. Although this will offer additional challenges regarding the care of the deceased, it is important for funeral directors and embalmers to remain neutral when families are making decisions regarding donation, and then supportive of the final decision. Embalmers must be prepared to execute our professional responsibility with respect to preparation and restoration in these cases. The realization of organ and/or tissue donation does not exclude the opportunity for viewing. In this section, we identify the various organs and tissues that are commonly donated, consider post-recovery restorative considerations, and offer suggestions for restorations. Although elements associated with embalming may be mentioned, our focus is on surface restoration.

Organs and tissues recovered

Although the fundamental purpose for donating organs and tissues is comparable and treatments at times may be similar, they are not the same. Tissue is defined as a collection of similar cells and intercellular substances surrounding them. Common tissue donations include epithelium (skin and cornea), connective tissues (blood, bone, tendons, and cartilage), muscle tissue, and nerve tissue. An organ is defined as any part of the body exercising a specific function such as respiration, secretion, and digestion; examples include kidney, heart, liver, lungs, pancreas, and eyes (Mayer, 2012).

As a result of the procedures required to donate both organs and tissues, the embalmer must keep a keen eye on the remains for certain post-recovery considerations that can develop into concerns with respect to the preparation and restoration of the body. Here is a list of such considerations:

Post-recovery restorative considerations

- Edema – abnormal accumulation of fluids in tissues or body cavities
- Discoloration – any abnormal color in or on the human body
- Lacerations – an irregularly torn or jagged wound

- Abrasions – antemortem and/or postmortem injuries resulting from friction of the skin against a firm object resulting in the removal of the epidermis
- Hair damage – anytime damage to hair is sufficient to require restoration
- Dehydration – the loss of moisture from body tissue
- Desiccation – extreme dehydration often resulting in post-embalming discolorations
- Prosthetic devices – any device that helps replace, correct, or support a body part or function of a body part
- Leakage – any blood or fluid that escapes the area in which it is normally contained
- Distention – a state of stretching out or becoming inflated

Treatments

As indicated previously, our central focus here is the surface restoration that may be required after a donation. It is important to acknowledge that a great deal of the treatments required in these cases are more consistent with the embalming procedure. Therefore, timelines associated with various restorations often consider embalming. It is also true that beyond concerns related to the embalming process, most major organ donations require little additional surface treatment beyond cauterizing, sealing, packing to secure normal contour, suturing, and application of appropriate plastic garments to prevent leakage. For this reason, the following section only considers bone, skin, total eye enucleation, and cornea donation.

Treatment for Bone Donors

One of the most common donations is that of bone. When this is the reality, certain protocol can assist the embalmer in the restoration. Here is the presentation of such protocol:
- Clean and bathe the body.
- Proceed with embalming as normal, disinfecting mouth, nose, eyes, and setting the features.
- Remove temporary sutures and any packing materials.
- Arterially inject the area using any available arteries using an increased strength of solution for the affected areas. It is necessary to clamp off any vessels that exhibit a loss of fluid during injection. Then utilize additional embalming techniques (hypodermic and surface embalming) as necessary to secure preservation. Pre-injection is not suggested for these cases.
- Aspirate and inject the cavity.
- Clean, dry, and cauterize the area, followed by application of preservative and absorbent powders.
- Use prosthetics such as PVC pipes and packing material to restore the area and achieve normal surface contour.

- Secure the area with a durable suture, most commonly the baseball stitch, and be sure to use incision sealing powder and/or cotton in these areas to further prevent leakage.
- Complete the final bathing of the deceased.
- If necessary, place mortuary adhesive on the sutured areas covered by cotton to provide an additional barrier against leakage.
- Use appropriate plastic garments to further protect against damage that may be caused by leakage.
- Proceed with any required cosmetic applications and then dress and casket.

Treatment for Skin Donors

Skin is also a common tissue donated. Donation areas typically include the thighs, back, and chest. The use of a dermatome to remove the skin should not cause any major damage to the vascular system or other deep structures such as muscles, bones, and joints. The main concern with skin donation is leakage. Again, specific protocol can assist the embalmer when dealing with these cases. Here is such suggested protocol:

- Embalm the body based on case analysis, and let exposed dermis drain during the procedure.
- Bathe the entire body and towel dry.
- Treat exposed areas with a surface compress containing an appropriate preservative/drying chemical (or preservative gel), and this compress should remain on the tissue for at least 30 minutes.
- Clean and dry affected areas.
- Apply mortuary sealing glue, and place cotton on top of the adhesive to help protect against leakage.
- Using mortuary tape, adhere sheets of plastic that extend a few inches beyond the affected areas.
- Use appropriate plastic garments.
- Proceed with any required cosmetic applications and then dress and casket.

Treatment for Eye Enucleation

As presented in Chapter 8, the growth in donation has led to an increase in cases requiring restoration following complete eye removal, or **enucleation**. In these cases, restoration will begin during arterial injection. First, remove any temporary packing placed in the orbital cavity by the harvesting organization. Open and gently stretch the palpebrae, and then dry each eye socket. Care should be taken to avoid swelling and discolorations, because these are more common due to the trauma already experienced by the tissue in the area. After drying, the orbital cavities should be packed with cotton soaked with a cauterizing chemical. An eyecap should then be placed over the cotton to keep the proper form during injection. Do not use pre-injection, and consider the use of a restricted cervical injection; in all cases a lower than normal rate of flow and pressure setting should be used. This will reduce the likelihood of swelling. After embalming, remove the temporary packing and dry the eye sockets again. Using wax or mortuary putty, recreate the form of the eyeball and set into each empty cavity. Then, place an eyecap on top, and close the palpebrae using an adhesive, if necessary (Klicker, 2002).

Treatment for Cornea Donation

It is also common for the embalmer to encounter the donation of the cornea only. When this is the case, work must be performed that will eliminate leakage. Note that most of the eye's interior is filled with vitreous, a gel-like substance that helps the eye maintain a round shape. The procedure required to remove the cornea creates a wound that allows the vitreous to evacuate; in other words, this creates a leakage concern. Therefore, it is necessary to remove this substance (prior to embalming if embalming is authorized) using digital pressure or aspiration. Clean and dry the area. Then, place rounded cotton saturated with a cauterizing agent directly on the eye. Also, place an eyecap on top of the cotton to help the eyelid maintain natural convexity during embalming. When the embalming is concluded, remove the cotton and eyecap and once again clean and dry the area. Then, create supplemental support using cotton, wax, or mortuary mastic and place it on the remains of the natural eye. Cover this material with an eyecap to assist with creating the natural convexity of the eyelid. Close the eye, making sure the eyelids abut in the lower 1/3 of the eye socket, and if necessary, use an adhesive to maintain the line of closure.

Hanging

Hanging, the execution or suicide by strangling or breaking the neck by a suspended noose, is a specific cause of death that the embalmer will encounter. When treating a body that has died of hanging, the restorative artist will employ a collection of treatments presented in this book that are necessary for that specific case. All injuries will be matchless and require a unique restoration. Depending on the specific case, the embalmer may need to use the treatments associated with the following injuries, all or in part when addressing the restoration: abrasions, lacerations, discolorations, stains, burns, distention, swelling, desquamation, as well as the techniques discussed when talking about providing stability for the orthopedic decapitation. The reality is that the restorative artist has a wide variety of techniques available for various restorations, and it is their professional responsibility to utilize the techniques on any given case that will provide the most positive viewing opportunity for the family.

Jaundice

Jaundice is a condition that is characterized by an excessive concentration of bilirubin in the skin and tissues and deposition of excessive bile pigment in the skin, cornea, body fluids, and mucous membranes with a resulting yellow appearance (Mayer, 2012). Jaundice is a feature of various conditions such as hepatitis and cirrhosis. Most embalmers consider jaundice one of the biggest challenges commonly encountered in the prep room. To add to the challenge, it is also possible that the yellow of the bilirubin may convert to the green of biliverdin as a result of a strong acidic environment (not strictly because of the use of a strong arterial fluid) causing additional problems (Mayer, 2012). It was once thought that if a funeral service professional encounters a body with jaundice, they would be wise to dress the remains in warm colors (and avoid yellow and white clothing); this is not a position supported in this text. Regardless of treatment (using jaundice fluids to remove the excessive bilirubin, counterstaining to create a more predictable base color, or performing cosmetic work) a restorative artist will be able to create a pleasant memory picture for the family without dictating they bring in warm-colored clothing. Although jaundice is more appropriate for an embalming textbook, we include this information here because jaundice is indeed considered one of the biggest challenges commonly found in the prep room and restoring natural color is a central part of restorative art. It is the responsibility of the embalmer to utilize professional treatments to treat bodies with jaundice. These include removal of the excessive bilirubin, counterstaining the tissue, or concealment with cosmetic applications. It is important for embalmers to remain mindful that the most important goal to achieve when embalming jaundice cases is preservation. Here, we present suggested protocol as related to the embalming procedure:

Pre-embalming

- Thoroughly bath the body with soap and warm water, as it is possible to remove some of the yellow discoloration from the surface of the skin.
- Liberally apply massage cream to viewable areas (face, neck, hands) and cover with a warm wash cloth. Allow the warm cloth to remain on the area for 10-15 minutes, and then gently wipe off the massage cream, as it is

possible to remove additional amounts of the yellow discoloration from the surface.

Concurrent with embalming
- Pre-injection is suggested as long as the body is not also exhibiting edema.
- Reapply massage cream to the viewable areas.
- Using a specific jaundice fluid (typically low index), inject a high volume of the solution **or** inject a normal strength of solution based on case analysis, but add sufficient dye to counterstain the tissue to create a more predictable foundation for cosmetic application. Regardless of the technique utilized, make sure the body experiences good distribution and drainage.
- The restricted cervical injection technique may be beneficial, as this will allow the embalmer to inject stronger solutions to the trunk.

Post-embalming

- Remove any massage cream that was applied during embalming to ascertain current condition of the bilirubin discoloration.
- Wait at least 24 hours for cosmetic application in order to obtain the most predictable skin color, as well as to make sure the remains are adequately preserved. It is also true that some chemicals require time to work properly.
- Proceed with cosmetic application as indicated in chapter 13, Mortuary Cosmetology, and use opaque cosmetics, as required.

Remains in which it is Suggested to Not View

Regardless of skill level and professional techniques available, sometimes it is the professional suggestion to families that remains should not be viewed. This is common as a result of trauma, disease, decomposition, bodies that have experienced third and fourth degree burns, drowning victims, bodies with tissue gas, or mutilation.

Klicker (2002) indicates the four most common body conditions that are beyond post-embalming restorative art treatments:

- Gas Bacillus
- Third degree burns
- Drowning
- Mutilated and crushed cases

Although viewing may not be appropriate, the embalmer can still achieve some degree of preservation; here, we suggest appropriate protocol:

- Remove the body from the disaster pouch.
- Clean and disinfect the pouch.
- When possible, embalm (using a strong solution) to the best of your ability using any available arteries, surface compresses, and hypodermic chemical injection.
- Place a liberal amount of preservative powder in the disaster pouch.
- Place the body in the pouch.
- Place more preservative powder on and around the remains in the pouch.
- Zip the disaster pouch closed and add glue to the zipper to aid in the containment of odors.

Another option would be to wrap the body in a sheet soaked with strong preservative fluid and place the wrapped body in the disaster pouch and place into the casket or Ziegler case. Regardless of the treatment applied, it is best to keep the casketed remains in the cooler as long as possible.

Chapter Conclusion

This chapter presented the general restorative treatments utilized to prepare remains for viewing and concluded with suggestions for cases that should not be viewed. This included the classifications of various cases that may require such treatment as well as appropriate timeframes associated with these treatments. Also, the importance of comprehending the connection between setting features and the restorative process was considered. The central purpose has been for the reader to understand this set of general restorative treatments and develop a foundation that will allow the reader to replicate these treatments in practice.

References

Professional Experience and Educational Presentations:
A great deal of the content of this book has been derived from years of professional experience as an embalmer, funeral director, and funeral service educator.

Klicker, R. (2002). *Restorative art and science*. Buffalo, NY: Thanos Institute.

Mayer, J. S. (1980). *Restorative art*. Dallas, TX: Professional Training Schools.

Mayer, R. G. (2012). *Embalming: History, theory, and practice* (5th ed.).

   New York, NY: McGraw-Hill.

Prager, G. J. (1955). *Postmortem restorative art*. Amelia, OH: G. Joseph Prager.

Spriggs, A. O. (1964). *Champion restorative art* (6th ed.). Springfield, OH: The

   Champion Company.

RESTORATIVE ART: FOUNDATION & PRACTICE: CHAPTER 11

Chapter Eleven

Sutures

Chapter Author: Steve Spann, M.S.

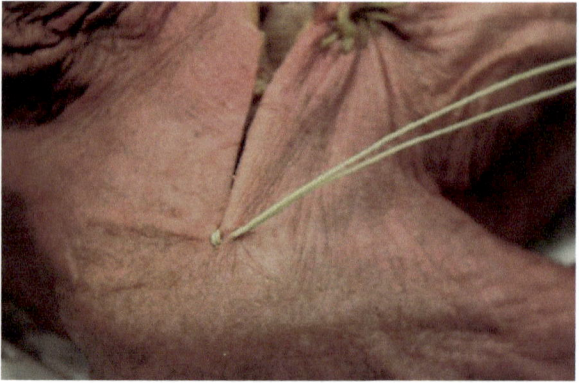

Images in this chapter courtesy of: Anthony Fleege, MBA, & Sydney Baumeister

Chapter Learning Objectives

Upon completion of the study of this chapter students should:

- Recall the instruments necessary to perform various sutures
- Be able to identify the various sutures utilized in restorative work, and be able to indicate in which situations each suture would be appropriate
- Be able to demonstrate how to employ each suture

Suture is a word used to describe two very different terms in the medical/restorative art professions. First, related to skeletal anatomy, the term refers to the union or articulation of two bones of the skull. Second, the term **suture**, defined as the act of sewing or bringing together the skin by using ligature, also may mean the completed stitch. Sutures will be required to close incisions, lacerations, and various openings in the skin. The main purpose of the closed suture is to return the skin to the natural position and to prevent leakage. There are various other needs for the suture such as to form an anchor for wax, securing the margins for a deep wound, to encircle the margins of a hole, or to attach a severed limb or other body part.

The ligature, thread, cord, or wire is used for tying vessels, tissues, or bones. Each time an embalmer performs a suture, the ligature used must be long enough to complete the suture without interruption. Ligature types include waxed or non-waxed silk and linen as well as nylon thread. Some special cases requiring hidden sutures and small ligature may use clear dental floss. Various types of needles are required for suturing. Mortuary needles include "U" shaped or full curve needles, "S" curve/autopsy needles, as well as numerous other shapes. Each one may be useful for performing specific sutures (see page 19 for images of various needles). Needle selection will depend on the location and length of the suture.

There are six types of sutures used in restorative art. Selection of the correct suture depends on the location and size of the suture area as well as the purpose and specific injury or incision the restorative artist will be closing.

The Six Sutures

TEMPORARY: (Interrupted or Bridge Suture) This suture is applied prior to embalming to hold surface areas in place for the embalming process. These sutures are intended to be removed post-embalming. These are single or multiple stitches knotted on the surface to hold the skin in place.

Performing the temporary suture

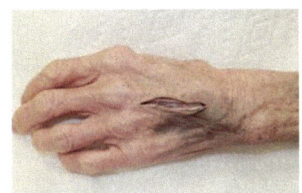  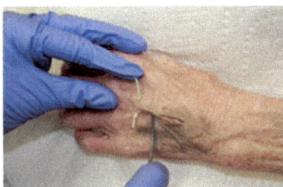

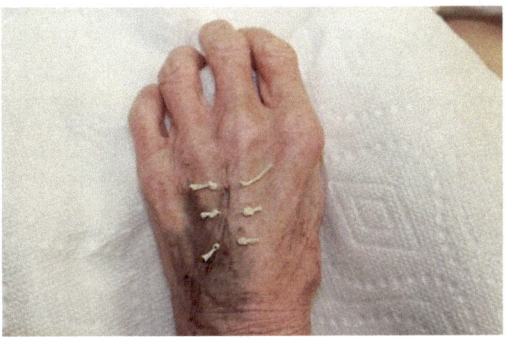

The Temporary Suture – The Completed Stitch

INTRADERMAL SUTURE: (Subcutaneous or Hidden Stitch) There are two types of intradermal sutures: Single Intradermal Suture and Double Intradermal Suture. This suture process is used to close an incision that appears on an area that will be visible, for example, facial lacerations. These sutures, therefore, are often referred to as a hidden sutures. When completed, this style will provide a surface that is better for the application of wax to conceal the incision.

SINGLE INTRADERMAL: The needle is inserted into one end of the incision leaving the ligature loose and exposed. Then, the needle is inserted into the margins of the incision from side to side and does not reach the surface of the skin. When the suturing reaches the opposite end of the incision, the ligature is passed from the end of the incision through the skin a short distance from the terminal end. DO NOT PULL the ligature tight until the suture is complete. Gently pulling on both ends of the ligature will pull the margins of the skin together. Pulling too tight will cause the margins to pucker. If the embalmer chooses, a small amount of fast acting adhesive may be applied across the incision prior to pulling the ligature to help secure the incision.

Performing the single intradermal suture

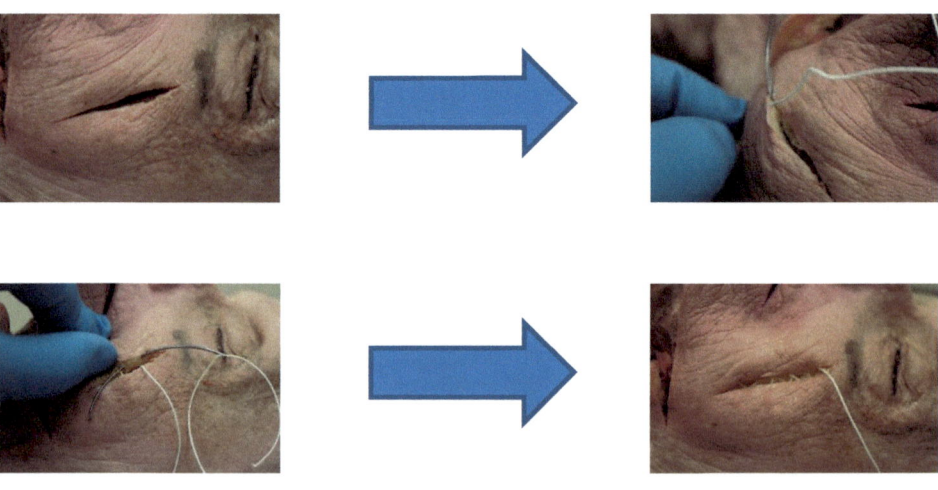

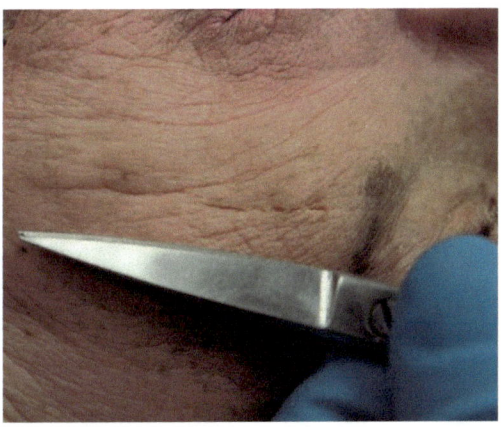

The Single Intradermal – The Completed Stitch

DOUBLE INTRADERMAL: The double intradermal suture is made with one ligature and two needles. A needle is placed on each end of the single ligature. The suture begins by inserting one needle into the derma of the incision. Each needle is alternated across the incision much like lacing up your shoes. At the end of the incision, both needles are inserted through the skin, leaving the ligature exposed. Gently pulling on both ends of the ligature will pull the margins of the skin together. Pulling too tightly will cause the margins to pucker.

Performing the double intradermal suture

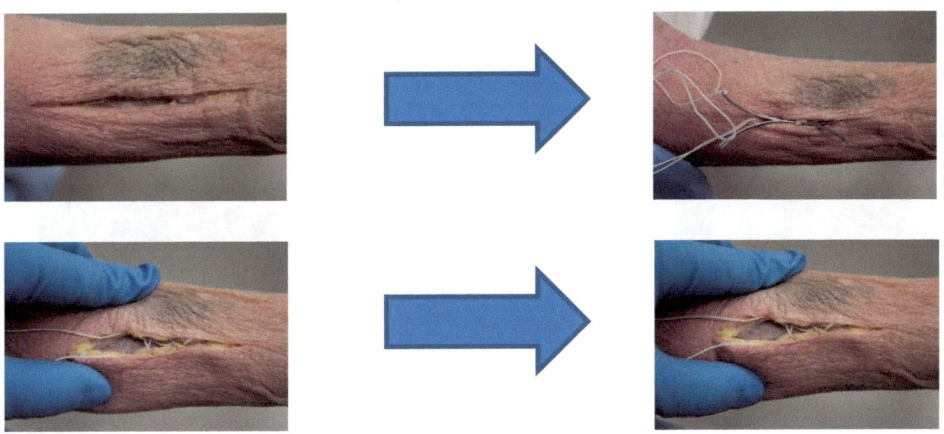

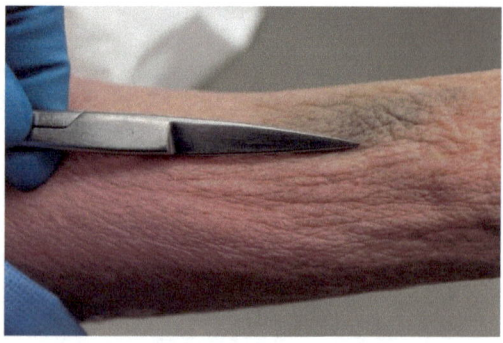

The Double Intradermal – The Completed Stitch

BASEBALL SUTURE: The baseball suture is commonly utilized for autopsy incisions as well as standard incisions made during the embalming procedure. The baseball suture can provide a very tight and secure suture for strength and sealing qualities. The needle is placed in the incision, through the skin, and a knot is tied to begin the suture. The needle is then placed in the incision, making a cross stitch motion from side to side of the incision. Care should be taken to keep the loose end (non-needle end) of the ligature under the cross stitch for the first half inch. This will hide the beginning ligature. Continue with the cross stitch motion from side to side, holding the ligature with the non-needle hand to keep the suture tight. Continue this stitch until the end of the incision, and then insert the needle through the skin at the end of the incision, and tie a double knot. To hide the end of the suture ligature, insert the needle into the skin next to the knot, and exit half an inch from the knot, then cut with scissors.

Performing the baseball suture

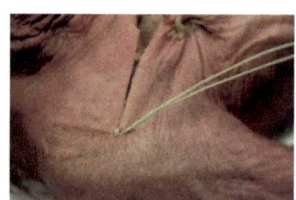  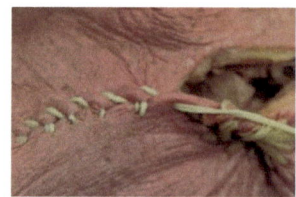

RESTORATIVE ART: FOUNDATION & PRACTICE: CHAPTER 11

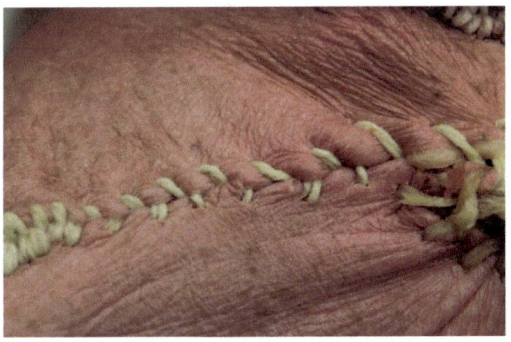

The Baseball Stitch – The Completed Stitch

WORM SUTURE (INVERSION; DRAW): The worm suture is much like the single intradermal suture in that it is conducive for wax restorations, but it stays on the outside of the incision. The needle is inserted into the skin at one end of the incision and a knot is tied. The ligature is crossed over the top of the incision from side to side, creating a worm diagram on top of the skin. Each stitch is to be pulled tightly as the stitches are made. At the end of the incision, insert the needle through the skin and tie a double knot in the ligature. To hide the end of the ligature, insert the needle into the skin next to the knot, exit half an inch from the knot, and cut with scissors. This suture will turn under the edges of the incision providing a good surface for wax restorations, as it will eliminate the raised area associated with the baseball stitch. Care should be taken to space each stitch at equal distances.

Performing the worm suture

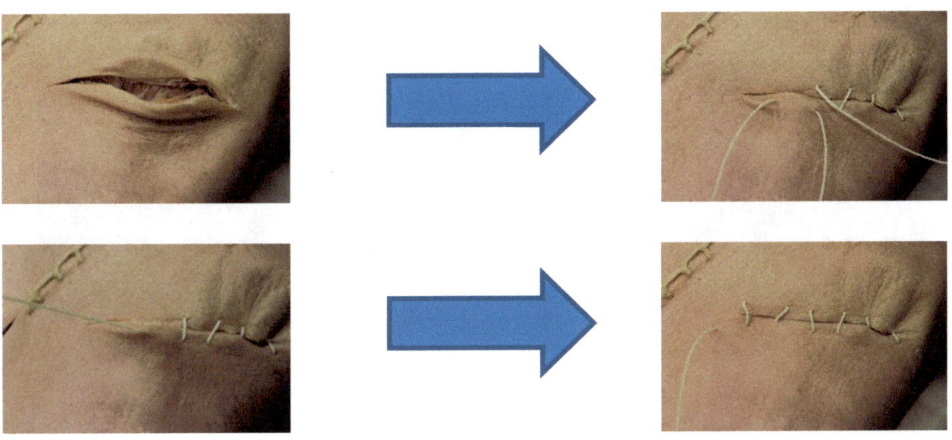

RESTORATIVE ART: FOUNDATION & PRACTICE: CHAPTER 11

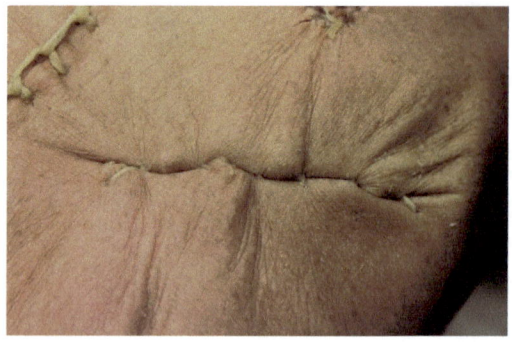

The Worm Suture – The Completed Stitch

PURSE STRING SUTURE: The purse string suture is used to close round holes in the skin such as the trocar insertion site, colostomy location, or the area where a surgical drain was removed. This suture provides for a tight leak-proof closure for a round opening. The needle is inserted into the skin a quarter of an inch from the opening and exits the skin a half inch from the entry point. Repeat this process around the diameter of the site and conclude the suture by exiting at a point beside the beginning entry location. Draw both pieces of ligature together and tie a double knot.

Performing the purse string suture

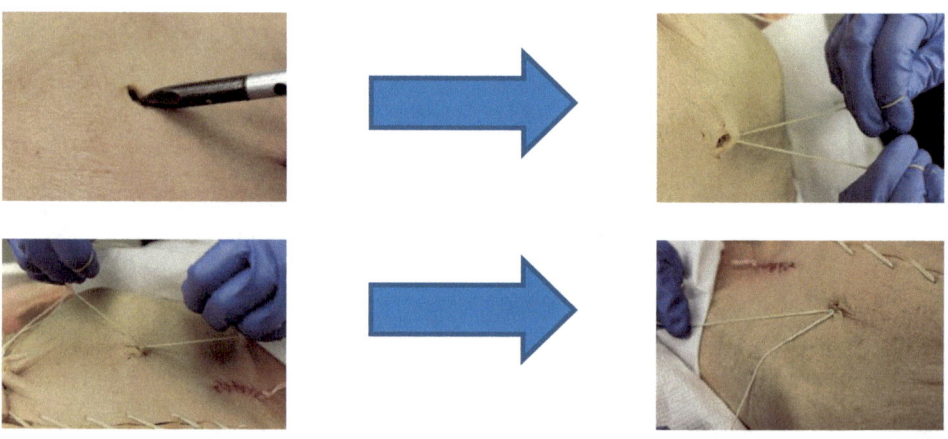

216

RESTORATIVE ART: FOUNDATION & PRACTICE: CHAPTER 11

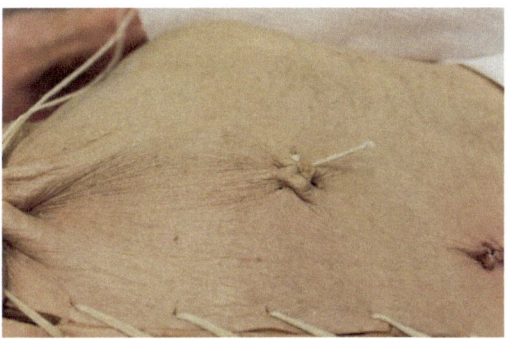

The Purse String Suture – The Completed Stitch

BASKET-WEAVE SUTURE: (Cross Stitch) the basket weave suture is commonly used in restorative art, not as a closure suture but as part of deep wound restorations. This suture in created under the surface of the skin and provides an attachment for both the margins of the wound as well as a base anchor for wax restoration. This suture begins and ends inside the wound by inserting the needle and ligature inside the margins of the wound, and tie a knot. The suture progresses in a crisscross fashion inside the wound multiple times to create the basket effect.

Performing the basket-weave suture

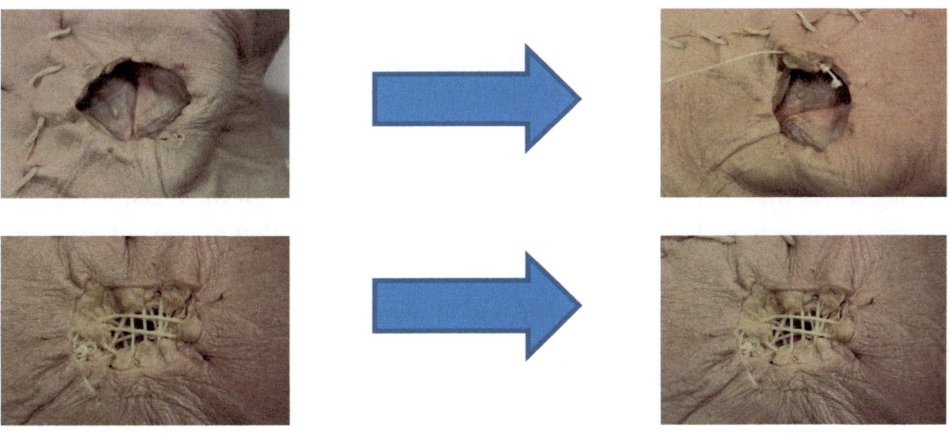

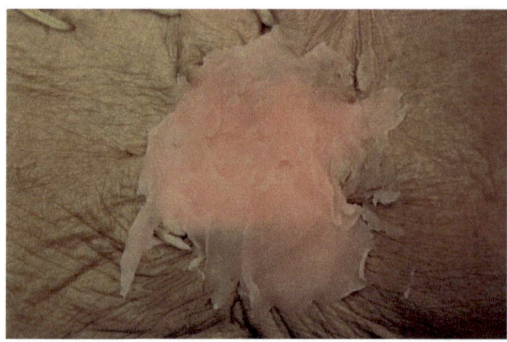

The Basket-weave Suture – Starting to apply wax after the Completed Stitch

Two additional sutures the embalmer may encounter are the **Whip Suture** and the **Lock Suture**. These sutures are not used in restorative art but are commonly used by the medical field to close autopsy incisions or close an incision when the patient dies during surgery. These sutures prevent leakage during the transport process. To begin the whip suture, place the needle in one end of the incision and through the skin; a knot is tied to begin the suture. The needle is placed in the outside of the skin and across the incision and exits the skin on the opposite side of the incision. Continuously, keep the ligature tight with the hand that does not hold the needle. This process is continued to the conclusion of the incision. Then, you should tie a double knot to secure end of the suture. The lock suture and the whip suture are used for closing long incisions. The lock suture process is the same as the whip suture but adds one step of periodically locking the suture for safety. The lock suture requires, after several inches of suturing, to "lock" the suture by passing the needle through the piece of ligature before completing the stitch. This process will secure and lock the suture.

There are times when the condition of the skin or the location of the incision does not allow for suturing. These situations require special attention to prevent leakage and prepare for restoration. **Adhesives** are commonly used in these situations. The adhesive can be used to seal the incision and hold the tissue in place. Some embalmers may also use adhesives to close embalming and cranial incisions. This process is only recommended in special cases to hide the incision.

RESTORATIVE ART: FOUNDATION & PRACTICE: CHAPTER 11

Chapter Conclusion

This chapter started by defining and exploring reasons we employ sutures. The instruments and supplies required were identified prior to examining the sutures. Then, the reader was presented the various sutures utilized for restorative work and situations that typically require the various sutures. The chapter then provided specific information related to the how to perform each suture, the temporary, intradermal (single and double), baseball, worm, purse string, and basket-weave. This should allow the restorative art student adequate information and imagery to start working to learn all sutures. The next unit of the book will turn to color and cosmetics as the process of providing families with a positive memory picture is further outlined.

References

Professional Experience and Educational Presentations:
A great deal of the content of this book has been derived from years of professional experience as an embalmer, funeral director, and funeral service educator.

Klicker, R. (2002). *Restorative art and science*. Buffalo, NY: Thanos Institute.

Mayer, J. S. (1980). *Restorative art*. Dallas, TX: Professional Training Schools.

Mayer, R. G. (2012). *Embalming: History, theory, and practice* (5th ed.).

New York, NY: McGraw-Hill.

Unit 5
Color Theory and Mortuary Cosmetology

- **Chapter 12:**
  Color Theory

- **Chapter 13:**
  Mortuary Cosmetology

Chapter Twelve

Color Theory

Chapter Learning Objectives

Upon completion of the study of this chapter students should:

- Be able to demonstrate an understanding of the history of color theory as well as the impact of the perception of color
- Comprehend aspects of light theory including information about the visible spectrum and principles associated with this theory
- Understand the Prang system and be able to repeat this color wheel
- Have a general knowledge of color in illumination.

Color Associations

Red - is the color of fire and blood, so it is associated with energy, war, danger, strength, power, determination as well as passion, desire, and love.

Orange - combines the energy of red and the happiness of yellow. It is associated with joy, sunshine, and the tropics. Orange represents enthusiasm, fascination, happiness, creativity, determination, attraction, success, encouragement, and stimulation.

Yellow - is the color of sunshine. It's associated with joy, happiness, intellect, and energy.

Green - is the color of nature. It symbolizes growth, harmony, freshness, and fertility. Green has strong emotional correspondence with safety. Dark green is also commonly associated with money.

Blue - is the color of the sky and sea. It is often associated with depth and stability. It symbolizes trust, loyalty, wisdom, confidence, intelligence, faith, truth, and heaven.

Purple - combines the stability of blue and the energy of red. Purple is associated with royalty. It symbolizes power, nobility, luxury, and ambition. It conveys wealth and extravagance. Purple is associated with wisdom, dignity, independence, creativity, mystery, and magic.

White - is associated with light, goodness, innocence, purity, and virginity. It is considered to be the color of perfection.

Black - is associated with power, elegance, formality, death, evil, and mystery.

- Color Wheel Pro (2020)

The importance of color, color theory, and how it impacts the funeral service profession is well established. Initially, students in this discipline trend toward the importance of this knowledge as it relates to the preparation and dressing rooms, and the direct impact on the appearance of the deceased. No doubt this is central to our work, but color theory expands into almost every area of our work. This includes the paint in the funeral home, lighting in various rooms, merchandising, décor, and of course, cosmetic application. Therefore, in this chapter, we explore a wide-range of topics as related to color theory. First, general information is covered followed by specific information about light theory, pigment theory, and color in illumination. As you read this material, remain mindful of the significant impact color has on the daily operation and success of a funeral home.

General Information

Color is a visual sensation perceived by the eye and mind due to the activity and vibration of light. Furthermore, color is the response to light of specific wave lengths of radiant energy, which strike the retina of the eye. Radiant energy is energy traveling through space in the form of electromagnetic waves of various lengths.

When considering color, it is valuable to revisit the cones and rods of the eye. The cones of the eye are sensory nerves in the retina of the eye having to do with color detection. The rods are long, rod-shaped sensory bodies of the retina of the eye that are responsive to light but not to color. As we explore the various elements of color theory, this information may assist in grasping a more complete understanding of the theories and how this impacts our world.

The reality is that we are immersed in a domain of color, and it impacts all people although people do vary in their perception of color. People vary in their ability to perceive color; they are influenced by past experience or associations, aesthetic preference, eye fatigue, sharpness of vision, and color blindness (Mayer, 1986). It is also true that the source of and amount of illumination will impact the perception of color as well as objects viewed at the same time or that are presented adjacent to other objects. As we continue this journey, keep in mind that without light we would not perceive color.

History of Color Theory

In 1666 Sir Isaac Newton discovered that sunlight is composed of pure colors, which are so balanced that no color is predominant. The process of breaking up a beam of sunlight into its individual colors is known as dispersion. When Newton placed a prism in the path of the beam of sunlight, the ray was spread out into a band of pure colors. This band of pure colors is called the visible **spectrum**. Spectrum, the visible band, is considered the original standard of color; it is the progressive arrangement of colors, red, orange, yellow, green, blue, indigo, violet or ROYGBIV, seen when a beam of white light is broken down into its component colors. Newton noted that the spectrum appeared similar in **brilliance**, brightness, and in the same sequence as the colors of a rainbow. Physicists have since eliminated Newton's indigo because of its closeness to blue and violet (Mayer, 1986). The visible spectrum is constructed of rays that can be seen, but there are rays that are out of the boundaries of this spectrum. For example, ultraviolet represents invisible rays of the spectrum lying outside the violet end of the visible spectrum, and infrared is part of the invisible spectrum adjacent to the red end of the visible spectrum. It was through the process of dispersion that the components of white light were detected. **White light** is a ray of light that contains all the hues of the visible spectrum in such proportion that the light appears colorless or natural, such as daylight or sunlight. Newton's experiment also revealed that each color of the spectrum could not be separated further by refraction.

Light Theory

As discussed above, a central element of light theory was the discovery of the visible spectrum, ROYGBIV. As we consider light theory, it is important to define the word light. **Light** is to shine, a form of electromagnetic radiation that acts upon the retina of the eye to make sight possible. Remember, without light we are unable to perceive color.

So how is color perceived? Fundamental to the perception of color are the concepts of absorption and reflection. **Absorption** is the process of taking in, as in a colored object that absorbs certain rays of light and reflects other rays, giving the object its recognizable color. For example, an apple is called red if the red rays are reflected and the other rays in the light are absorbed. **Reflection** is simply the return of light waves from surfaces, and as mentioned above, it is this that will determine what color objects are perceived to be.

When studying light color theory, to more fully understand white light, it is necessary to consider additional elements discovered by Sir Isaac Newton. He later disclosed that of the seven colors of the visible spectrum, three could be used to reproduce the other colors of the spectrum as well as new colors that resulted from their mixtures. These three colors are considered the primary colors of the visible spectrum; they are red, blue, and green. They are considered the primary colors because their mixtures will produce all of the other light colors but cannot be reproduced from the mixtures of any other colors of the spectrum.

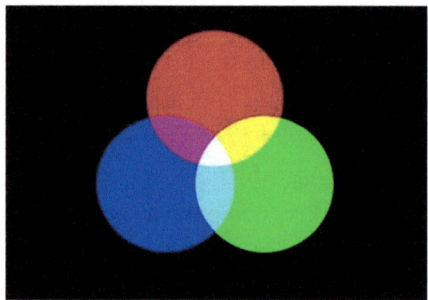

As is indicated in the Venn diagram above, the mixture of red, blue, and green light results in white light. Furthermore, the secondary colors of light theory are revealed. The secondary colors are yellow, green/blue or cyan, and magenta. Yellow is created by mixing red and green light. Cyan is created by mixing blue and green light and magenta is created by mixing red and blue light. The mixture of light is an additive process. **Additive method** is a process of mixing colored lights on a surface on which the wave lengths of each are combined, or adding two or more colored lights together to create another color of light. Although the mixture of light is considered an additive process, it is important to acknowledge the reality of a subtractive method related to light theory. This **subtractive method** is a method of diminishing the wave lengths of light by superimposing two or more color transparencies over the same light source, causing the light to be gradually reduced by adsorption of colors in the light.

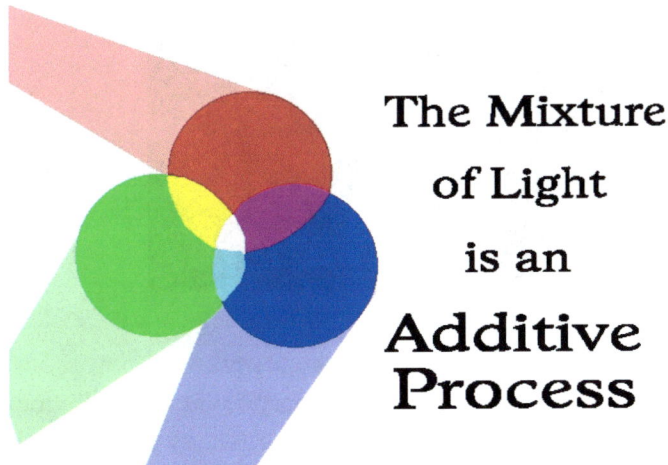

The Mixture of Light is an Additive Process

As we conclude light theory and prepare to move into pigment theory, it is valuable to identify two important terms: chromatic and achromatic colors. A **chromatic color** is a color having hue, a color of the visible spectrum, while an **achromatic color** is a color not found in the visible spectrum, a neutral color such as white, black, gray, silver, and gold.

Pigment Theory/Prang System Color Wheel

Thus far, the presentation has been about light theory and the mixture of colored lights. Another important theory important to the restorative artist is pigment theory. Unlike light theory, pigment theory is considered a subtractive method. When pigments are mixed, they absorb some of the light waves while the mixture of reflected light combines light waves. **Pigment** is defined as a coloring matter that can be applied to an object when combined with some type of vehicle. The first image that probably comes to mind is the application of cosmetics. **Pigment theory** is the Prang system, which theorizes that all visible colors originate from three primary colors or hues. In order to fully explore pigment theory, it is important to initiate the conversation with a presentation of the Prang color wheel. Presented on the next page, this color wheel is a combination of three primary colors, three secondary colors, and six intermediate colors. The primary colors, with respect to pigment theory, are red, yellow, and blue. A **primary hue** is one of three pigmentary hues (red, yellow, and blue), which can be combined to make all other hues, yet none of the primary colors can be produced from mixtures of the other color pigments; recall in light color theory the hues red, blue, and green can be combined to make all other hues.

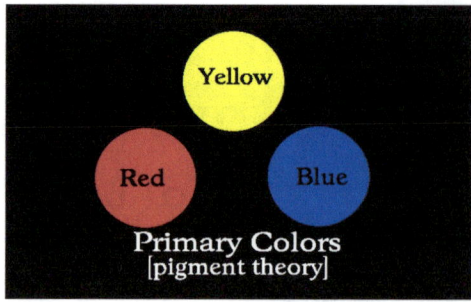

A **secondary hue** is an equal mixture of two primary colors that will produce pigmentary hues (orange, green, and purple). The secondary colors with respect to pigment theory are orange, green, and purple. An **intermediate hue** is a pigmentary hue produced by mixing, in equal quantities, a primary hue with its adjacent secondary hue on the color wheel. The intermediate colors with respect to pigment theory are yellow-green, blue-green, blue-purple, red-purple, red-orange, and yellow-orange. Collectively, the primary, secondary, and intermediate hues constitute the Prang color wheel.

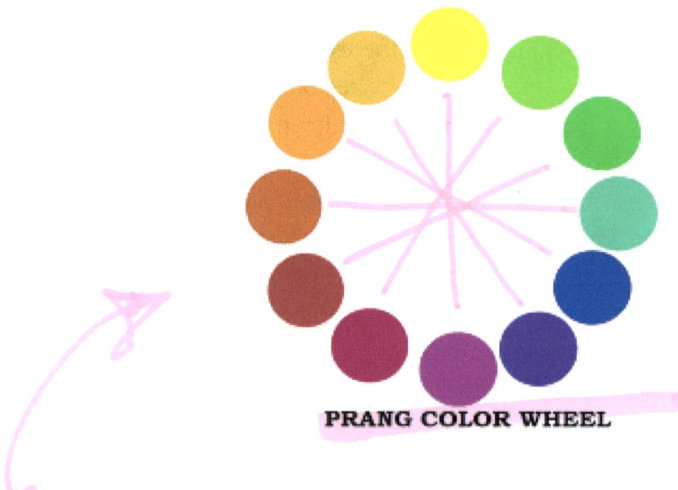

PRANG COLOR WHEEL

Complements are directly opposite hues on the color wheel; any two pigmentary hues which, by their mixture in equal quantities, produce gray.

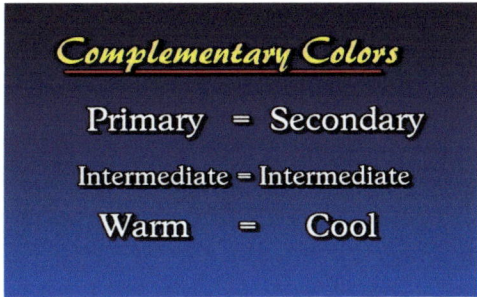

Each pigmentary hue is categorized as either warm or cool. A **Cool hue,** such as blue, green, purple, or any intermediate pigmentary hue in which they predominate; these are receding hues, which create the illusion of distance from the observer; a color of short wave-lengths. Blue is considered the coolest hue. A **warm hue** is a color that appears in the spectral band, characterized by long wave-lengths; a color which makes an object appear closer and larger; a color which reflects warmth, for example red, orange, yellow, and other colors in which they are predominate. Orange is considered the warmest hue.

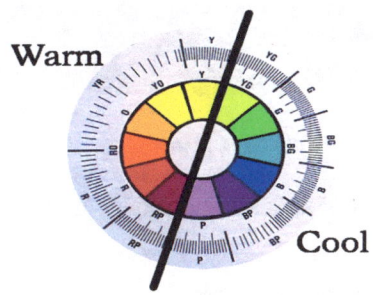

Exploring Pigment Theory further we consider Three Dimensions of Color:

Hue: The property of a color by which it is distinguished from other colors.

Value: The lightness or darkness of a hue.

Chroma (Intensity): Brightness or dullness of a color.

Changing the Value of a Hue

Tint: A hue into which various quantities of white are mixed; the lightened hue

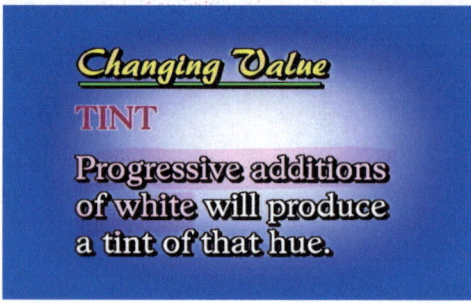

Shade: A hue into which various quantities of black are mixed; the darkened hue

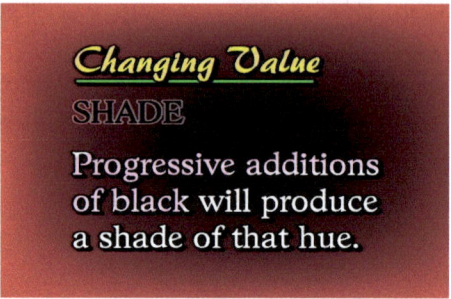

Changing the Intensity (Chroma) of a Hue

Tone: A hue mixed with either a small quantity of gray or the complement of the hue, resulting in dulling the hue

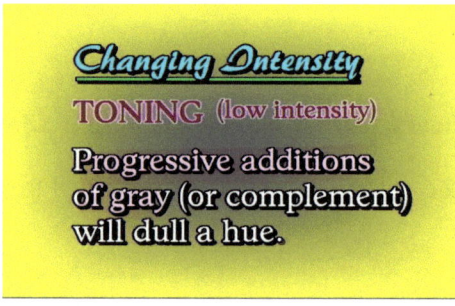

Juxtaposition: Any two hues seen together which modify each other in the direction of their complements

Juxtaposition: Any two colors seen together... modify each other in the direction of their complements.

If the hues are complements, they enrich each other, and if they are not complements they will dull each other.

Harmony Considered: Certain aesthetically pleasing color combinations

Monochromatic: Variations of one hue; tints, tones, and shades of one hue

Analogous: In color harmony, two or more hues which have the same hue in common

Complementary: Colors opposite each other on the color wheel. The high contrast of complementary colors creates a vibrant appearance.

Contrast non-complementary: A color scheme of contrasting but non-complementary hues. These can be pleasant, although not as vivid as complements. For example red and blue show contrast but are not complements.

Other Color Items to Consider

Saturation: A visual aspect indicating the vividness of the hue in the degree of difference from a gray of the same lightness

Tertiary hue: The hue that results from the mixture of two secondary pigmentary hues or an unbalanced proportion of compliments with the warm hue or cool hue predominating.

Color in illumination

The color of an object not only depends on the hue it reflects but also on the illumination it receives. The reality is that an increase or decrease of the illuminant raises or diminishes the vividness of the hue. Therefore, we need to discuss various sources of lighting commonly found in the funeral home. Fritch and Altieri (2017) indicate the lighting in any room should enhance the experience, but it is essential to consider the function of various rooms in a funeral home in order to ascertain appropriate lighting strategies. Poor lighting will diminish a family's ability to perceive the exact qualities of various caskets or other merchandise and even possibly make the client consider what the funeral home is trying to hide or make real the belief that these are dark troubling spaces. Appropriate lighting will highlight merchandise and enhance any unique qualities various products offer. A combination of both **direct** (illumination directly shining on an object) and **indirect** (reflected illumination of an object) **lighting** is best in a selection room. The indirect lighting can offer a general appeal to the room, and the direct lighting will highlight color, form, shadow and any distinctive elements of the products. A final comment on lighting revolves around the reality that various types of lighting will impact overall appearance. For example, **fluorescent lighting** is illumination produced by a tubular electric discharge lamp; the fluorescence of phosphors coating the inside of a tube will generate light that will appear cold and cause objects to appear flat, while **incandescent lighting**, the illumination resulting from the glowing of a heated element, has a warmer appearance but does have a yellowing impact. **Halogen lighting**, a high intensity light source that produces a clean bright white light approximating natural daylight, is also commonly used in the selection room to most approximate the exact color of products and the intricate details offered by many of our products. The newest type of lighting is **LED** which is a light-emitting diode (**LED**). This is a very energy-efficient light source, but it will also impact the appearance of our products, as LED produces a very bright light source. Many consider the LED source to be the top "green" light source, as they last a long time (as long as ten years), come with a warranty, and are the most energy-efficient lighting option available. The important element to grasp here is that light, both style and type, impact the appearance of objects and we must consider this when designing the spaces in our funeral homes.

In addition to the various sources of illumination, the impact of colored lights on perception must be considered. Colored lights indeed will impact the perception of color. For a discussion on this topic, see the effects of colored light and white light on colored objects presented in Chapter 13 as related to mortuary cosmetology.

Chapter Conclusion

This chapter started with a presentation of the history of color theory as well as the impact of the perception of color. Next, specific aspects of light theory were examined, taking into consideration the visible spectrum and principles associated with light theory. After the discussion of light theory, pigment theory and the Prang color wheel were explored. The last section introduced general information about various sources of light found in funeral homes. Chapter 13 explores mortuary cosmetology, and this includes the effects of colored light and white light on colored objects.

References

Professional Experience and Educational Presentations:
A great deal of the content of this book has been derived from years of professional experience as an embalmer, funeral director, and funeral service educator.

Fritch, J. B. & Altieri, J.C. (2017). *Fundamentals of funeral directing: Building*

a professional cornerstone. Oklahoma City, OK: Funeral Service

Education Resource center.

http://www.color-wheel-pro.com/color-meaning.html retrieved February 18, 2020

Klicker, R. (2002). *Restorative art and science.* Buffalo, NY: Thanos Institute.

Mayer, J. S. (1986). *Color and cosmetics.* Dallas, TX: Professional Training

Schools.

Mayer, J. S. (1980). *Restorative art.* Dallas, TX: Professional Training Schools.

Mayer, R. G. (2012). *Embalming: History, theory, and practice* (5th ed.).

New York, NY: McGraw-Hill.

Chapter 13: Mortuary Cosmetology

Chapter Author: Cody L. Lopasky, M.A.

Image courtesy of the Dodge Company

Chapter Learning Objectives

Upon completion of the study of this chapter students should:

- Understand the theory of mortuary cosmetology
- Be able to distinguish the different skin pigments and types of cosmetics
- Be able to explain different methods of cosmetic application
- Understand how to cosmetize embalmed and unembalmed remains
- Be able to describe the effect of lighting on cosmetics

Introduction

Cosmetology is the study of beautifying and improving the complexion, skin, hair, and nails of the living. **Mortuary Cosmetology** is the study of the materials and techniques of applying colorants to simulate a natural appearance for the deceased. A **colorant** is simply any substance used to impart color to an object. In general, mortuary cosmetology strives to achieve naturalism without any hint of artificiality.

RESTORATIVE ART: FOUNDATION & PRACTICE: CHAPTER 13

By natural, it is meant that the decedent should look as they did in life. For some, this means an appearance that seems free of cosmetics, and others need to be "done up" to appear as they did in life.

Knowledge, skill, and professionalism are paramount in achieving the goal of a natural appearance. The necessary knowledge is the foundational principles of mortuary cosmetology, and this is gained through both academic study and experience. Skill is acquired over time through the hands-on, practical application of the techniques used in mortuary cosmetology. Finally, professionalism is key to ensuring that each decedent is cosmetized in a way that is appropriate for them. Sloppy or rushed cosmetic application rarely results in a natural appearance. Also, a "one-size-fits-all" approach to cosmetizing is unethical and will inevitably lead to disappointment and unhappiness on the part of client families. Case analysis should determine which specific cosmetics and application techniques are used on each individual case. When a restorative artist is knowledgeable, skillful, and professional, positive results can be achieved. Examples of the desired results include:

- Replacing the color lost in death and disease
- Replacing any color lost through embalming
- Compensating for the effect of lighting
- Presenting a well-groomed appearance
- Creating a memory picture for the family and friends
- Accenting or de-emphasizing parts of the face if needed
- Concealing discolorations

Biologically, the color of complexion is the result of three distinct skin pigments. The interplay of these three pigments, in differing amounts, produces the wide range of natural human skin tones. Following death, complexion is restored using a variety of cosmetic media. Internally, color is imparted to the skin tissue through the use of active dyes in the embalming solution. This is known as **internal coloring** and creates a base for further restoration. However, the color can be splotchy due to uneven fluid distribution in the tissues (Klicker, 2002). Externally, color is imparted by applying cosmetics to the viewing areas (the face and hands). This process of **cosmetizing** a decedent is known as **external coloring**. Additionally, light can play a major factor in the complexion of the deceased, and this must be addressed as well. This chapter will discuss in detail these areas of skin pigments, cosmetics, application methods, cosmetizing, and lighting. The use of cosmetics on unembalmed remains is also examined.

Skin Pigments & Complexion

Human skin receives its color from within. The three pigments that combine internally to create skin color are: **melanin**, **carotene**, and **hemoglobin**.

Melanin

Melanin is a pigment in the epidermis and hair which ranges in color from brown to brown-black. It is the determinative pigment of all races. Those with lighter or fair skin have very little melanin present, while those with darker skin have more. In other words, racial differences in skin tone are simply a byproduct of the amount of melanin produced in the skin. Certain skin characteristics and anomalies are created by melanin as well. These are explained in the chart below.

Characteristics Caused by Melanin	
Freckles	An uneven distribution of melanin; common in children and tend to fade with age in the absence of constant sunlight exposure
Tanning	An increase in pigment cells (melanin) to protect the deep tissues from the sun's ultraviolet rays; a physiological reaction
Albinism	A complete absence of melanin due to heredity; affects skin, hair, and eyes
Vitiligo	Patches of skin that are free of melanin; may affect hair and/or eyes as well
Age/Liver Spots	Small spots of increased melanin pigmentation common in older adults; found on areas most exposed to the sun like hands, forearms, shoulders, etc.

Carotene

Carotene is the yellowish pigment of the skin, and it is not a dominant skin pigment. The human body obtains carotene from ingesting certain vegetables (Cohen & Taylor, 2009). It is then stored in the adipose tissue cells, which in turn aids in their yellow color. The amount of carotene a person has varies depending on age, diet, and health. In older individuals, the skin may become more translucent and allow the yellow color to appear more abundant. In extreme cases, the complexion may become a sickly, yellowish color. This is known as a **sallow** complexion.

Hemoglobin

The third pigment in human skin is the hemoglobin. Although it is known as the red pigment in the skin, it is not a true skin pigment. Hemoglobin is the iron-containing protein in the blood; giving blood its red color. It is the hemoglobin in the red blood cells that conveys oxygen to the tissues (Cohen & Taylor, 2009). In doing so, the red color shows through the dermis and is visible on the surface. Though not an actual skin pigment, the influence of hemoglobin on the skin's appearance is quite apparent; especially in the superficial capillaries.

Complexion

The interplay of the three aforementioned skin pigments aids in producing the wide range of human complexions. Each individual's complexion is a result of their skin pigments, age, environmental conditions, health, and other factors. Age can lead to a duller and grayer complexion, and climate effects are dependent on the amount of sunshine (Klicker, 2002). Abnormal complexion coloring may be the result of disease like yellow from jaundice or bronze from Addison's Disease. Some postmortem conditions like decomposition (green) and postmortem stain (purple) produce abnormal complexion coloring as well. Certain common complexions even receive a descriptive moniker. For example: A **ruddy** complexion has a healthy reddish color and is quite vivid, a **florid** complexion is flushed with red though not as vivid as ruddy, and **swarthy** is a dark-colored complexion associated with the tropical sun.

Cosmetic Media

The cosmetics used in funeral service can be either mortuary cosmetics or consumer cosmetics available to the general public. The former are formulated specifically for deceased tissue and purchased through mortuary supply companies like Dodge, ESCO, Pierce, etc. The latter are created for the living and can be purchased by anyone at innumerable retail stores like WalMart, Target, Ulta, etc. It is always advisable to use mortuary cosmetics, because they are created for specific conditions associated with the deceased, such as loss of natural moisture and skin oils and being at room temperature versus warm. There was a time when the Dodge Company sold cosmetics to actors and dancers, but the demand slowed when users discovered that the products "run" as result of high body heat, like that created during live performances (Rogalsky, 2019).

Admittedly, most restorative artists have, and sometimes use, regular consumer cosmetics. It is very common to use consumer cosmetics when brought in by the family of a decedent. When a decedent's own cosmetics are available, they should always be used or at the very least incorporated into the cosmetizing of that person.

Whether mortuary or consumer, cosmetics come in three main varieties: cream, liquid, and powder. Additionally, these three are produced in varying densities and/or consistencies:

> **Transparent** – light rays pass through, anything behind or beyond can be distinctly seen
>
> **Translucent** – light may pass through but diffusion of distinct images occurs, only somewhat transparent
>
> **Opaque** – no light passes through, neither transparent nor translucent

Cream

Cream cosmetics are semi-solid and tend to be either translucent or opaque. In other words, they range in consistency from fairly thin to very thick. The thickest cream cosmetics are routinely referred to as "opaques" by some practitioners. Creams are a mixture of pigment powder, vehicle(s), and other ingredients. The vehicle used in a cream often does not evaporate (Mayer, 1986). The benefits of cream cosmetics include ease of blending, the ability to mix with or adhere to wax, the inhibition of dehydration, and the ability to properly conceal discoloration or other faults. Conversely, creams do have negative attributes. They can become matted in facial hair, eyebrows, cilia, and head hair, which requires removal to reduce artificiality. Creams are also easily removed or rubbed off, thus creating a hazard for casket interiors and decedents' clothing. Last, the appearance of being "caked on" is a common complaint regarding opaque creams and results from their overapplication (Mayer, 1986). Cream cosmetics can be applied in numerous ways, such as stippling and sponging. However, care must be taken to avoid simply painting them on. This often results in visible brushstrokes and bristle lines.

Liquid

Liquid cosmetics are fluid, non-solid colorants in which pigments are dissolved or suspended in a vehicle, or combination of vehicles. These tend be transparent or translucent, and some practitioners refer to them simply as "tint." Most liquids flow easily and have an evaporating vehicle. Normally, liquid cosmetics must be shaken vigorously to properly mix the pigment and vehicle, which separate in the container due to density and gravity. After shaking, the liquid is painted on. Note that the cosmetic may need to be re-shaken if ingredients begin to separate during cosmetizing. Immediately after application, the appearance may not be desirable, but this is corrected after the vehicle evaporates. A positive aspect of liquid cosmetics is the fact that they indeed dry after evaporation of the vehicle. Also, they can be applied in and around the eyebrows, cilia, facial hair, and head hair without much worry. They do not generally cling to the hair or colorize it. Negative aspects exist as well though. Liquids are not suited for concealing discolorations; they can stain clothing and casket interiors; they are not compatible with wax, and their pigments may collect in shallow areas or crevices of the face (Mayer, 1986).

Powder

Powder is a type of cosmetic medium composed of fine particles of ground pigment that are either loose or compressed. These particles are commonly ground and mixed with chalk, zinc oxide, talcum, or titanium dioxide (Mayer, 1986). The main purposes of powder cosmetics are setting cosmetics and reducing sheen. Using powder to set cosmetics is akin to using hairspray to set a charcoal or colored-pencil piece of artwork; it helps to reduce smearing. Many types of cream and liquid cosmetics replace the oils and/or moisture that is natural to living skin, but they can leave a visible sheen in the process. Powder will lessen the sheen and reduce the chances of a moist appearance for the deceased. For application, powder is most often applied lightly with a powder brush or puffed on with an atomizer and then tapped with a powder brush.

Other/Miscellaneous

In addition to the previous three, other cosmetics exist as well. Things like eyeshadow, mascara, eyeliner/eyebrow pencil, and blush/rouge may all be used when cosmetizing a decedent. Their application will mimic that of the living. **Lip color** is another area that does not fall neatly into one of the three above categories. It can be achieved through several cosmetic options that include both consumer and mortuary cosmetics. The former normally involves using the specific lipstick or lip liner brought in by the family of a decedent. Restorative artists also acquire these over time, and they use them as needed to recreate the lip color of a decedent that wore such cosmetics in life. Mortuary lip color comes in two main varieties: cream and liquid. Cream lip colors resemble opaque cream cosmetics but in much smaller containers and obviously different colors. Cream mortuary lip colors and consumer lipsticks are both applied using a small lip brush. Note – do not apply lipstick by hand as a decedent would have in life! Liquid mortuary lip color, sometimes referred to as lip tint, often comes in containers that resemble nail polish. It is applied in a similar manner with a built-in brush on the cap, and care must be taken to avoid running. Notably, the color is usually less vivid after the cosmetic dries, much like liquid cosmetics.

Regardless of type, all cosmetics will come in a host of shades and colors needed to match all complexions, ethnicities, and any variations. These will differ based on

RESTORATIVE ART: FOUNDATION & PRACTICE: CHAPTER 13

the type and manufacturer. However, all cosmetics will in some way utilize the four colors necessary to reproduce the color of human skin: white, red, yellow, and brown. Complexion is always a combination of these four principle colors.

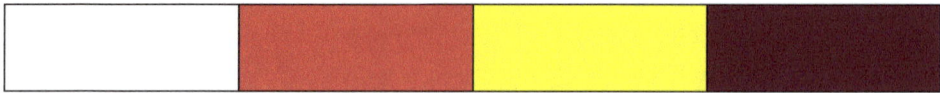

Methods of Application

As discussed in the previous section, cosmetics come in many varieties and consistencies, which all require different application methods. Cosmetics are often applied using a type of brush. Brushes are produced with either natural (animal) or synthetic hair. The type of brush needed will be based on the type of cosmetic or application technique that is used. A brush's type is determined by its bristles and the shape of the ferrule, the metal piece that holds the bristles in place (Klicker, 2002). Many types exist, but they can be simplified into five main categories: spreading, blending, stipple, lip, and powder.

Images courtesy of The Dodge Company

Cosmetic Brushes

Spreading brushes are used as their name implies, to spread cosmetics. This can be cream cosmetics or liquid, but the latter should ideally be done with a smoother, less-coarse brush. Blending brushes are used to blend different shades of cosmetic or different types of cosmetics into one another. **Stipple brushes** are used to apply thick cream cosmetics. The name is derived from the action for which they are used, stippling. This is a slight stabbing or patting motion as opposed to using broad painting strokes which can leave signs of artificiality. When used on human skin, stippling pushes cosmetic media into the pores, which reduces the likelihood of the skin "soaking up" cosmetics; forcing later reapplication. On wax, stippling recreates the effect of pores on human skin. **Lip brushes** are small in size and used to apply either mortuary lip color or consumer lipstick. Powder brushes, as mentioned earlier, can be used either independently or in conjunction with an atomizer to apply powder. Some restorative artists prefer to tap the brush directly in powder and then lightly pat the face. For this method, tap the brush lightly with a finger to ensure that excess powder is knocked off to eliminate any splotchy application. Others prefer to first puff powder on the face using an atomizer and then set it by patting with the powder brush.

Powder Atomizer

A **powder atomizer** is simply a tool comprised of a reservoir (filled with powder), a nozzle, and a bulb. When the bulb is squeezed, it forces through air that pulls powder from the reservoir which is then puffed out through the end of the nozzle. Before using an atomizer, point away from the decedent and squeeze the bulb. This will clear the nozzle and eliminate any clogs that could create an uneven application.

Sponges

Some practitioners prefer to use a sponge when applying cosmetics, often with creams. Sponges are normally round or triangular (like a wedge of cheese). However, they may be in any shape or form and can be purchased from numerous stores and suppliers. When using a sponge, it is patted or tapped on the area to be colorized. Larger areas, though, may allow for a swiping motion. Sponges can be of particular value when concealing discolorations.

Aerosol & Airbrush

Airbrush Cosmetic Kit

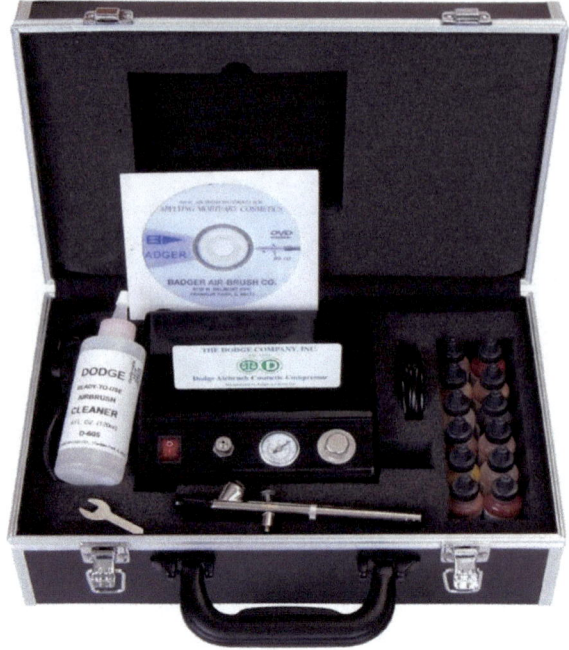

Image courtesy of the Dodge Company

Aerosol and **airbrush** cosmetics both exist and do not require any additional application instruments. Aerosols are solutions that are dispensed as a mist directly from the container. Airbrush cosmetics work in the same fashion but are sprayed from a pressurized atomizer, normally with electric power. Cosmetic colorants are mixed in a reservoir and then transformed into a mist before being released through the nozzle. These types of cosmetics work well for hiding large, discolored areas. Before applying to the viewing areas, though, it is recommended to spray a non-viewed portion of the body to ensure that the desired color has been created (Klicker, 2002). Also, cleaning and maintenance are of great importance with airbrush systems. The previously used color should be thoroughly cleaned out so that it does not affect the color created for the next decedent. Similarly, leftover and dried colorant can clog the nozzle, creating an uneven spray as well.

Other Methods

Certain consumer cosmetics will come with their own puff or pad that may be used for application, powders and blushes for example. Also, some restorative artists prefer to use their hands for the application of certain cosmetics. Overall, the application method that is used should be that which will correctly recreate the appearance of the deceased.

Cosmetizing Basics

The process of cosmetizing is a post-embalming restorative treatment. In general, the areas that will be cosmetized are the face, neck, and hands, termed the viewing areas. These areas should be thoroughly cleaned, washed, and dried before any cosmetic application. Additionally, the face and neck should be shaved on all cases. However, leave any facial hair desired by the family. This task seems obvious on men, but it is equally important on women and children. In children, and some women, a downy-type lanugo hair is common. This type of hair can negatively impact the application of certain cosmetics and needs to be removed, especially when using cream cosmetics, but communication is the key, it is best practice to receive authorization prior to shaving remains if you have any doubt with respect to the desires of the family.

Base/Foundation

Once the decedent is clean and preliminary grooming is complete, cosmetizing can then be done. The average case will receive a base or foundation color first. For liquid cosmetics, this usually suffices as the majority of color. Cream cosmetics will necessitate more. If the foundation color does not achieve the desired result, then the addition of an overtone coloring may be required to adjust the complexion. Also, it is generally advised that the foundation color used on the face should be used on the hands as well.

Highlights & Shadows

Once a base has been applied, **highlights** and **shadows** may be added for **corrective shaping**. These are created to accentuate certain features and de-emphasize others. This is often done in cases with trauma where major restoration has occurred. In these instances, certain aspects of the face may need to be accented in order to conceal or draw attention away from others. Also, corrective shaping on normal cases can be achieved through the use of highlights and shadows. A highlighted or lightened area creates emphasis and the illusion of projection. A shadowed or darkened area lessens emphasis and gives the appearance of recession or distance (Klicker, 2002). These two methods are not required on every case but can be of importance when a decedent has lost their natural face shape due to age, disease, etc. The appearance of a decedent's normal geometric head shape can be restored by corrective shaping through the addition of highlights, shadows, or a combination of both.

Warm Color Areas

Unlike highlights and shadows, **warm color areas** will need to be created for most cases. These are the areas of the face and hands that appeared redder during life due to the presence of blood closer to the skin surface (i.e. superficial capillaries).

The warm color areas include the following locations:

- Forehead
- Cheeks
- Tip & wings of the nose
- Mucous membranes
- Chin
- Ears
- Knuckles of the fingers
- Fingernails/cuticle

When creating the warm areas, start with less and add more, if needed. It is much easier to add more than to remove unwanted excess. Remember that these areas should be subtle so that color appears less artificial. For decedents that wore blush in life, more may be used but only to accurately match the appearance seen in photographs. Therefore, some cases will need warm areas that appear natural while others will require a more ornamental approach.

Two main techniques exist for recreating the warm color areas. With the first method, blush or rouge can be applied with a small pat or dab to the referenced areas. The second method for creating warm areas entails mortuary lip color. Some restorative artists will use the lip color that they used/will use on the decedent and place a small dab of it on each of the warm areas. Then, a stipple brush is taken to the area to stipple the red color into the surrounding foundation cosmetic. The mucous membranes will receive their own unique cosmetizing. For these, use either a mortuary lip cosmetic color or lipstick. Apply with a lip brush, and match the shade and shape as dictated by current photographs of the deceased. Normally, a redder color is needed for females. Be mindful that powder may tone down lips that appear too vivid. When a decedent exhibits misshapen lips, it is often the result of a breathing tube or other medical apparatus. The normal issue in need of restoration is one or both lips curling inward on the affected end. In mild cases, this can sometimes be corrected with lip color. A restorative artist can "cheat" the margins of the mucous membranes by extending them into the integumentary lip simply with lip color. A natural outline is then restored.

Many practitioners erroneously pay little or no attention to the hands. In a 2019 article encouraging consideration of the hands, Dodge representative Matt Black explains, "The loved one's hands play an important part in creating a natural appearance in the open casket or in an ID viewing. This effort to restore the hands will pay off as we aim to satisfy the needs of a grieving family." The fingernails and cuticles may receive their warm color through arterial injection during embalming. If they do not, then the above methods for warm areas will not fix them. Fingernail polish may be required in these instances but always with the permission of the family. For the knuckles of the hands, either of the two methods for creating warm color areas may be used. Doing so will greatly enhance the appearance of the deceased. In theory, all three joints of each finger should receive attention, two for the thumb. However, the distal joint will normally require less color than the others.

Cosmetized Warm Color Areas of the Hand

Image courtesy of Anthony Fleege, MBA, & Sydney Baumeister

Powder

As a final step in the cosmetizing process, powder should be applied to set and dry the cosmetics and reduce any sheen. In addition to its main uses, powder may be used as a color corrective. It can be used to tone color down or add more color. For example, white powder will lesson a color. Conversely, using a powder color that is similar to that of the face will increase that color (Klicker, 2002). Be aware that powder can remain visible on dark-colored clothing. Therefore, powder should be applied with care in areas adjacent to any garments.

Discolorations

Discolorations of an internal, intravascular nature will generally clear during the arterial embalming process. Extravascular or external discolorations normally require post-embalming treatments such as bleaching. These restorative treatments (discussed in another chapter) may eliminate, or greatly reduce, the appearance of any discolorations or stains. When they do not, however, cosmetics should be used. Avoid using liquid cosmetics for this task, because their translucent or transparent appearance will allow discolorations to remain visible. The main cosmetic of choice for concealing discolorations is an opaque cream. When applied in sufficient amount, creams will not let a discoloration show through. A color different from the foundation may be needed due to the ways in which colors interact. Often, discolorations require the use of a color lighter than the base color. Complimentary color knowledge is beneficial. For example, a purple discoloration should be covered with yellow first in order to neutralize it. Normal complexion coloring can then be applied over the area. When base and concealment colors differ, ensure that the edges are feathered to reduce any obvious signs of artificiality.

Lighting & Cosmetics

Light can play a major role in the funeral environment. **Funeral lighting** is the quality and quantity of illumination used for the presentation of casketed remains. Typically, two main types of lighting exist that will affect cosmetics and the deceased: white light and colored light.

White Light

White light is produced by fluorescent bulbs as well as the sun. **Fluorescent light** is created by an electrical discharge reacting with the coating inside a tubular bulb. It is ideal for the preparation room due to its brightness and crispness. The downside to fluorescent light is that it drowns out cosmetics and makes the deceased appear pale. Therefore, this type of lighting is not traditionally used in the viewing/reposing areas of a funeral home. When a church or other service venue uses white light, be sure to prepare a family that the decedent may appear paler than they did at the funeral home. Some practitioners prefer to "over-cosmetize" such cases to counteract the effect of fluorescent lighting.

Treat sunlight in a similar manner to fluorescent lighting. The former will void cosmetics just like the latter. Be mindful of any viewing rooms in which windows or skylights exist. The influence of sunlight will affect the appearance of the deceased by lessening the color of cosmetics. Also, be aware of such circumstances as the time of day. In the evening or at night, a decedent will appear perfectly cosmetized in a room with windows. However, the decedent will appear paler in that same room during the day. Remember to explain these differences to a family when such locations are used. One example is the narthex or foyer of a church. A decedent in state there the evening before a service will appear different the following day. When a location and certain logistics are under the funeral home's control, consider slight adjustments like closing the blinds, drawing the curtains, or perhaps using a different orientation of the casket.

Colored Light

Colored lighting is produced by **incandescent** bulbs. These produce light through an electric current heating a filament inside the bulb. This type of lighting is softer and "warmer" than white lighting. Incandescent lights are well-suited for viewing purposes. They give color to the deceased and enhance the appearance of cosmetics. Most viewing and reposing rooms will employ some style of colored light. Normal incandescent bulbs produce what is often termed yellow light even though the bulbs are in fact white.

In certain rooms where viewing will occur, especially the funeral home chapel, it is very common to use a special type of colored lighting known as cosmetic lights. Cosmetic lights are colored incandescent bulbs arranged in a way that enhances the appearance of the decedent, their clothing, the casket, and even the flowers. Recessed lighting that is parallel to the casket and floral arrangements is an ideal setup. Adequate space should be left between individual lights so that light beams can overlap and blend. Usually, blue and red/pink are the colored lights of choice, but others can be added as well. These lights work together by way of the **additive method** of lighting. A key aspect of cosmetic lighting is adjustment. In other words, the ability to make specific lights brighter or dimmer based on the appearance of each decedent. This is paramount.

It must be noted that colored light can have an effect on colored objects. Certain colors can be changed, become less vivid, or voided entirely. For example, a pink casket interior will be voided by bright red/pink cosmetic lighting, producing the appearance of a less pink or even white interior. Care should be taken to avoid anomalies like this. When necessary for the appearance of the deceased, though, an explanation should be offered to the family. For reference, the effects of red and blue light (the two most common cosmetic lights) on colored objects are shown in the following table.

	Effect of Red and Blue Lighting on Colored Objects	
	Red Light	Blue Light
Red Object	Fades out	Darkens
Orange Object	Lightens	Darkens greatly
Yellow Object	Turns white	Turns orchid
Green Object	Darkens greatly	Lightens
Blue Object	Darkens to dark gray	Turns to pale blue
Violet Object	Darkens to black	Turns orchid

Table adapted from *Restorative Art and Science* (Klicker, 2002).

Cosmetizing Unembalmed Remains

When a family chooses not to embalm their loved one, viewing may still be allowed and possible. In these instances, cosmetizing should be done in order to improve appearance. It is also recommended that basic feature setting be done, but authorization from the family should be obtained first. This is due to the invasive techniques of certain eye and mouth closure methods.

After feature setting, the first step in cosmetizing unembalmed remains is to evaluate and prepare the surface of the skin tissue. Ensure that the areas to be cosmetized have been properly washed, disinfected, and dried. Any surface debris, natural or foreign, should be removed. As with embalmed remains, the face should be shaved, with appropriate authorization from the family/authorized agent.

The tissues of unembalmed remains do not receive the benefit of firming provided by injected chemicals during embalming. Due to this, extra care should be taken in both the selection of cosmetics and their application. Liquid cosmetics may be used, but be aware that the pigment in the liquid may settle into crevices and other areas, causing an uneven appearance. Cream cosmetics are a common choice, but stippling may be difficult on tissues that are not firm. This is especially true on cases with excess adipose tissue on the face and hands. If available, aerosols and airbrush cosmetics are desirable options, because they are not affected by tissue flaccidity and can mask vascular discolorations that remain due to a lack of embalming. Create any necessary highlights and shadows, the warm color areas, and apply powder as dictated by the conditions of the decedent. Remember that unembalmed remains do not receive internal coloring from active dyes used during the embalming process. Therefore, regardless of the cosmetic type used, know that more cosmetic media or even a darker color may be required to achieve naturalism.

Chapter Conclusion

In this chapter, the basics of mortuary cosmetology were discussed. The foundational knowledge of human skin pigments and other complexion variables were introduced first. Then, each standard type of cosmetic was described along with application methods. The principles of cosmetizing were explained, and the importance of lighting was included too. Due to the increase in viewing unembalmed remains, this chapter also touched on the basic tenets of cosmetizing such cases. Overall, the information provided comprises the basis for which color is restored to the deceased.

References

Professional Experience and Educational Presentations:
A great deal of the content of this book has been derived from years of professional experience as an embalmer, funeral director, and funeral service educator.

Black, M. (2019, Summer). Under the blanket. *Dodge Magazine, 111*(3), 4-6.

Cohen, B., & Taylor, J. (2009). *Memmler's structure and function of the human body* (9th ed.). Baltimore, MD: Lippincott Williams & Wilkins.

Klicker, R. (2002). *Restorative art and science*. Buffalo, NY: Thanos Institute.

Mayer, J. S. (1986). *Color and cosmetics*. Dallas, TX: Professional Training Schools.

Rogalsky, R. (2019, Summer). Cosmetic choices. *Dodge Magazine, 111*(3), 8-9.

GLOSSARY

Abrasion – antemortem and/or postmortem injuries resulting from friction of the skin against a firm object resulting in the removal of the epidermis

Abscess – a localized accumulation of pus

Absorption – the process of taking in, as in a colored object which absorbs certain rays of light and reflects other rays giving the object its recognizable color. (e.g., An apple is called red if the red rays are reflected and the other rays in the light are absorbed.)

Abut – to bluntly adjoin another structure; for example, the line of eye closure

Acetone – dimethyl ketone; a colorless liquid which is used to soften and remove scabs; a solvent for restorative wax, or a stain remover

Achromatic color – a color not found in the visible spectrum; a neutral color such as white, black, gray, and silver and gold (for decorative purposes)

Acquired facial markings – facial markings that develop during one's lifetime, primarily as a result of repetitious use of certain muscles

Additive method – a process of mixing colored lights on a surface on which the wave lengths of each are combined; adding two or more colored lights together to create another color of light

Adhesive – sticking to or adhering closely; substances which may be applied in order to sustain contact of two surfaces

Aerosol – a colloidal solution dispensed as a mist

After-image – psychological; a visual impression remaining after the stimulus has been removed

Airbrush – a pressured atomizer utilized for spraying liquid paint or cosmetic upon a surface

Alveolar processes – a bony ridge found on the inferior surface of the maxilla and the superior surface of the mandible which contains the sockets for the teeth

Alveolar prognathism – an abnormal protrusion of the alveolar process(es)

Analogous – in color harmony, two or more hues which have the same hue in common

Angle of the mandible – a bony angle formed by the junction of the posterior edge of the ramus of the mandible and the inferior surface of the body of the mandible; marks widest part of lower 1/3 of face

Angulus oris eminence – the small convex prominence found lateral to the end of the line of closure of the mouth; a natural facial marking

RESTORATIVE ART: FOUNDATION & PRACTICE: GLOSSARY

Angulus oris sulcus – the groove found at each end of the line of closure of the mouth; a natural facial marking

Anterior – before or in front of; an anatomical term of position and direction which denotes the front or forward part

Anterior nares – the external openings of the nostrils

Antihelix – the inner rim of the ear

Antitragus – a small eminence obliquely opposite the tragus on the superior border of the lobe of the ear

Aquiline – curved, as the beak of an eagle; as viewed from the profile, a nasal profile which exhibits a "hook" or convexity in its dorsum

Arch of the wing – the inferior margin of the nasal wing, which forms a distinct concave arc superiorly

Armature – framework; a material, commonly of pliable metal or wood, employed to provide support for a wax restoration

Aspiration – to draw out liquids or gases by means of suction

Asymmetry – lack of symmetry, balance, or proportion

Base – (1) in cosmetology, the vehicle in a cosmetic (oil base); the initial application of cream or cosmetic; (2) the lower part of anything, the supporting part

Basic pigment – four hues that correspond to the pigments of the skin

Basket-weave suture – a network of stitches, which cross the borders of a cavity or excision to anchor fillers and to sustain tissues in their proper position

Bilateral – two sides

Bilateral differences – dissimilarities existing in the two sides or halves of an object

Bilateral view – an inferior or superior viewpoint, which permits the comparison of the two sides or halves of an object or facial feature

Blanch – to whiten by removing color; to make pale

Bleaching – the act of lightening a discoloration by hypodermic means or by surface compress

Bleaching agent – a chemical which lightens or blanches skin discolorations

Body of the mandible – the horizontal portion of the lower jaw

RESTORATIVE ART: FOUNDATION & PRACTICE: GLOSSARY

Bridge – a raised support; the arched portion of the nose, which is supported by the nasal bones; a structure or span connecting two parts of a mutilated bone

Bridge stitch – (interrupted suture) a temporary suture consisting of individually cut and tied stitches employed to sustain the proper position of tissues

Brilliance – brightness; in colored illumination, the quantity of illumination passing through a color transparency

Buccal cavity – the space between the lips and the gums and teeth; the vestibule of the oral cavity

Buccal depressions – natural, shallow concavities of the cheeks which extend obliquely downward from the medial or lateral margins of the cheekbones

Buccinator – the principle muscle of the cheek which compresses the cheeks and forms the lateral wall of the mouth

Bucco-facial sulcus – the vertical furrow of the cheek; an acquired facial marking

Burn – to oxidize or to cause to be oxidized by fire or equivalent means; a tissue reaction or injury resulting from the application of heat, extreme cold, caustic material, radiation, friction, or electricity

Carmine – purple-red in coloration; (aka crimson)

Carotene – the yellow pigment of the skin

Cartilage – a specialized type of dense connective tissue; attached to the ends of bones and forming parts of structures, such as the nasal septum and the framework of the ear

Cauterizing agent – a chemical capable of drying tissues by searing; caustic

Cement – a substance used to promote the adhesion of two separated surfaces, such as the lips, the eyelids, or the margins of an incision

Channeling – creation of dermal and subdermal passageways , through a single entry point in the tissue, in order to allow for the removal of watery fluids and gasses

Charred – reduced to carbon; the state of tissues destroyed by burning

Chroma – **(Intensity)** brightness or dullness of a color

Chromatic color – a color having hue; a color of the visible spectrum

Cilia – the eyelashes

Collodion – a clear syrup-like liquid which evaporates, leaving a contractile, white film; a liquid sealer

RESTORATIVE ART: FOUNDATION & PRACTICE: GLOSSARY

Color – a visual sensation perceived by the eye and the mind due to the activity and vibration of light

Color corrective – a category of concealer that neutralizes discoloration and pigmented blemishes by using opposing colors from the color wheel

Color rendering index (CRI) – a measurement of light quality of a light source as compared to sunlight

Colorant – in cosmetology, a substance used to impart color to an object; dye, pigment, ink, or paint

Colored filter – colored glass, gelatin, or other substances that transmit light of certain wave lengths while absorbing the others

Colored light – illumination of an identifiable hue

Color wheel – a circle in which the primary, secondary, and intermediate hues are arranged in orderly intervals

Columna nasi – the fleshy termination of the nasal septum at the base of the nose; located between the nostrils; the most inferior part of the mass of the nose

Complements – directly opposite hues on the color wheel; any two pigmentary hues which, by their mixture in equal quantities, produce gray

Complexion – the color and texture of the skin, especially that of the face

Compound fracture – a broken bone that pierces the skin

Compress – gauze or absorbent cotton saturated with water or an appropriate chemical and placed under or upon tissues to preserve, bleach, dry, hydrate, constrict, or reduce swelling

Concave – exhibiting a depressed or hollow surface; a concavity

Concave-convex profile – a facial profile variation in which the forehead protrudes beyond the eyebrows while the chin recedes from the plane of the upper lip

Concave nasal profile – a depressed profile form, which may dip concavely from root to tip (also see retrousse and infantine)

Concave profile – a basic facial profile form in which the forehead protrudes beyond the eyebrows while the chin protrudes beyond the plane of the upper lip (e.g. infantine, retrousse, and least common)

Concave-vertical profile – a facial profile variation in which the forehead protrudes beyond the eyebrows while the upper lip and chin project equally to an imaginary vertical line

Concha – the concave shell of the ear; the deepest depression of the ear

RESTORATIVE ART: FOUNDATION & PRACTICE: GLOSSARY

Concurrent – treatments of a restorative nature performed during the embalming operation

Condyle – a rounded prominence at the end of a bone forming an articulation; on both the mandible and occipital bone

Contour – the outline or surface form

Contusion – a bruise often accompanied with distention

Convex – curved evenly; resembling a segment of the outer edge of a sphere

Convex-concave profile – a profile variation in which the forehead recedes from the eyebrows while the chin protrudes beyond the plane of the upper lip

Convex nasal profile – (Roman, aquiline) a nasal profile that exhibits a hump in its linear form. e.g. Roman, aquiline

Convex profile – a basic profile form in which the forehead recedes from the eyebrows while the chin recedes from the plane of the upper lip (most common)

Convex-vertical profile – a profile variation in which the forehead recedes from the eyebrows while the chin and upper lip project equally to an imaginary vertical line

Cool hue – blue, green, purple, or any intermediate pigmentary hue in which they predominate; a receding hue which creates the illusion of distance from the observer; a color of short wave lengths

Cords of the neck – vertical prominences of the neck; an acquired facial marking

Coronal plane – anatomical plane dividing the anterior of the body from the posterior

Coronoid process – the anterior, non-articulating process of the ramus of the mandible, which serves as the insertion for the temporalis muscle

Corpulence – having an abnormal amount of fat on the body

Corrective shaping – a cosmetic technique that consists of highlighting those parts of the face or individual features to enlarge or bring them forward or shadowing them to reduce the appearance of size or deepen a depression

Corrugator – a pyramid-shaped muscle of facial expression, which draws the eyebrows inferiorly and medially

Cosmetic – a media for beautifying the complexion and skin, etc.

Cosmetic compound – a cosmetic medium composed of two, three, or all four basic pigments

Cosmetizing – the process of applying cosmetics to a surface

RESTORATIVE ART: FOUNDATION & PRACTICE: GLOSSARY

Cosmetology – the study of beautifying and improving the complexion, skin, hair, and nails

Cranium – that part of the human skull that encloses the brain

Cranial sutures – non-moveable joints that connect the bones of the cranium together

Cream cosmetic – a semi-solid cosmetic

Cribriform plate – the horizontal plate of the ethmoid bone separating the cranial cavity from the nasal cavity

Crown – (**Vertex**) the topmost part of the head

Crows feet – (Optic facial sulcus) the furrows radiating from the lateral corner of the eye; acquired facial markings

Crura of the antihelix – the superior and anterior bifurcating branches of the antihelix of the ear

Crus of the helix – the origin of the helix which is flattened in the concha

Decapitation – separation of the head from the body; to decapitate is the act of such separation

Decomposition – separation of compounds into simpler substances by the action of microbial or autolytic enzymes

Deep - below the surface, or toward the central part of a structure

Dehydration –the loss of moisture from body tissue

Density – the thickness of the applied cosmetic

Dental prognathism –oblique insertion of the teeth

Dental tie – ligature around the superior and inferior teeth employed to hold the mandible in a fixed position

Depression – a hollow or shallow concave area in a surface

Depressor anguli oris – a muscle of facial expression which depresses the angle of the mouth

Depressor labii inferioris – a muscle of facial expression which draws the lower lip inferiorly and slightly lateral

Derma – (dermis, skin) the corium, or true skin

Desquamation – (**Skin slip**) the separation of the epidermis from the dermis as a result of putrefaction

RESTORATIVE ART: FOUNDATION & PRACTICE: GLOSSARY

Desiccation – extreme dehydration, often resulting in post-embalming discolorations

Diamond – a facial shape in which the cheeks are the widest point accompanied by a narrowing forehead and chin

Digastric – a double bellied muscle, which draws the hyoid bone superiorly

Dimples – shallow depressions located on the cheek or chin in a rounded or vertical form; e.g. one of the natural facial markings

Discoloration – any abnormal color in or on the human body; may be removed by arterial injection

Distal – away from the center of the body or point of attachment

Distention – a state of stretching out or becoming inflated

Distortion – a state of being twisted or pushed out of natural shape or position

Dorsum – top; the anterior protruding ridge of the nose from the root to the tip of the lobe

Dusky – swarthy; somewhat dark in color; when used to describe the complexion color

Edema – abnormal accumulation of fluids in tissues or body cavities

Electric spatula – an electrically-heated blade used to dry moist tissues, reduce swollen tissues, and restore contour to natural form

Emaciation – a wasted condition resulting in sunken surfaces of the face

Embed – to fix or fasten in place

Eminence – a prominence or projection

Emollients – heavy moisturizer; creamy, thick, helps to retain moisture

Enucleation – the removal of an entire mass or part, especially a tumor or the eyeball, without rupture

Epicranius (Occipitofrontalis) – the muscle that draws the scalp posteriorly and inferiorly and raises the eyebrows

Epidermis – the outermost layer of skin; the cuticle or scarf skin

Excise – to remove as by cutting out

External auditory meatus – the opening or passageway of the ear

External pressure – weight applied to a surface

RESTORATIVE ART: FOUNDATION & PRACTICE: GLOSSARY

Eyebrows – (**Supercilia**) superficial hairs covering the superciliary arches

Eyebrow pencil – a cosmetic in pencil form for coloring the hairs of the eyebrow, or creating an eyebrow where the hairs were removed

Eyecap – a thin, dome-like shell made of hardened cloth, metal, or plastic placed beneath eyelids to restore natural curvature and to maintain the position of posed eyelids

Eyelids – (**Palpebrae**) two movable flaps of skin which cover and uncover each eyeball.

Eye shadow – a cosmetic color applied to the upper eyelid

Eye socket – the bony region containing the eyeball; the orbital cavity

Face – anatomically, the region from the eyes to the base of the chin; physiognomically, the region from the normal hairline to the base of the chin

Facial markings – the "character" lines of the face and neck; wrinkles, grooves, cords, and dimples

Facial profiles – the silhouettes of the face from the side view

Facial proportions – mathematical relationships of the facial features to one another and/or to the head and face

Feather – to reduce gradually to an indistinguishable edge; to "taper"

Feature builder – (**tissue builder**) a substance used to elevate sunken (emaciated) tissues to normal level by hypodermic injection

Firmness – the degree of rigidity or stability; a condition of the tissues necessary for the application of wax

Firm wax – the most dense and least adhesive type of wax; a putty-like material used to fill large cavities or model features

First degree burn – an injury caused by heat that produces redness of the skin

Florid – flushed with red, when describing a complexion; not as vivid as ruddy

Fluorescent light – the illumination produced by a tubular electric discharge lamp; the fluorescence of phosphors coating the inside of a tube

Fold – an elongated prominence adjoining a surface

Foramen magnum – an opening in the occipital bone through, which the spinal cord passes from the brain

Forehead – that part of the face above the eyes

RESTORATIVE ART: FOUNDATION & PRACTICE: GLOSSARY

Form – external shape; a mold for casting; produce a certain shape; to constitute existing elements

Foundation – the complexion cosmetic in ornamental cosmetology

Fourth degree burn – total evacuation (absence) of tissue

Fracture – broken bone

Frenulum – the vertical restraining fold of mucous membrane on the midline of the inside of each lip connecting the lip with the gum

Frontal – anterior; the anterior view of the face or features

Frontal bone – the anterior third of the cranium, forming the forehead and the anterior portion of the roof of the skull

Frontal eminences – paired, rounded, unmargined prominences of the frontal bone found approximately one inch beneath the normal hairline

Frontal plane – see **Coronal plane**

Frontal process of the maxilla – the ascending part of the upper jaw that gradually protrudes as it rises beside the nasal bone to meet the frontal bone; the ascending process of the upper jaw

Funeral lighting – the quality and quantity of illumination used for presentation of casketed remains

Furrow – a crevice in the skin accompanied by adjacent elevations

Geometric – the shape of a plane figure determined by its outline

Glabella – a single bony prominence of the frontal bone located between the superciliary arches in the inferior part of the frontal bone above the root of the nose

Grecian – a nasal profile form in which the dorsum exhibits a straight line from the root to the tip; a straight nasal profile

Groove – an elongated depression in a relatively level plane or surface

Hairline – the outline of hair growth on the head or face; the lowest centrally located part of the hair of the cranium

Hard palate – the anterior portion of the roof of the mouth

Height – the vertical measurement of a feature or part of a feature; the distance above the base

Helix – the outer rim of the ear

RESTORATIVE ART: FOUNDATION & PRACTICE: GLOSSARY

Hemoglobin – red pigment; the protein coloring matter of the red blood corpuscles, which serves to convey oxygen to the tissues forming oxyhemoglobin

Hidden stitch – (**Intradermal suture**); type of suture used to close incisions in such a manner that the ligature remains entirely under the epidermis

Highlight – a surface lying at right angles to the source of illumination, which reflects the maximum amount of light; the brighter part

Horizontal – parallel to the plane of the horizon

Hue – the property of a color by which it is distinguished from other colors

Hunting bow – shaped as a bent wood weapon with a central belly; resembling a "cupid" bow; the five arcs in the line of the lip closure resemble the design of the classic hunting bow

Hypodermic injection – the insertion of chemicals directly into the tissues through the use of a syringe and needle

Hypodermic tissue building – the injection of special creams or liquids into the tissues through the use of a syringe and needle to restore natural contour

Illumination – giving or casting of light

Incandescent Light – the illumination resulting from the glowing of a heated filament

Incision – a clean cut into tissue or skin

Incisive fossa – the depression between the mental eminence and the mandibular incisors

Incisor teeth – the four teeth located anteriorly from the midline on each jaw

Inclination – slope; deviation from the horizontal or vertical; oblique

Infantine – babyish, childlike in regard to much adipose tissue; also refers to a facial shape or nasal profile

Inferior – beneath; lower in plane or position; the undersurface of an organ or indicating a structure below another structure; toward the feet

Inferior palpebral sulcus – the furrow of the lower attached border of the inferior palpebra; an "acquired" facial marking

Infranasal prognathism – a form of prognathism in which the base of the nasal cavity protrudes abnormally

Inner canthus – eminence at the medial corner of the closed eyelids

RESTORATIVE ART: FOUNDATION & PRACTICE: GLOSSARY

Integumentary lips – superiorly, the skin portion of the upper lip from the attached margin of the upper mucous membrane to the base of the nose; and inferiorly, the skin portion of the lower lip from the attached margin of the lower mucous membrane to the labiomental sulcus

Intensity – see **Chroma**

Interciliary sulci – the vertical or transverse furrows between the eyebrows; "acquired" facial markings

Intermediate hue – a pigmentary hue produced by mixing, in equal quantities, a primary hue with its adjacent secondary hue on the color wheel

Internal decapitation – trauma that occurs when the skull base separates from the spine

Interrupted suture – see **Bridge stitch**

Intertragic notch – a notch or opening between the tragus and the antitragus of the ear

Intradermal suture – see **Hidden stitch**

Inversion – turned in an opposite direction or folded inward

Inverted triangle – a facial shape with a wide angular forehead, angular jaw, and pointed chin

Jawline – the inferior border of the mandible

Juxtaposition – any two hues seen together that modify each other in the direction of their complements

Labia – lips

Labial sulci – the vertical furrows of each lip extending from within the mucous membranes into the integumentary lips; acquired facial markings

Labiomental sulcus – the junction of the lower integumentary lip and the superior border of the chin, which may appear as a furrow; a natural facial marking

Laceration – an irregularly torn or jagged wound

Lanugo – the downy hair of a fetus, children, or women

Lateral – a position or direction away from midline; to the side

LED lighting – light emitting diode lighting; a semiconductor device that converts electricity into light; noted for its high energy savings and long-lasting durability

Length – a vertical dimension

Leptorrhine – a nasal index having a long, narrow, and high-bridge

RESTORATIVE ART: FOUNDATION & PRACTICE: GLOSSARY

Levator anguli oris – a muscle of facial expression that elevates the angle of the mouth

Levator labii superioris alaeque nasi – a muscle of facial expression that elevates the upper lip and dilates the nostril opening; the common elevator

Levator labii superioris – a muscle of facial expression that elevates and extends the upper lip

Levator palpebrae superioris – a muscle of facial expression which raises the upper eyelid

Ligature – thread, cord, or wire used for tying vessels, tissues, or bones

Light – to shine; a form of electromagnetic radiation that acts upon the retina of the eye to make sight possible

Line of closure – the line that forms between two structures, such as the lips or the eyelids when in a closed position, which marks their place of contact with each other

Linear sulci – eyelid furrows that are short and broken, extending horizontally on the palpebrae themselves, and which may fan from both the medial and lateral corners of the eyes

Lip brush – a small, flat brush having soft hairs of uniform length

Lip wax – a soft restorative wax, usually tinted, used to surface the mucous membranes or to correct lip separations

Liquid cosmetic – a fluid, colorant in which pigments are dissolved or suspended

Liquid sealer – a quick-drying fluid adhesive

Lobe – the inferior part of the ear or the projection of the nose overlying the lower lateral cartilages

Loop stitch – a single, noose-like suture, not pulled taut before knotting, which stands from the skin and anchors restorative materials

Major restoration – restorative art procedures with greater time requirements, higher skill level, and authorization

Mandible – the horseshoe-shaped bone forming the inferior jaw

Mandibular fossa – the small oval depression on the zygomatic process of the temporal bone into which the condyle of the mandible articulates, just anterior to the external auditory meatus

Mandibular notch – a relatively deep indentation between the condyle and coronoid process of the mandible

Mandibular prognathism – jaw protrusion of the inferior jaw

RESTORATIVE ART: FOUNDATION & PRACTICE: GLOSSARY

Mandibular sulcus – the furrow beneath the jawline, which rises vertically on the cheek; an acquired facial marking

Mandibular suture – type of mouth closure that utilizes the mandible for the inferior anchor and the nasal septum for the superior anchor

Margins – the boundaries or edges

Mascara – a cosmetic preparation used to darken the eyelashes

Mask – anything that hides or conceals, as cosmetics

Massage cream – a soft, white, oily preparation used as a protective coating for external tissues; a base for cream cosmetics and a wax softener; an emollient

Masseter – muscles of mastication that close the mandible

Mastoid process – the rounded projection on the inferior portion of the temporal bones just posterior to the lobe of the ear

Matte – having a dull finish; created by the application of loose powder, lack of sheen

Maxilla – a paired bone with several processes that form the skeletal base of most of the superior face, roof of the mouth, sides of the nasal cavity, and floor of the orbit

Maxillary prognathism – superior jaw protrudes

Medial – nearer to the midline; opposite of lateral direction

Medial lobe – tiny prominence on the midline of the superior mucous membrane

Median plane – **(mid-sagittal plane)** situated or placed in the middle of the body dividing it into the right and left halves

Melanin – the brown to black-brown pigment in the epidermis and hair

Mental eminence – a triangular projection on the inferior portion of the anterior mandible

Mentalis – the muscle that elevates and protrudes the inferior lip, wrinkles the skin over the chin

Mesorrhine – a nasal index which is medium broad and medium-low bridged

Mid-sagittal plane – see **Median plane**

Minor restoration – restorative art procedures that require minimal time and basic skill

Modeling – constructing a form with a pliable material such as wax or clay

Monochromatic – variations of one hue; tints, tones, and shades of one hue

RESTORATIVE ART: FOUNDATION & PRACTICE: GLOSSARY

Mottle – to diversify with spots or blotches of a different color or shade

Mouth former – a device used in the mouth for shaping the contour of the lips

Mucous membranes – the visible red surfaces of the lips; the lining membrane of body cavities which communicate with the exterior

Musculature suture – type of mouth closure that utilizes the mentalis muscle for the inferior anchor and the nasal septum for the superior anchor

Mutilated – disfigured by a loss of a natural part by force

Nasal bones – directly inferior to the glabella and forming a dome over the superior portion of the nasal cavity

Nasal cavity – the orifice in the bony face bounded by the margins of the nasal bones and the maxilla

Nasal index – the ratio of nasal width to nasal height multiplied by 100

Nasal spine of the maxilla – the sharp, bony projection located medially at the inferior margin of the nasal cavity

Nasal sulcus – the angular area between the posterior margin of the wing of the nose and the nasolabial fold; a natural facial marking

Nasolabial fold – the anterior fold of the cheek which descends laterally along the upper lip from the wing of the nose; a natural facial marking

Nasolabial sulcus – the furrow lying medial and adjacent to the nasolabial fold; an acquired facial marking

Naso-orbital fossa – the concavity superior and medial to the inner corner of the eye

Natural facial markings – those that are present at birth, hereditary

Natural shadows – areas of color in the tissues normally darker than the adjacent areas

Needle injector – an instrument used to impel specially designed metal pins (with wire attached to each pin) into bone

Neoplasm – a new and abnormal formation of tissue, as a tumor or growth

Norm – the most common characteristics of each feature; typical, common, average

Oblique – slanting or inclined, neither perpendicular nor horizontal

Oblique palpebral sulcus – the shallow, curving groove below the medial corner of the eyelids; a natural facial marking

RESTORATIVE ART: FOUNDATION & PRACTICE: GLOSSARY

Oblong – a facial shape in which the head is long and narrow throughout.

Occipital bone – lowest part of the back and base of the cranium, forming a cradle for the brain.

Occipital protuberance – the prominence at the center of the external surface of the occipital bone.

Occipitofrontalis – (see **Epicranius**)

Opaque – not transparent or translucent; not allowing light to pass through a concealing cosmetic.

Optic facial sulci – see **Crows feet**.

Oral cavity – the mouth; the orifice containing the teeth and tongue.

Orbicularis oculi – the muscle that closes the eyelids; compresses the lacrimal sacs.

Orbicularis oris – the muscle that closes and puckers the lips.

Orbital cavity – see **Eye socket**.

Orbital pouch – bags under the eyes; the fullness between the inferior palpebrae and the oblique palpebral sulcus.

Ornamental – an adornment or embellishment; to artificially beautify the face.

Oval – a facial shape with a rounded forehead, cheeks, and chin and is longer than it is wide; most common geometric head form.

Palatine bone – one of the bones forming the posterior part of the hard palate and lateral nasal wall between the interior pterygoid plate of the sphenoid bone and the maxilla.

Palpebrae – see **Eyelids**.

Parietal bones – two bones that form the posterior 2/3 of the vault of the cranium and part of the sides of the skull.

Parietal eminence – the rounded peak of the external convexity of the parietal bones; determines the widest part of the cranium.

Pathological condition – diseased; due to disease.

Penetrating wounds – wounds that cause a puncture of the skin, a cavity, or an organ.

Phenol – disinfectant employed to dry moist tissues and to bleach discolored tissues.

Philtrum – the vertical groove located medially on the superior lip; a natural facial marking

RESTORATIVE ART: FOUNDATION & PRACTICE: GLOSSARY

Physiognomy – the study of the structures and surface markings of the face and features

Pigment – a coloring matter that can be applied to an object, when combined with some type of vehicle

Pigment theory – the Prang system; system which theorizes that all visible colors originate from three primary colors or hues

Planes – surfaces having very little curvature

Plaster of Paris – calcium sulfate; a white powdery substance which forms a quick-setting paste when mixed with water

Platyrrhine – a nasal index which is short and broad and has the minimum of projection

Platysma – thin layer of muscle covering anterior aspect of neck

Platysmal sulci – the transverse, dipping furrow of the neck; an acquired facial marking

Point of entry – point of insertion for hypodermic injection or channeling

Pores – minute depressions in the surface of the skin, as in the openings of the sweat glands

Post-embalming – treatments of a restorative nature performed after the embalming operation

Posterior – position of direction; toward the back

Powder – any solid substance in the state of fine, loose particles as produced by crushing or grinding

Powder atomizer – a device used to blow powder onto a surface

Powder brush – a device containing hairs or bristles set in a handle; used to apply and/or remove powder

Pre-embalming – treatments of a restorative nature performed before the embalming operation

Primary hue – one of three pigmentary hues (red, yellow, and blue), which can be combined to make all other hues; in light color theory the hues red, blue, and green can be combined to make all other hues

Procerus – the muscle that draws the skin of the forehead inferiorly

Professional portrait – a photograph or painting in which the subject has been posed and lighted flatteringly by a professional photographer or artist

Profile – the side view of the human head

RESTORATIVE ART: FOUNDATION & PRACTICE: GLOSSARY

Prognathism – projection of the jaw(s) beyond the projection of the forehead

Projection – the act of throwing forward; a part extending beyond the level of its surroundings

Proportions – the relationships of the size of one feature as compared with another feature or with the width or length of the face

Protruding lobe – the rounded, anterior projection of the tip of the nose

Protrusion – the state or condition of being thrust forward or projecting

Proximal – a structure that is closer to the center of the body or point of attachment

Puncture – a hole or wound resulting from piercing

Purse string suture – a suture made around the circumference of a circular opening or puncture to close it or to hold the margins in position

Radiate – to spread out from a common point

Ramus – the vertical portion of the mandible

Razor burn – a darkened, air-dried area on the skin resulting from removal of the epidermis while shaving

Recession – a type of surface formed by the withdrawal of a part from its normal position

Rectangle – a facial shape with a flat forehead, cheeks, and jaw that are all the same width, and the length is longer that it is wide

Reflection – the return of light waves from surfaces; the bending or folding back of a part upon itself

Restorative art – the care of the deceased to recreate natural form and color

Retrousse – a nose which is turned up superiorly at its tip; a concave nasal profile

Risorius – the narrow superficial band of muscle that pulls the angle of the mouth laterally

Rods of the eye – the long, rod-shaped sensory bodies of the retina of the eye responsive to light but not color

Roman – the aquiline profile of the nose

Root – the apex (top) of the pyramidal mass of the nose, which lies directly inferior to the forehead; the concave dip inferior to the forehead (profile view)

Round – **(infantine)** a facial shape in which the vertical distance and the width between the cheekbones are equal and the cheeks and chin are rounded

RESTORATIVE ART: FOUNDATION & PRACTICE: GLOSSARY

Ruddy – red complexion; having a healthy reddish color, said of the complexion, more vivid than florid

Sagittal – anatomical plane dividing the body into right and left sides

Sallow – a yellowish, sickly color of the complexion

Saturation – a visual aspect indicating the vividness of the hue in the degree of difference from a gray of the same lightness

Scapha – fossa between the inner and outer rims of the ear; the shallowest depression of the ear

Sealer – a quick-drying material which leaves a hard, thin transparent coat or layer through which moisture cannot pass

Second degree burn – those resulting in acute inflammation of the skin and blisters

Secondary hue – equal mixture of two primary light colors that will produce pigmentary hues (orange, green, and purple); a mixture of yellow, magenta, and cyan (green-blue)

Septum – vertical cartilage dividing nasal cavity into two chambers, responsible for asymmetry of the nose

Severed – to have been cut or broken apart; disjoined

Shade – a hue into which various quantities of black are mixed; the darkened hue

Shadow – surfaces which do not lie at right angles to the source of illumination or are obscured by other surfaces and which reflect little or no light

Sheen – shine; as of the reflection of natural oils of the skin

Sides of the nose – the lateral walls of the nose between the wings and the bridge

Simple fracture – fractured bone which does not pierce the skin

Skin slip – see **Desquamation**

Soft wax –wax that is softer and more pliable than modeling wax; less adhesive than lip wax

Spatula – a flat, blunt, knife-like instrument used for mixing cosmetics and modeling; a palette knife

Spectrum – visible band; the original standard of color; the progressive arrangement of colors (ROYGBIV) seen when a beam of white light is broken down into its component colors

Sponge – an elastic, porous mass of interlacing horny fibers which are permanently attached; remarkable for its power of absorbing water and becoming soft when wet without losing its toughness

RESTORATIVE ART: FOUNDATION & PRACTICE: GLOSSARY

Squama – the vertical surface of the temporal bone

Square – a facial shape in which the vertical and horizontal measurements are equal, the hairline is straight, and the jaw is angled

Stain – to discolor with foreign matter; an area so discolored

Stain removers – any substances or agents which will cause an external discoloration to be removed or lessened

Sternocleidomastoid – a muscle of the neck that is attached to the mastoid process of the temporal bone and by separate heads to the sternum and clavicle; marks the widest part of the neck

Stipple brush – A small, rounded, stiff brush, all bristles the same length, used to simulate pores on wax; stencil brush; could be used for cosmetic application

Straight nasal profile – a nasal profile in which the dorsum exhibits a straight line from the root to the tip; the most common nasal profile

Subcutaneous – situated or occurring beneath the skin

Sublingual suture – type of mouth closure that anchors inferior to the tongue and utilizes the nasal septum for the superior anchor

Submandibular – describing those portions that lie immediately inferior to the mandible

Submental sulcus – the junction of the base of the chin and the submandibular area, which may appear as a furrow, a natural facial marking

Subtractive method – method of diminishing the wave lengths of light by superimposing two or more color transparencies over the same light source; the light is gradually reduced by absorption of colors in the light

Sulcus – a furrow, wrinkle, or groove

Superciliary arches – the inferior part of the forehead just superior to the median ends of the eyebrows

Supercilia – eyebrows

Superficial – closer to the surface

Superior – more elevated in place or position; higher; upper; anatomically towards the head.

Superior palpebral sulcus – the furrow of the superior border of the upper eyelid; an acquired facial marking

Supraorbital area – region between the supercilium and the superior palpebrae

RESTORATIVE ART: FOUNDATION & PRACTICE: GLOSSARY

Supraorbital margins – the superior rim of the eye sockets

Surgical reduction – restoration to a normal position or level through surgical excision

Suspension – a substance in which particles of ground pigments are mixed with a fluid but are undissolved

Suture – act of sewing; also the completed stitch

Swarthy – dark-colored complexion, as a face made swarthy by the tropical sun

Symmetry – correspondence in size, shape, and relative position of parts that are on opposite sides of the face

Taper – a form that receded away from a given point; a form that becomes gradually smaller toward one end; to reduce gradually from the center

Temporal bones – inferior portion of the sides and base of the cranium, inferior to the parietal bones and anterior to the occipital bone

Temporal cavity – the concave surface of the head overlying the temporal bone

Temporalis – muscles of mastication which help to close the mandible

Tertiary hue – the hue that results from the mixture of two secondary pigmentary hues or an unbalanced proportion of complements with the warm hue or cool hue predominating

Texturizing brush – a brush with a relatively large tuft of good quality, fine bristles, such as black sable or finch; used to blend and stipple cosmetics or powder into the applied (cream) cosmetic, and clean out deposits impacted in pores

Third degree burn – destruction of cutaneous and subcutaneous tissues; seared or charred tissue

Three-quarter view – in reference to a photograph, a view that reveals the fullness of the cheeks

Tint – a hue into which various quantities of white are mixed

Tip – the extremity of anything which tapers (e.g. the tip of the nose; the termination of the forward projection of the nose)

Tissue builder – see **feature builder**

Tone – a hue mixed with either a small quantity of gray or the complement of the hue, resulting in dulling the hue

Toupee – a small wig or patch of false hair covering a bald spot; a hairpiece

Tragus – elevation protecting the ear passage (external auditory meatus)

RESTORATIVE ART: FOUNDATION & PRACTICE: GLOSSARY

Translucent – transmitting light but causing sufficient diffusion to eliminate perception of distinct images; somewhat transparent

Transparent – having the property of transmitting rays of light through its substance so that bodies situated beyond or behind can be distinctly seen.

Transverse frontal sulci – furrows that cross the forehead; acquired facial markings

Trauma – a physical injury or wound caused by external force or violence

Triangle – a facial shape in which the forehead is pointed, the sides widen inferiorly, and the jaw is the widest point; (least common geometric head form)

Triangular fossa – depression between the crura of the ear; the second deepest depression of the ear

Tumor – a spontaneous new growth of tissue forming an abnormal mass

Undercut – the angled cut of the borders of an excision, made so that the skin surface will overhang the deeper tissues

Undertones – underlying colors in the skin

Value – the lightness or darkness of a hue

Vehicle – a material combined with pigments so they may be applied more easily

Vertex – see **Crown**

Vertical – perpendicular to the plane of the horizon; balanced

Vertical-concave profile – one in which the forehead and the eyebrows project equally to a vertical line and the chin protrudes more than the upper lip

Vertical-convex profile – one in which the forehead and the eyebrows project equally to a vertical line and the chin recedes from the projection of the upper lip

Vertical (balanced) profile – one in which the forehead, upper lip, and chin project equally to an imaginary vertical line; e.g. balanced

Vomer – bone of the nasal cavity situated between the nasal passages on the median plane; it forms the inferior and posterior portion of the septum of the nose

Warm color areas – areas of the skin surface which, during life, are naturally reddened; places where cosmetics will be applied to restore the appearance of warmth that red hemoglobin will give

Warm hue – a color that appears in the spectral band, characterized by long wave-lengths; a color that makes an object appear closer and larger; a color that reflects warmth; i.e. red, orange, yellow, and other colors in which they are predominate

RESTORATIVE ART: FOUNDATION & PRACTICE: GLOSSARY

Wax – a restorative modeling or surfacing material composed of beeswax, spermaceti, paraffin, starch, and a coloring pigment that will soften at body temperature and will reflect light in a manner similar to normal skin

Weather line – the line of color change at the junction of the wet and dry portions of each mucous membrane

White light – a ray of light that contains all the hues of the visible spectrum, in such proportion that the light appears colorless or "natural"; as daylight or sunlight

Width – the dimension of an object measured across from side to side

Wings of the nose – lateral lobes of the nose

Wire bridging – the length of wire employed to connect two structures that are undamaged such as remaining parts of a bone; a wire mesh placed within an aperture to hold other restorative fillers

Worm suture – (aka inversion suture, draw stitch); a method of sewing an incision along the edges without entering the opening whereby the suture becomes invisible and the line of suture becomes depressed, which lends it ease of concealment by waxing

Zygomatic arch – the processes on the temporal and zygomatic bones; determines the widest part of the face

Zygomatic arch depression – one of the lesser concavities of the face located on the lateral portion of the cheek inferior to the zygomatic arch

Zygomatic bones – bones of the cheeks

Zygomaticofrontal process – the lateral rim of the eye socket formed by a process of the frontal bone and a process of the zygomatic bone

Zygomaticus major – muscles of the face that draw the superior lip posteriorly and superiorly

Zygomaticus minor – muscles of the face that draw the superior lip superiorly and anteriorly

INDEX

A

Abrasion: 141, 149, 154, 157, 176, 177, 187, 192, 203, 205, 248

Abscess: 184, 185, 248

Achromatic color: 225, 248

Acquired facial marking: 92, 104, 105, 111, 112, 113, 116, 152, 248

Additive method: 224, 245, 248

Airbrush: 122, 240, 246, 248

Alveolar processes: 70, 81, 83, 96, 144, 248

Angulus oris eminence: 34, 96, 97, 98, 109, 110, 248

Angulus oris sulcus: 34, 110, 249

Anterior nares: 140, 141, 142, 249

Antihelix: 52, 53, 156, 157, 249

Antitragus: 52, 53, 156, 157, 249

Aquiline: 139, 249

Aspiration: 153, 191, 205, 249

Asymmetry: 105, 122, 135, 140, 143, 249

B

Basket-weave suture: 14, 185, 217, 218, 249

Bilateral: 8, 10, 116, 118, 135, 150, 152, 249

Bleaching: 22, 154, 157, 174, 180, 181, 191, 244, 249

Body of the mandible: 83, 84, 102, 149, 249

Bridge Suture: 184, 211

Brilliance: 223, 250

Buccinator: 95, 96, 109, 114, 250

Bucco-facial sulcus: 100, 114, 250

C

Carotene: 234, 250

Cartilage: 140, 155, 202, 250

Cauterizing agent: 17, 22, 177, 178, 179, 183, 187, 188, 191, 192, 205, 250

Channeling: 148, 153, 191, 250

Chroma: 225, 229, 250

Chromatic color: 225, 250

Cilia: 152, 153, 154, 160, 163, 164, 236, 250

Colored light: 245, 251

Color wheel: 225, 230, 251

Columna nasi: 27, 28, 108, 140, 141, 168, 251

Complements: 226, 228, 229, 251

Concave: 7, 27, 74, 129, 130, 139, 140, 150, 156, 251

Concha: 52, 53, 156, 157, 251

Condyle: 72, 74, 83, 84, 252

Contusion: 198, 199, 252

Convex: 7, 73, 80, 109, 252

Cool hue: 227, 229, 252

Cords of the neck: 102, 116, 252

Coronoid process: 83, 84, 90, 252

Corrugator: 92, 112, 252

RESTORATIVE ART: FOUNDATION & PRACTICE: INDEX

D

Decapitation: 186, 187, 188, 205, 253

Dehydration: 147, 154, 173, 176, 179, 180, 181, 183, 185, 194, 203, 236, 253

Desquamation: 192, 205, 253

Digastric: 102, 254

Distention: 173, 174, 190, 191, 199, 200, 203, 205, 254

Dorsum: 27, 139, 140, 254

E

Edema: 147, 172, 173, 183, 190, 192, 202, 207, 254

Emaciation: 172, 173, 194, 254

Enucleation: 155, 203, 204, 254

Epicranius: 88, 254

Excise: 158, 183, 184, 185, 199, 254

External auditory meatus: 74, 156, 158, 254

Eyecap: 21, 153, 154, 155, 204, 205, 255

Eyelids: 21, 44, 91, 92, 109, 135, 150, 151, 152, 154, 175, 195, 205, 255

F

Facial profiles: 116, 118, 129, 135, 136, 148, 255

Facial proportions: 26, 116, 118, 124, 125, 129, 135, 141, 148, 149, 155, 158, 255

Feature builder: 22, 194, 255

Frontal bone: 75, 76, 77, 80, 81, 88, 150, 256

G

Glabella: 28, 77, 79, 112, 140, 256

Grecian: 139, 256

H

Helix: 52, 53, 156, 157, 195, 256

Hemoglobin: 234, 235, 257

Hidden stitch: 212, 257

Highlight: 3, 21, 80, 123, 124, 149, 174, 229, 230, 241, 242, 246, 257

Hypodermic injection: 17, 22, 154, 180, 181, 199, 257

Hypodermic tissue building: 9, 174, 194, 195, 257

I

Illumination: 123, 221, 222, 223, 229, 230, 244, 257

Incandescent light: 230, 245, 257

Infantine: 133, 139, 257

Inferior palpebral sulcus: 114, 152, 153, 257

Integumentary lips: 34, 115, 144, 146, 258

Interciliary sulci: 44, 92, 94, 112, 113, 258

Intermediate hue: 226, 258

Intertragic notch: 52, 53, 156, 157, 258

Inverted triangle: 133, 152, 163, 164, 258

J

Juxtaposition: 228, 258

L

Labial sulci: 115, 258

Labiomental sulcus: 34, 110, 143, 149, 258

Laceration: 149, 154, 176, 179, 187, 202, 205, 210, 212, 258

RESTORATIVE ART: FOUNDATION & PRACTICE: INDEX

Leptorrhine: 139, 258

Levator anguli oris: 98, 259

Levator labii superioris alaeque nasi: 97, 259

Levator palpebrae superioris: 93, 154, 259

Levator superioris: 97, 98, 259

Linear sulci: 153, 259

Lip wax: 14, 147, 154, 259

Liquid cosmetic: 236, 237, 241, 244, 246, 259

M

Major restoration: 2, 9, 27, 122, 189, 241, 259

Mandibular fossa: 74, 158, 259

Mandibular notch: 84, 259

Mandibular sulcus: 100, 114, 115, 260

Masseter: 90, 98, 260

Mastoid process: 74, 75, 100, 101, 158, 260

Maxilla: 79, 81, 83, 90, 91, 96, 98, 140, 144, 150, 260

Melanin: 160, 161, 234, 260

Mental eminence: 83, 149, 260

Mentalis: 99, 149, 260

Mesorrhine: 139, 260

Minor restoration: 9, 27, 260

Monochromatic: 229, 261

Mouth former: 21, 146, 147, 175, 261

N

Nasal bones: 79, 93, 140, 142, 261

Nasal cavity: 77, 79, 81, 140, 144, 261

Nasal index: 139, 261

Nasal sulcus: 27, 28, 109, 261

Nasolabial fold: 35, 96, 98, 108, 109, 112, 143, 167, 261

Nasolabial sulcus: 35, 98, 112, 261

Naso-orbital fossa: 44, 152, 261

Natural facial markings: 104, 105, 107, 108, 116, 261

O

Oblique palpebral sulcus: 44, 109, 114, 152, 153, 261

Occipital bone: 69, 72, 74, 77, 88, 187, 262

Occipitofrontalis: 88, 89, 254, 262

Opaque: 14, 15, 154, 207, 236, 237, 244, 262

Optic facial sulci: 45, 92, 113, 152, 262

Orbicularis oculi: 91, 92, 113, 262

Orbicularis oris: 94, 95, 96, 98, 262

Orbital cavity: 150, 153, 155, 204, 262

Orbital pouch: 45, 153, 262

P

Palpebrae: 93, 151, 152, 153, 154, 155, 163, 204, 205, 255, 262

Parietal bones: 69, 73, 74, 76, 262

Penetrating wounds: 198, 262

Philtrum: 35, 95, 108, 263

Physiognomy: 2, 5, 11, 127, 263

Pigment theory: 222, 225, 226, 227, 230, 263

Platyrrhine: 139, 263

Platysma: 100, 115, 263

Platysmal sulci: 100, 115, 263

Primary hue: 225, 226, 263

Procerus: 93, 113, 263

Prognathism: 143, 144, 146, 264

Protrusion: 7, 127, 144, 153, 264

Puncture: 192, 198, 264

Purse string suture: 216, 217, 264

R

Ramus: 83, 84, 91, 264

Reflection: 224, 264

Risorius: 98, 264

Roman: 139, 252, 264

S

Scapha: 52, 53, 156, 265

Second degree burn: 183, 265

Secondary hue: 226, 265

Septum: 77, 140, 265

Shade: 228, 229, 265

Shadow: 3, 123, 124, 230, 237, 241, 242, 246, 265

Sheen: 237, 243, 265

Simple fracture: 193, 265

Skin slip: 183, 192, 253, 265

Soft wax: 14, 154, 265

Spatula: 15, 18, 147, 148, 154, 191, 265

Spectrum: 221, 223, 224, 225, 230, 265

Squama: 74, 266

Sternocleidomastoid: 100, 101, 266

Stipple brush: 17, 20, 238, 242, 266

Straight nasal profile: 139, 266

Subcutaneous: 104, 116, 183, 212, 266

Submental sulcus: 110, 149, 266

Superciliary arches: 76, 77, 266

Supercilia: 160, 165, 166, 255, 266

Superior palpebral sulcus: 45, 113, 152, 267

Supraorbital area: 113, 152, 197, 267

Supraorbital margins: 76, 165, 267

T

Temporal bones: 69, 74, 75, 267

Temporal cavity: 74, 90, 267

Temporalis: 83, 90, 91, 201, 267

Third degree burn: 183, 184, 207, 267

Three-quarter view: 123, 267

Tint: 14, 15, 21, 228, 229, 236, 237, 267

Tissue builder: 147, 153, 175, 195, 255, 267

Tone: 228, 229, 267

Tragus: 52, 53, 156, 157, 195, 268

Transverse frontal sulci: 89, 112, 268

U

Undercut: 185, 268

V

Value: 227, 228, 268

Vertex: 69, 126, 127, 128, 132, 268

Vomer: 140, 268

W

Warm hue: 227, 229, 269

Weather line: 144, 147, 175, 269

Worm suture: 215, 216, 269

Z

Zygomatic arch: 74, 75, 80, 90, 91, 126, 128, 158, 269

Zygomatic arch depression: 80, 269

Zygomatic bones: 74, 75, 79, 80, 95, 98, 150, 269

Zygomaticofrontal process: 80, 150, 269

Zygomaticus major: 95, 269

Zygomaticus minor: 97, 269